WALKING
WITH THE
GIANTS

A Minister's Guide to
Good Reading and Great Preaching

WARREN WIERSBE

BAKER BOOK HOUSE
Grand Rapids, Michigan

Every published writer
is indebted to some
who have encouraged him along the way
and helped open doors for him.
I dedicate this book
with deep appreciation
to four such friends
Ken Anderson
Bob Cook
Ted Engstrom
Ken Taylor
and also to the memory
of my first editor
Mel Larson

Contents

List of Illustrations

Preface

These chapters first appeared in "Insight for Pastors," a column in *Moody Monthly,* that fine magazine published by The Moody Bible Institute in Chicago. Since 1971 when the column first appeared, I have received encouraging letters from people all over the world telling me that these brief excursions into Christian biography and bibliography have helped them. I want to express here my deep appreciation to the *Moody Monthly* staff for their patience and kindness, particularly to Wayne Christianson (who invited me to write the column) and Calvin Biddle (who wrestled with my prose).

Since the inception of "Insight for Pastors," my good friend Herman Baker has encouraged me to compile and publish the series. Baker Book House, of which he is founder and president, has done a monumental piece of work in reissuing the great books of the past that need to be known and used by today's pastors. I trust that all evangelical publishers will find it possible to reprint more of the great works of the past; this generation of Christians needs them!

The following generously supplied pictures from which the sketches were made of E. M. Bounds—Mrs. Myles L. Greene, Washington, Georgia; B. H. Carroll—Southwestern Seminary, Fort Worth, Texas; Edwin C. Dargan—Historical Commission of the Southern Baptist Convention, Nashville, Tennessee; Charles E. Jefferson—Congregational Library, Boston, Massachusetts; and W. E. Sangster—The Evangelical Library, London, England.

Part 1

Great Preacher-Authors

When I start to read a biography, I often think of what Solomon wrote: "He that walketh with wise men shall be wise" (Prov. 13:20). Phillips Brooks amplified that truth when he wrote (in 1886): "A biography is, indeed, a book; but far more than a book, it is a man. . . . Never lay the biography down until the man is a living, breathing, acting person to you." We who are in the ministry, of all people, ought to read biography. We minister to real people, and the better we understand great men and their times, the better we can minister to our people in our times. A truly good biography of a great person has a universal quality about it that makes it touch life at many points. Whenever I read a good biography of a Christian leader, especially of a preacher, it makes me glad that God called *me* to preach! I feel a new sense of awe as I begin my sermon preparation and contemplate standing in the pulpit to minister to my people.

We must never, after reading a biography of a great man, merely imitate him. Our day is cluttered with men who are carbon copies of greater men. I do not think God is interested in cookie-cutter pastors and preachers. He wants each man to be himself and, with fear and trembling, to "work out his own salvation." But each of us can learn from the lives of those whom God has singularly gifted and used. To quote Brooks again, "The object of reading biography . . . is not imitation but inspiration." And if biography teaches us anything, it teaches us that God calls and uses different kinds of men in a variety of ministries. There is no need for us to imitate when God has a work for each of us to do in his own special way.

Let me make a few suggestions that might help you profit the most from your reading of religious biography. First, *read widely.* If you read only the lives of the people with whom you totally agree, then you will have a very small biography section in your library! The man we disagree with most may very well teach us something new that we might have otherwise missed. Brooks suggested that while we should read the lives of those who are the most like us in character and vocation, we also should read about those who are the most unlike us. ". . . read the first sort for light and intensity; . . . read the second for sympathy and breadth." In other words, a life of Spurgeon could well make us better pastors and preachers, but a life of Cromwell could improve our understanding of human needs and problems. It is for this reason that I have included in this book chapters on men with whose theology I disagree. I selected my biographical subjects primarily on the basis of how interesting and helpful to the reader the person's life and ministry would be.

Second, *read wisely.* "Popular" biographies that read like press releases will contribute little to your intellectual or spiritual treasury. Be sure the author, whether or not he knew his subject personally, really entered into his life and work. (By the way, the wife or husband often writes the poorest biography, partly because love can be blind and partly because the writer stands too close to the subject for proper perspective. I may stand alone in this, but I have always felt that the biography of Dwight L. Moody written by his son Will suffers in this way, in spite of the fact that it is well-written and interesting.)

Finally, *read honestly.* None of us will be another J. Hudson Taylor or G. Campbell Morgan, but we can learn much from their lives just the same. The ideals and principles that governed their ministries are valid today. The important thing is to look beyond the accidentals to the essentials and imitate them. Morgan was a great preacher not because he ate very little and smoked cigars but because he was at his desk early every morning and permitted nothing to interfere with his study of the Word of God. To read a biography and then ignore it because its subject differs from us, in either theology or life style, is to reveal immaturity and prejudice. Let us "walk with wise men" to learn from them first, and to criticize them afterward (if, indeed, we have the right to be critical). After we have entered into their thinking and ministering we can evaluate their contribution and take for ourselves whatever is helpful and inspiring.

Brooks concluded that "while it is good to walk among the living, it is good also to live with the wise, great, and good dead. It keeps out of life the dreadful feeling of extemporaneousness, with its conceit and its despair. It makes us always know that God made other men before He made us. It furnishes a constant background for our living. It provides us with perpetual humility and inspiration." As we walk together with the great ministers of the past, I trust that all of these blessings—and more—will come to us. The possibilities of Christian biography are limitless, and obviously I have only scratched the surface in the chapters that follow. But my purpose is simply to get you the reader to start discovering Christian biography for yourself.

1

Samuel Rutherford

(1600-1661)

An English merchant, traveling in Scotland in the seventeenth century, made this entry in his journal: "In St. Andrews I heard a tall, stately man preach, and he showed me the majesty of God. I afterwards heard a little fair man preach, and he showed me the loveliness of Christ. I then went to Irvine, where I heard preach a well-favoured, proper old man, with a long beard, and that man showed me all my heart." The first preacher was Robert Blair, who ministered at St. Andrews in Edinburgh for more than a quarter of a century. The third preacher was the great Covenanter and professor of theology, David Dickson, whose commentary on the Psalms has been reissued by Banner of Truth and is worth owning. The "little fair man" was Samuel Rutherford, one of the most paradoxical preachers Scotland has ever produced.

"For generations Rutherford has inspired the best preaching in Scotland," wrote Alexander Whyte in 1908; and yet today the man is almost forgotten. He should be known as the saintly writer of *The Letters of Samuel Rutherford,* but most people associate the name with Mrs. A. R. Cousin's song "The Sands of Time Are

Sinking," which was inspired by statements found in his letters. (This happened to be D. L. Moody's favorite song.)

Rutherford was born in the little village of Nisbet, in the shire of Roxburgh, about 1600. Apparently he lived a rather careless life during his youth. "I must first tell you that there is not such a glassy, icy, and slippery piece of way betwixt you and heaven, as Youth," he wrote to his friend William Gordon. "The old ashes of the sins of my youth are new fire of sorrow to me." To another friend he wrote, "Like a fool, as I was, I suffered my sun to be high in the heaven, and near afternoon, before ever I took the gate by the end." He entered the university in Edinburgh in 1617, began his theological studies in 1626, and in 1627 was licensed to preach. That same year he was called to Anwoth. His life and ministry there put that little village on the map.

Thirty years before, the congregation at Anwoth had enjoyed the ministry of another man of God, John Welsh, the son-in-law of the famous John Knox. Welsh often left his bed in the middle of the night, wrapped himself in a warm plaid, and interceded for the people of his parish. When his wife would beg him to go back to sleep, he would say, "I have the souls of three thousand to answer for and I know not how it is with many of them." It is interesting that both Welsh and Rutherford were exiled because of their preaching and their opposition to the king's encroachments upon the church. When he was on his deathbed, Welsh received word that the king had lifted the ban; so he arose, went to the church and preached a sermon, returned to his bed, and died two hours later!

I visited Rutherford's church at Anwoth and was surprised to find the ruins of a barn-like building, sixty by twenty feet. It could not have seated more than 250 people; and yet Rutherford faithfully ministered there for nine years. "I see exceedingly small fruit of my ministry," he wrote after two years at Anwoth. "I would be glad of one soul, to be a crown of joy and rejoicing in the day of Christ." Mrs. Cousin put it this way in her song:

> *Fair Anwoth by the Solway,*
> *To me thou still art dear!*
> *E'en from the verge of Heaven*
> *I drop for thee a tear.*
> *Oh, if one soul from Anwoth*
> *Meet me at God's right hand,*
> *My Heaven will be two Heavens,*
> *In Immanuel's land.*

The people of the congregation knew that God had sent them a dedicated pastor. They said to their friends, "He is always praying, always preaching, always visiting the sick, always catechizing, always writing and studying." Often he fell asleep at night talking about Christ, and often he spoke of Christ while sleeping. (Spurgeon once preached a sermon in his sleep. His wife wrote down the main points and gave the outline to him the next morning—and he went to the tabernacle and preached it!)

In 1630 Rutherford's wife died; he was also to lose two children during his Anwoth ministry. But in spite of difficulties and the smallness of the place in which he ministered, Rutherford never sought to put himself into a larger place. "His own hand planted me here," he wrote in 1631. "And here I will abide till the great Master of the Vineyard think fit to transplant me." "Transplanted" he would be, but not in the manner he anticipated. For in 1636 Rutherford published *An Apology for Divine Grace,* a book that assailed the weak theology of that day and aroused the opposition of Archbishop Laud's party. Rutherford was tried in Edinburgh on 27 July 1636 and was banished to Aberdeen and warned never to preach in Scotland again. He remained in Aberdeen from 20 August 1636 to June 1638, where he was known as "the banished minister." It is important to note that Rutherford was not imprisoned or made to suffer physically. He was exiled from his ministry and made to suffer in an even greater way by being forbidden to preach.

But history repeated itself; for out of the exile came one of the most spiritual devotional books ever written. Out of Paul's imprisonment came Ephesians, Philippians, and Colossians; out of Bunyan's imprisonment came *Pilgrim's Progress;* and from Rutherford's exile in Aberdeen came *The Letters of Samuel Rutherford.* Of course Rutherford did not write these letters with any thought of publication.

He died on 29 March 1661; and in 1664 an edition of 284 letters was published in Rotterdam, edited by a former student and secretary to Rutherford, Robert McWard. The title of this first edition was *Joshua Redivivus, or, Mr. Rutherfoord's Letters. Joshua Resurrected* seems at first to be a strange title; but if you think about it and read some of the letters, it begins to make sense. McWard considered Rutherford to be a second Joshua who spied out the spiritual land of Canaan and came back to share the precious fruits with others. The third edition of the book, issued in 1675, contained 68 additional letters; and the 1848 edition added 10 more. By the 1863 edition there were 365 letters, one for each day of the year.

Why would anyone want to preserve and read these letters? After all, they were never written for the public eye: they were intimate letters, written from a pastor's heart, to help people he could no longer minister to publicly. Two-thirds of the letters were written during Rutherford's years of exile, when his ministerial burden for his people was especially heavy. But here, I think, is the value of the letters: they are "heart to heart" and focus on the specific needs of real people. Rutherford's encouragement and spiritual counsel are just as helpful today as they were three centuries ago.

Let me confess that there are times when Rutherford's writings are a bit too effeminate for me. I am sure the problem is with me and not with the saintly author. Rutherford, of course, steeped his writing in Scripture, quoting primarily from Isaiah and the Song of Solomon. I started keeping a list of references and allusions while reading the letters, but I finally gave up. There were just too many of them.

Rutherford had three favorite images of the church in his letters: the bride of Christ, the vineyard of the Lord, and the ship. There are hundreds of references to the bride, and Mrs. Cousin included a few of them in her song. There is no question that Samuel Rutherford had an intimate communion with his Lord and that he was not afraid to talk about it.

> *The Bride eyes not her garment,*
> *But her dear Bridegroom's face;*
> *I will not gaze at glory,*
> *But on my King of Grace—*
> *Not at the crown He giveth,*
> *But on His pierced hand:*
> *The Lamb is all the glory*
> *Of Immanuel's land.*

The allusions to the vineyard are not surprising since Anwoth was situated in farming country; and the nautical image stems from Anwoth's proximity to the Solway on the River Fleet. "Have all in readiness against the time that ye must sail through the black and impetuous Jordan," he wrote to John Kennedy in 1632, "and Jesus, Jesus, who knoweth both those depths and the rocks, and all the coast, be your pilot." He wrote to his close friend Lady Kenmure, "Look for crosses, and while it is fair weather mend the sails of the ship."

Rutherford's letters were not written for speed-readers or

frantic pastors looking for sermon outlines. These letters must be read slowly, meditatively, prayerfully. This perhaps explains why this priceless collection is almost ignored today: we are too busy and too pragmatic. If a book today can be read quickly and easily, without demanding too much thinking, and if it contains two or three outlines or promotional ideas, then it is well on its way to popularity. However, if a book, like *The Letters of Samuel Rutherford,* can only minister to the interior life, make Jesus Christ very wonderful, and create in the reader a deeper love for God and the souls of men, then it may have to fight for survival.

Before you dismiss Rutherford as an impractical mystic, let me share with you the other side of his life and ministry which prompted my earlier reference to him as "one of the most paradoxical preachers Scotland ever produced." Rutherford was not only the writer of devotional letters; he was also the author of a number of theological works that placed him among the leading thinkers and apologists of his day. In addition to *An Apology for Divine Grace,* the book that precipitated Rutherford's exile, he also helped write the famous Westminster Confession of Faith, and tradition states that he wrote the famous Shorter Catechism that is based on that great confession. The story is worth telling.

In March 1638 it was possible for Rutherford to leave Aberdeen and return to Anwoth. His last letter from exile is dated 11 June 1638, and his first letter from Anwoth is dated 5 August 1638. In November of that year, he was officially "vindicated" by the Assembly, so he settled down to minister again to his beloved flock. But in 1639 he was commissioned to take the chair of divinity at St. Mary's College, Edinburgh, and reluctantly he obeyed. Then in 1643 he was sent to London to represent the Scottish church at the Westminster Assembly. He took Robert McWard, one of his students, to be his secretary, little knowing that one day McWard would give the world the classic book of letters. He remained in London until November 1647, when he returned to Edinburgh to become principal of St. Mary's.

However, while in London he had published in 1644 a book that was to take Great Britain by storm, a book that almost led Rutherford to the gallows. It was called *Lex Rex* (Latin for "The Law and the Prince"). In that day, anybody who wrote about the monarchy had better be loyal or prepared to make a quick getaway to Europe; Rutherford was neither. When he was involved in controversy, his stubbornness and devotion to truth could be as strong as the mysticism of his letters. He was an ardent apologist, and he could wield the sword with deadly blows. No doubt his deep love for Christ and the church gave him courage and daring in the theological arena.

What he wrote in *Lex Rex* would cause little excitement today because we are accustomed to democracy and civil rights; but in the days of Charles I and Charles II, a call for democracy and constitutional rights was a summons for the hangman. In fact, when Charles II was crowned in Scotland in 1651, Rutherford opposed his policies and, because of his convictions, broke with his two close friends, Blair and Dickson. Rutherford wrote to Lady Kenmure, "The Lord hath removed Scotland's crown, for we owned not His crown." On 16 October 1660 the common hangman burned *Lex Rex* at the cross of Edinburgh; and on 28 March 1661 the "Drunken Parliament" indicted Rutherford and three other Christian leaders. But by that time the author of *Lex Rex* was on his deathbed; and his reply to the official summons was: "I behoove to answer my first summons, and ere your day come, I will be where few kings and great folk come." He died on 29 March 1661. His last words were, "Glory, glory dwelleth in Immanuel's land!"

Should you want to get acquainted with Rutherford, I suggest you begin with the excellent essay by Marcus Loane in his *Makers of Religious Freedom in the Seventeenth Century.* You might also read the chapter on Alexander Henderson, another "man of the Covenant." Then secure the edition of *Rutherford's Letters* edited by Andrew Bonar, because this is by far the best: it is complete; the biographical and historical notes help the reader identify people, times, and places; the glossary of Scottish terms is invaluable; and the letters are arranged in chronological order. Do not plan to read this book at one sitting; read a letter or two a day and let the Spirit of God quietly speak to your heart. Granted, Rutherford is not for everyone; but if he is for you, then enjoy this first meeting as long as you can.

Alexander Whyte preached a series of sermons from *Rutherford's Letters,* and they were published under the title *Samuel Rutherford and Some of His Correspondents.* You should read the first two sermons before you begin the *Letters* themselves; they are excellent introductions to the book and its author. After reading several of the letters, you can see how Whyte interprets them in his sermons. By the way, Whyte also brought out an edition of the Shorter Catechism in his "Handbooks for Bible Classes" series. And in the same series is John Macpherson's fine history of the Westminster Confession entitled *The Westminster Confession of Faith.*

One of the best studies of Rutherford's life and character is that by A. Taylor Innes in "The Evangelical Succession" series. It is called simply *Samuel Rutherford,* and Alexander Whyte himself called it "the finest thing that has ever been written on Rutherford." Alexander Smellie's classic volume, *Men of the Covenant,* also should be consulted.

"I look not to win away to my home without wounds and blood," Rutherford wrote in 1630; and shortly before his death thirty-one years later, he wrote, "For me, I am now near to eternity.... Fear not men, for the Lord is your light and your salvation."

It is best that we remember Samuel Rutherford not as the courageous apologist or the dogmatic theologian but as the man who lived so close to the Savior's heart. His pen was always ready to write of the things "touching the King." In this day of headache and haste, perhaps it is good for us to heed his invitation to a closer communion with our Lord. Then we can join the testimony Mrs. Cousin put upon his lips:

> *With mercy and with judgment*
> *My web of time He wove,*
> *And aye the dews of sorrow*
> *Were lustred with His love.*
> *I'll bless the hand that guided,*
> *I'll bless the heart that planned,*
> *When throned where glory dwelleth*
> *In Immanuel's land.*

Bibliography

Innes, A. Taylor. *Samuel Rutherford.* The Evangelical Succession, series 2. Edinburgh: MacNiven and Wallace, 1883.

Loane, Marcus L. *Makers of Religious Freedom in the Seventeenth Century.* Grand Rapids: Eerdmans, 1961.

Macpherson, John. *The Westminster Confession of Faith.* Edinburgh: Clark, 1882.

Rutherford, Samuel. *An Apology for Divine Grace.* 1636.

————. *Joshua Redivivus, or, Mr. Rutherfoord's Letters* ... 1664.

————. *Letters.* 2 vols. Edited by Andrew A. Bonar. Edinburgh: Kennedy, 1863.

————. *Lex Rex: The Law and the Prince.* London: Field, 1644.

Smellie, Alexander. *Men of the Covenant.* London: Marshall, Morgan, and Scott, 1924. Reprinted—Edinburgh: Banner of Truth, 1975.

Whyte, Alexander. *Samuel Rutherford and Some of His Correspondents.* Edinburgh: Oliphant, Anderson, and Ferrier, 1894.

2

F. W. Robertson

(1816-1853)

It is 3 August 1841. A young British preacher is visiting Geneva, hoping to restore both his faith and his broken health. He visits the celebrated Henri Caesar Malan, the Swiss evangelical leader whose fearless ministry has aroused the resentment of the established church. The young preacher opens his heart to the man for he, too, finds his position in the established church an uncomfortable one. As the two pastors discuss matters theological and ministerial, the godly Malan looks at his visitor, shakes his head, and announces: "You will have a sad life and a sad ministry!"

The prophecy was fulfilled. The young man died at the age of thirty-seven after only thirteen years of ministry; and when he died, he considered himself a failure. Nevertheless within a few years of his death, his printed sermons were making an impact on thinking Christians (and even unbelievers) that has not diminished to this day. He lived a sad, almost tragic life, and his ministry was filled with pain, both physical and emotional; yet Frederick W. Robertson is known as "the preacher's preacher," and his failure has turned into success.

Robertson was born on 3 February 1816 in London, His father was a captain in the Royal Artillery, and Robertson spent his first five years at Leith Fort, near Edinburgh. In 1821 Captain Robertson retired and moved the family to Yorkshire, where young Frederick grew up enjoying the outdoors and dreaming of a soldier's life. Both his father and grandfather had served gallantly in the army; his three younger brothers were to follow in their steps. But not Frederick. Though he prepared himself and applied for his commission, two years passed before he heard from the Crown. But before that, something interfered.

In March 1837 a neighbor introduced him to Mr. Davies, a devoted clergyman who asked Robertson what he planned to do with his life. When told that the young man planned to enter the army and was even then waiting for his commission, Davies asked, "Have you ever considered the church?" Robertson replied, "No, never! Not that! I am not fit for that!" After further conversation Robertson asked Davies what he should do; the wise pastor said, "Do as your father likes, and pray to God to direct your father aright." In true military fashion Robertson followed his counsel; and Captain Robertson decided that the place for his son was the church. On 4 May 1837 Robertson entered Oxford. Five days later his army commission arrived.

Robertson was disappointed in Oxford. The students, having little sense of duty or devotion, jested about sacred things; and the Anglican church was seething with division and debate. John Henry Newman was preaching at Oxford at that time, and the famous Tractarian movement that ultimately led Newman back to Rome was getting underway. Robertson's studies were not too systematic, nor did he strive to win prizes. He did focus attention on the Bible, and each morning while shaving he tried to memorize certain portions. His biographer claimed that Robertson memorized *all* of the New Testament in English and much of it in Greek!

Upon leaving college he plunged into his ministerial career and on 12 July 1840 was ordained by the Bishop of Winchester. Interestingly enough, the text of the ordination sermon was "Endure hardness as a good soldier of Jesus Christ." That was exactly what Robertson would have to do for the next thirteen years, and at times he would be tempted to quit. His first sermon, given a week later, was on Isaiah 55:1, "Ho, every one that thirsteth!"

Apparently he and Mr. Nicholson, the rector, got along beautifully, for the young man had a mind to work. Nicholson was in poor health, and many of the pastoral responsibilities fell to his young assistant, who performed them with sympathy and success.

Unfortunately Robertson developed the bad habit of "unwise self-dissection" during that year, and the constant examination of his spiritual condition did not make for spiritual health. He became overly sensitive to his faults and gradually over-critical of the faults of others. He lived, too, under a self-induced conviction that he was going to die soon, and this outlook tended to make him melancholy.

His morbid attitude only made his symptoms worse. The doctors recommended that he tour the Continent, and in July 1841 he set off for Geneva. It was there he met Malan. It was also there that he met Helen Denys, daughter of a British noble; they were married after a brief acquaintance.

The Robertsons returned to England, and in 1842 he began his ministry at Christchurch, Cheltenham, working with Mr. Archibald Boyd, the rector. Boyd was what was known in those days as "a pulpit giant," and Robertson learned much about preaching and studying during his five years at Christchurch. Up to this point Robertson had been somewhat careless about sermon preparation, sometimes leaving it until Saturday! Now he saw that real preaching was born of painstaking work and agonizing prayer and study.

But he had his problems in Cheltenham. To begin with, Robertson was ministering to the wealthy, and his heart was with the poor. The city was "a resort for the lame and lazy and rich," and Robertson had no desire to be a popular preacher to a pleasure-seeking society. But his most difficult problem was with the evangelicals in Cheltenham. Robertson himself had been brought up in the evangelical tradition, but he was pained by the bitterness, narrowness, and downright meanness that seemed to characterize some of their leaders. Their publications seemed to thrive on name-calling, tests of orthodoxy, and the reaffirming of traditional truths in the same traditional language. When Robertson's preaching did not completely conform to their standards, they began to shoot at him. "I stand nearly alone," he wrote, "a theological Ishmael!" He was too conservative for the liberals and too liberal for the conservatives.

At this point, "the sudden ruin of a friendship . . . accelerated the inward crisis," and Robertson was plunged into a spiritual conflict that shook him to the very foundations. "It is an awful moment," he wrote, "when the soul begins to find that the props on which it has blindly rested so long are, many of them, rotten, and begins to suspect them all. . . ." It was his "dark night of the soul."

He left his wife and children in England, took a leave of absence from the church, and headed once again to the Continent, to struggle alone with himself and his God. Even his dreams afflicted him. He dreamed that members of the church were gossiping about him and tearing down his work. He would awaken, go back to sleep, and then dream that he was being reproached for work left undone. Neither change of scenery nor strenuous exercise up and down the mountains could cure his deep melancholy and the painful conviction that his ministry was a failure. He returned home, resigned from the church, served as interim at another church for two months, and then moved to Trinity Chapel, Brighton, where he was to carry on a brave and noble ministry for six brief years.

Brighton was a fashionable seaside resort of about seventy thousand people, one-fourth of them holiday vacationers. There were thirteen Anglican churches in the city, as well as nineteen independent churches, a Quaker meeting, a Jewish synagogue, and a Roman Catholic church. But the churches seemed to make little difference in the lives of the people, who were interested primarily in pleasure and money. Every weekend a new army of pleasure-seekers invaded the city from London, and the worldliness of Brighton became a burden on Robertson's heart.

He turned to the poor and to the workingmen of the city, and this upset the rich of the congregation. He refused to be labeled, and as a result he was libeled. His sermons were too pointed, and he dared to name the sins of the rich right in the presence of their servants! Anonymous letters attacked him; some of these even found their way into the local newspapers. Because he dared to search into the truth of the Bible and let the Bible open up its own message, he was condemned by those who rested on a secondhand faith and never knew the "dark night of the soul" through which he had won his own convictions.

One of the main organs of criticism was *The Record*, published by the evangelical party of the church. When one of his London pastor friends wrote to *The Record* to defend him, Robertson wrote to thank him and said: *"The Record* has done me the honor to abuse me for some time past, for which I thank them gratefully. God forbid they should ever praise me! One number alone contained four unscrupulous lies about me, on no better evidence than that someone had told them, who had been told by somebody else." But Robertson was human, and these barbs often penetrated deeply into his heart. A tinge of bitterness crept into his personality, though he was always kind to people—including those who differed with him.

In 1852 the young men of the congregation presented a public testimonial to their pastor, which he gratefully accepted. However, he confessed in a letter to a friend, "In the midst of the homage of a crowd, I felt alone, and as if friendless."

He sensed that the end was near; the physical demands of his ministry were too much for him, let alone the strenuous demands he made upon himself in sermon preparation. He suffered from splitting headaches; often he would sit alone for hours, gritting his teeth and silently waging war against indescribable pain. At night he slept with his head against the rung of a chair. There was an abcess in his brain, and nobody could do anything about it. A group of friends raised the money to provide an assistant for the church, but the vicar of Brighton rejected the man they chose because of a long-standing grudge between them!

Robertson's last sermon at Trinity concluded a series on II Corinthians; the text was, "Finally, brethren, farewell!" It proved to be prophetic. On 12 August 1853 he wrote his last letter; and his closing words were: "His will be done! I write in torture." When his physician and his wife tried to move him to a more comfortable position, he said, "I cannot bear it; let me rest. I must die. Let God do His work." On 15 August 1853 he finished his course. Two thousand persons attended his funeral, and all of Brighton was draped in mourning. Even some who had bitterly attacked him realized that he had taught them something important and, even more, that he had lived before them the message that he preached.

One is tempted to ask, "Why was such an effective preacher so constantly discouraged and overshadowed by a dark cloud of failure?" No doubt there were physical reasons: Robertson was not a robust man and the seeds of death were working in his body years before his friends knew they were there. A pastor's health may not be as important as his doctrine, but Paul does not separate the two in I Timothy 4:6-8. "I am impressed," said Phillips Brooks in his *Lectures on Preaching,* "with what seems to me the frivolous and insufficient way in which the health of the preacher is often treated." Bodily weakness need not be an obstacle to a successful ministry (witness McCheyne and Brainerd, for example), but certainly it is no advantage. It was when Elijah was weary and hungry that he entered the valley of despair and sat under his juniper tree.

A second factor in Robertson's attitude was, I believe, disappointment: he had always wanted to be a soldier, and when he was made a minister instead, he continued to live like a soldier. He read the "war news" of his day eagerly and often imagined himself leading a batallion to victory. He confessed to a friend that he could not witness military maneuvers without experiencing a choking sensation. He often wore a dragoon cloak, and the emphasis on *duty* in his preaching is obvious. He would have fled from Brighton the first year of his ministry had not a soldier's sense of duty kept him there. I am not suggesting that he was not dedicated to the ministry, or that he ministered in a half-hearted way; but rather that his concept of the ministry was primarily *militant* and in war you either win or lose. In the ministry the victories are not always that definite; so Robertson was never really able to evaluate honestly the good he was doing through his preaching.

Perhaps a chief cause of depression was his tendency to be a loner. He had few close friends or confidants, probably because he did not want to be crushed by another broken friendship as he had been in Cheltenham. Even his wife does not seem to have entered into his ministry the way a pastor's wife normally would. There are suggestions in his letters that he and his wife did not agree on church matters and that on more than one occasion she was right!

Because he could not find a group that agreed with him and because he had too much humility to start one of his own, he identified himself with no group and ultimately ended up criticizing all of them! His ministerial loneliness robbed him of the balance he needed, both emotionally and spiritually. "I would rather live solitary on the most desolate crag," he wrote, "shivering, with all the warm wraps of falsehood stripped off . . . than sit comfortably on more inhabited spots, where others were warm in a faith which is true to them, but which is false to me." It seems to me that his alternatives are not honest: a man can have convictions and still have companions. Again, this is the soldier in Robertson: he was on the defensive, always protecting his citadel of truth and never suspecting that others were trying to defend it too. The pastor is a lonely enough man without making the situation worse!

What is Robertson's contribution to our preaching today? Perhaps his "six principles" still have something to say to us: (1) establish positive truth instead of only destroying error; (2) since truth is made up of two opposite propositions, look for a doctrine large enough to include both; (3) preach suggestively, not exhaustively; (4) start with Christ's humanity, then move to His deity (Brooks would say, "Find the place where truth touches life"); (5) truth works from the inward to the outward; and (6) try to find the basis of truth even in error. We may not totally agree with all these propositions, but we must confess they give us a great deal to think about.

Robertson's weakness was in the area of systematic theology. His Oxford training was definitely inadequate here, and even during his own personal studies he never did arrive at concrete statements of the great doctrines of the faith. Principal A. M. Fairbairn wrote: "The very incompleteness of his work was the secret of his power. He said what many had been feeling, but he did not help the many to translate their feelings into a rational substitute for what he so vigorously swept away."[1] It is his vagueness that attracts people of different schools, but we must confess that this vagueness leaves the soul a bit dissatisfied.

Robertson was not, as is often claimed, the "father of the two-point sermon." He learned it from his beloved rector at Christ-church, Archibald Boyd. But it was Robertson who perfected the approach and made it popular. I fear I would tire of it week after week, as would my congregation; but it is worth studying and incorporating into our own kit of homiletical tools.

Before you rush out and purchase everything by and about F. W. Robertson, acquaint yourself with the man. I suggest you start with *The Preaching of F. W. Robertson* by Gilbert E. Doan, Jr., a volume in the excellent "Preacher's Paperback Library" published by Fortress Press. Along with a brief biography and a fine study of his preaching are ten of Robertson's best sermons. Do not read these sermons quickly! Read them carefully, slowly, meditatively, beginning with "The Loneliness of Christ," which is perhaps Robertson's most autobiographical sermon.

If you find yourself excited by what you read, then secure *The Soul of Frederick W. Robertson* by James R. Blackwood. This is the best brief study of Robertson you will find, based on careful scholarship and a fine sympathy for the man. (The author is a son of the eminent Princeton professor of homiletics, Andrew W. Blackwood.) You may also want to read Lewis O. Brastow's study of Robertson in his *Representative Modern Preachers.*

If at this point you are still interested, then purchase Stopford A. Brooke's definitive *Life and Letters of Frederick W. Robertson,* which is available in several different editions. Brooke spent eight years writing this book! At times it is tedious, but for the most part it permits the preacher to speak for himself. The author's

---

1. In A. W. W. Dale, *The Life of R. W. Dale* (London: Hodder and Stoughton, 1898), p. 705.

most subjective chapter is chapter 7 in the first volume, where some of his views need to be taken with a grain of salt. Of course you will then want to add all of Robertson's sermons and addresses to your library, index them, and refer to them as you study. You will also want to read a sermon now and then, just for your own edification.

In his monumental *A History of Preaching,* Edwin C. Dargan called Robertson "one of the most pathetic and powerful figures in all the history of English preaching. . . ."[2] Perhaps so; but could we not use in the church today a bit more of the "soldier spirit" that gives a man the courage to keep ministering in spite of the odds? Robertson once suggested that all clergy be "forced to serve in the army for five years previous to ordination, to make them men. . . ." We may not agree with this suggestion, but we do agree with Paul's admonition—and Robertson's ordination charge— "Endure hardness as a good soldier of Jesus Christ."

Bibliography

Blackwood, James R. *The Soul of Frederick W. Robertson.* New York: Harper, 1947.

Brastow, Lewis O. *Representative Modern Preachers.* London: Hodder and Stoughton, 1904. Reprinted—Plainview, N.Y.: Books for Libraries, 1975.

Robertson, F. W. *Life and Letters of Frederick W. Robertson.* Edited by Stopford A. Brooke. 2 vols. Boston: Ticknor and Fields, 1865. Reprinted—1 vol. New York: Harper, 1903.

———. *The Preaching of F. W. Robertson.* Edited by Gilbert E. Doan, Jr. Philadelphia: Fortress, 1964.

---

2. 2 vols. (New York: Armstrong, 1905-1912), 2:520.

3

Alexander Maclaren

(1826-1910)

Years ago, every Scottish father wanted a son in the ministry. David Maclaren was no exception. A gifted lay preacher and dedicated Christian businessman in Glasgow, Maclaren did all he could to encourage his son. One day he took him to see the Rev. Charles Stovel, a pastor friend.

"Do you think the lad would make a minister?" Maclaren asked.

The pastor thought for a while, then replied, "Well, perhaps he might."

It was a historic ecclesiastical understatement, for Alexander Maclaren became one of the greatest preachers of the nineteenth century, an era that gave us Charles H. Spurgeon, R. W. Dale, Joseph Parker, and Henry Liddon. His printed sermons are models of scholarly, yet practical, exposition. His monumental *Expositions of Holy Scripture* is an excellent homiletical tool that has continually proved its worth ever since the first volume on Genesis was published in 1904. "A man who reads one of Maclaren's sermons," said W. Robertson Nicoll, "must either take his outline—or take another text." One listener said, "This man is a prophet, and you must either listen and swallow, or flee." Parker said there was "no greater preacher than Alexander Maclaren in the English-speaking pulpit."

How did he do it? The answer is simple: through hard work, disciplined study, and concentration on the one important thing—preaching the Word. He turned down most speaking and social invitations. He stayed home, did his work, and built a great church. "I began my ministry," he told a group of young preachers, "with the determination of concentrating all my available strength on the work, the proper work of the Christian ministry, the pulpit. . . . I have tried to make my ministry a ministry of exposition of Scripture." Maclaren would weep if he saw how some pastors today rarely if ever preach; they prefer bringing in guest luminaries to disciplining themselves to study and preach the Word of God. Maclaren was known to devote sixty hours to the preparation of a single message.

He was born in Glasgow, Scotland, in 1826. His father was recognized as a capable expositor of the Word; and even though his business often took him away from home for long periods of time, David Maclaren had a godly influence on his son. (By the way, the family name was originally spelled "McLaren," but during his student days Alexander changed it. "I do not like the Highland way of spelling the name," he wrote to his family. You will see both spellings in homiletical literature.) After wrestling with the doctrine of election, young Alexander finally yielded to Christ and in 1840 was baptized into the fellowship of the Hope Street Baptist Church. (Some books, including the biography by Carlile, incorrectly give the year as 1838.)

The family moved to London, and Maclaren enrolled in Stepney College in 1842. He immediately proved to be a leading student. He loved Hebrew and Greek and graduated with honors in both. All his life, Maclaren read two chapters a day in the original, one from the Old Testament and one from the New. He did his sermonic work directly from the Hebrew and Greek.

In 1845 he was sent to preach at a run-down church in Southampton; the people were so impressed they called him to be their pastor. After graduation the following year he began his ministry at the Portland Chapel, a church that had suffered greatly under an incompetent pastor who had plunged them into debt and given the church a bad reputation in the community. The building needed repair, and the church was not even sure it could pay the new pastor's salary. "If the worst comes to the worst," Maclaren wrote home, "I shall at all events not have to reflect that I have killed a flourishing plant, but only assisted at the funeral of a withered one. . . . The difficulties will keep me busy and prevent my relapsing into idleness."

Years later he told ministerial students, "I thank God that I was stuck down in a quiet, little, obscure place to begin my ministry; for that is what spoils half of you young fellows. You get pitchforked into prominent positions at once, and then fritter yourselves away in all manner of little engagements that you call duties . . . instead of stopping at home and reading your Bibles, and getting near to God. I thank God for the early years of struggle and obscurity." It is worth noting that Joseph Parker, G. Campbell Morgan, and Charles H. Spurgeon began their ministries in small places, during those "hidden years" laying the foundation for their future work.

The work at Portland Chapel prospered. Debts were paid, the building repaired, and the district awakened to the young preacher. His hard work and godly life were paying spiritual dividends. In 1856 Maclaren married his cousin, Marion Maclaren; he claimed later that his ministry would have been impossible without her. Two years later he was called to preach at Union Chapel, Manchester. He accepted and began an amazing forty-five–year term that gave him the name "Maclaren of Manchester."

He loved nature, and yet he was placed in the midst of an ugly manufacturing city. He was shy and retiring, yet he was surrounded by thousands of people. He was a student of the Word, and yet the cosmopolitan population that would attend his church would expect a "message for the times." The demands would be heavy, and yet he must find time to study, meditate, and pray.

History repeated itself: the church grew and had to move into a new edifice that seated nearly two thousand. Maclaren had changed his location, but not his disciplines. He still refused most invitations and concentrated on studying the Word and feeding his people. He was not a visiting pastor, and he repeatedly challenged the adage that "A home-going pastor makes a church-going people." He reminded ministerial students that the adage is true only if, when the people come to church, they hear something worth coming for.

Maclaren's natural shyness led many to think he was proud and aloof. He rarely gave interviews to the press. His first was to Arthur Porritt, the noted Christian journalist, who tells about it in his charming book *The Best I Remember:* "Dr. Maclaren was rather an exasperating subject for an interviewer. He said the most interesting things, downright indiscreet things (which, of course, make the best 'copy'), but having said them he would purse his lips in a roguish way and say, 'I'm thinking that that will not have to go into the interview; you'll leave it out, won't you?' "

One vacation he had his picture taken by a local photographer who did not know how famous his customer was. The photographer put the portrait in his window and was amazed at the number of people who wanted to purchase copies—but he had destroyed the negative! "That man might have told me he was famous," he complained, "but he didn't look like it!" Maclaren was simply obeying his own admonition: "To efface one's self is one of a preacher's first duties. The herald should be lost in his message."

It was probably fear of becoming a popular idol that motivated him to refuse an invitation many wish he had accepted—the opportunity to deliver the Yale Lectures on preaching. He was begged to accept, but to this too he said no.

Surprisingly, Maclaren was haunted all his life by a sense of failure. Often he suffered "stage fright" before a service, but in the pulpit he was perfectly controlled. He sometimes spoke of each Sunday's demands as "a woe," and he was certain that his sermon was not good enough and that the meeting would be a failure. After accepting an invitation to preach at some special occasion, he would fret about it and wonder if there were any way to escape. After the meeting he would lament that he had done poorly. Sometimes he became depressed, but then he would say, "Well, I can't help it, I did my best, and there I leave it."

Maclaren was a perfectionist and an idealist. Hence he was never satisfied with his own work. Perhaps that is how the Lord keeps gifted people humble, and Maclaren was both. Maybe there is a warning here for preachers: let God evaluate your ministry, for often when we think we are doing our poorest, we are really doing our best. Woe to the man who becomes satisfied with his ministry.

To Maclaren, preparing messages was hard work. He often said he could never prepare sermons while wearing slippers: he always wore his outdoor boots. Studying was work, and he took it seriously. When you read his sermons, you can quickly tell that they were not "manufactured" between conferences and committee meetings. Maclaren was an expositor; he let the Bible do its own preaching. He studied a passage in the original language, meditated on it, sought its divine truth, and then "opened it up" in such a way that we wonder why we didn't see it before ourselves. No artificial divisions, no forced alliteration, nothing sensational; just divine truth presented so simply that any listener (or reader) could understand and apply it.

If you have not read Maclaren, start with *The Best of Alexander Maclaren,* edited by Gaius Glenn Atkins and published by Harper in 1949. Here are twenty of Maclaren's choice messages, a homiletical "sampler" that will whet your appetite for more. Then get the three-volume series *Sermons Preached in Manchester. Weekday Evening Addresses, The Secret of Power, A Year's Ministry, The Wearied Christ, Triumphant Certainties,* and *The God of the Amen* are other titles to watch for, and there are many more. His greatest literary achievement is the *Expositions of Holy Scripture,* recently republished by Baker Book House.

The standard biographies are: *Alexander Maclaren, D.D.: The Man and His Message* by John Charles Carlile; *Dr. McLaren of Manchester: A Sketch* by his cousin and sister-in-law, E. T. McLaren, who explains the spelling of the last name; and *The Life of Alexander Maclaren* by David Williamson. There is an article on him in *Princes of the Church* by W. Robertson Nicoll.

What was the "secret" of Maclaren's ministry? It could be summarized in two words: devotion and discipline. He was devoted to the Lord, and he walked with the Lord.

"Power for service is second," he told the Baptist World Congress in 1905. "Power for holiness and character is first. . . ." He said to a group of ministers, "The first, second and third requisite for our work is personal godliness; without that, though I have the tongues of men and angels, I am harsh and discordant as sounding brass, monstrous and unmusical as a tinkling cymbal."

He fed on God's Word, not as a book for sermons, but as the source of his spiritual life and power. He meditated long hours and sought to understand the heart and mind of God. When he discovered a truth, he first applied it to himself and then sought the best way to share it with his people. But devotion without discipline can become shallow mysticism, and this pitfall Maclaren avoided. He scheduled his time and saw to it that none of it was wasted. He knew how to enjoy a vacation or an evening of relaxation; but even those times were opportunities for meditation and preparation. He did more by doing less. He knew how to say no. He did not feel obliged to attend every meeting, sit at every table, or grace every platform.

"This one thing I do" characterized his life as it ought to characterize our lives today. We may not have Maclaren's gifts, but certainly we can seek to follow his example.

Bibliography

Carlile, John Charles. *Alexander Maclaren, D.D.: The Man and His Message.* New York: Funk and Wagnalls, 1902.

Maclaren, Alexander. *The Best of Alexander Maclaren.* Edited by Gaius Glenn Atkins. New York: Harper, 1949.

_____. *Expositions of Holy Scripture.* 32 vols. London: Hodder and Stoughton, 1904-1910. Reprinted—17 vols. Grand Rapids: Baker, 1974.

_____. *The God of the Amen.* London: Alexander and Shepheard, 1891.

_____. *The Secret of Power.* London: Snow, 1870.

_____. *Sermons Preached in Manchester.* 3 vols. London: Cambridge, 1865.

_____. *Triumphant Certainties.* London: Christian Commonwealth, 1897.

_____. *The Wearied Christ.* London: Alexander and Shepheard, 1893.

_____. *Week-day Evening Addresses.* London: Macmillan, 1877.

_____. *A Year's Ministry.* New York: Funk and Wagnalls, 1902.

McLaren, E. T. *Dr. McLaren of Manchester: A Sketch.* London: Hodder and Stoughton, 1912.

Nicoll, W. Robertson. *Princes of the Church.* London: Hodder and Stoughton, 1921.

Porritt, Arthur. *The Best I Remember.* London: Cassell, 1922.

Williamson, David. *The Life of Alexander Maclaren.* London: Clarke, 1910.

4

R. W. Dale

(1829-1895)

Whenever John Angell James stepped into the pulpit of the Carr's Lane Congregational Church in Birmingham, England, he silently prayed that God would give him a successor who would carry on the great work of the church. Carr's Lane was one of the most influential churches in Great Britain, and James had been its pastor over fifty years. He had a right to be concerned about his successor! How God provided that man is a remarkable story.

James wrote a religious best seller called *The Anxious Inquirer After Salvation* which sold some 200,000 copies within the first five years of publication. A copy of this book fell into the hands of an assistant schoolteacher in the little village of Andover in Hampshire, and the reading of that book led to the young man's conversion. Robert William Dale was fourteen years old at the time. Ten years later, in 1853, he was installed as copastor of the famous Carr's Lane Church; in 1859, when James died, Dale became the sole pastor. He devoted thirty-six years to that one church. When Dale died in 1895, the church called the famous John Henry Jowett to succeed him, and he remained there until

1911. It was during Jowett's ministry at Carr's Lane that A. T. Pierson made the statement that "Carr's Lane is the finest church in the world."

The transition from James to Dale was not easy, either for the church or for the young successor. James was Calvinistic in his leanings, although he preached the Word of God and not a doctrinal system. "I do not seem to find much about Calvinism in the Bible!" he once told a friend who asked him why he was not preaching more Calvinistic sermons. When Dale began questioning unconditional election, total depravity, and limited atonement, some of the saints were horrified. Were it not for the fact that James privately intervened and told his unhappy leaders to be patient with their associate, Dale probably would have been dismissed. In fact, early in his ministry as copastor, Dale felt he was definitely out of place at Carr's Lane. An opportunity opened in a church in Manchester, and some of Dale's friends urged him to accept the call; but loyal to his senior pastor, Dale laid the matter before James and asked him to make the decision. Without hesitation, James replied, "Stay!" And Dale stayed! Subsequent events would indicate that the decision was a wise one.

R. W. Dale was a perplexing combination of preacher, theologian, politician, and denominational leader. Most pastors are happy to encourage their members to get involved in matters of government while they themselves concentrate on matters spiritual. But Dale's convictions drove him right into the middle of some of England's most explosive political issues. Dale saw no difference between God's working in the church and His working in government. To him there was no separation between the secular and the sacred. God was just as concerned about the government of Birmingham as He was the government of Carr's Lane Church. For this reason, nearly one-third of the 750-page biography written by his son is devoted to matters of British politics. Those of us who have never been initiated into the mysteries of home rule, parliament, and the British educational system will probably read these pages dutifully but not very profitably.

It was as a theologian and a preacher of doctrine that Dale excelled. "I hear you are preaching doctrinal sermons to the congregation at Carr's Lane," an experienced preacher said to Dale one day when they met on the street. "They will not stand it." Dale replied, "They will *have* to stand it." And they did. From these doctrinal sermons came some of the books that helped make Dale a famous man: *The Atonement, Christian Doctrine, The Living Christ and the Four Gospels,* and *Christ and the Future*

Life. His books on the Ten Commandments, Ephesians, and James are familiar to most pastors who read.

There is an interesting story in connection with his book *The Living Christ and the Four Gospels.* Dale was preparing an Easter sermon when the truth of Christ's physical resurrection burst in upon him with compelling power. "Christ is alive!" he said aloud; "He is alive—alive!" He began to walk about the room saying to himself, "Christ is living! Christ is living!" Not only that following Easter Sunday, but for months afterward he exulted in the theme of the resurrected Christ. He even began the practice of having a resurrection hymn sung each Sunday morning, just to remind the people that they were worshiping a living Christ.

Dale wore his hair cut short, but he had a full beard and moustache. Some of the older people in his church were scandalized when the moustache appeared, and some people even wrote letters to the newspapers in protest! They felt it gave him "an air of levity and worldliness." There is no record that anybody was upset over his smoking. "Food and drink he could forego without a pang," wrote his son, "but cut off from tobacco, he was little better than a lost soul."

A dark thread of depression ran through Dale's life, and often he spoke of "the strange, morbid gloominess" that he had to battle, sometimes for weeks at a time. These periods of depression may have had their physical causes, but it is likely that Dale's own personal struggles with doctrine and duty were partly responsible. Once he wrote, "I do not envy those who walk through life with no questionings, no mental struggles." These seasons of depression would come without warning and often leave as suddenly as they came.

One day Dale was in a depressed mood, walking down a Birmingham street, when a poor lady passed him and said, "God bless you, Dr. Dale!" He asked her name, but she refused to give it.

"Never mind my name," she said, "but if you could only know how you have made me feel hundreds of times, and what a happy home you have given me—God bless you!"

As she hurried away she seemed to take the dark cloud with her. Dale said, "The mist broke, the sunlight came, I breathed the free air of the mountains of God." (Church members take note: sincere appreciation is good medicine for faithful pastors.)

Shortly after he became the sole pastor of Carr's Lane, Dale began to have sincere doubts about the traditional Christian doctrines of man's immortality and eternal punishment. When he attempted to preach on judgment, he found the experience "costly." Fifteen years later, in 1874, he publicly committed himself to the doctrine of annihilation, that only those possessing eternal life in Christ would live forever.

When Moody and Sankey came to Birmingham in 1875 for their first revival meeting, Dale threw himself into the effort with enthusiasm. Years later, Dale told G. Campbell Morgan that D. L. Moody was the only preacher that he felt had a right to preach about hell. "I never heard Moody refer to hell without tears in his voice." Many of the clergy in Birmingham were opposed to the Moody meetings, some because of his simple gospel message and others because of his "American methods." More than one preacher published rather severe criticisms, including Archibald Campbell Tait, the archbishop of Canterbury. Dale rose to Moody's defense and published a pamphlet called *The Day of Salvation: A Reply to the Letter of the Archbishop of Canterbury on Mr. Moody and Mr. Sankey.* No doubt Dale and Moody had their disagreements, but this did not keep them from being friends and laboring together to win souls. Dale reported that he received about two hundred new members from the meetings, and he concluded years later that about seventy-five percent of them "stood well."

Now for an interesting sequel to these events. Nine years later Moody returned to Birmingham, and again Dale cooperated with the meetings. But Dale thought he detected a change in the evangelist and in the converts. Moody's emphasis in 1875 had been the free grace of God, but now his emphasis seemed to be repentance "as though it were a doing of penance." Dale wrote that Moody was "just as earnest, as vigourous, as impressive as before. People were deeply moved. Hundreds went into the inquiry room every night. But the results, as far as I can learn, have been inconsiderable. . . . I have seen none of the shining faces that used to come to me after his former visit." Dale did the Christian thing and wrote to Moody, sharing his convictions; and the evangelist replied that Dale's letter had "set him a-thinking." Whether Moody's preaching or whether Dale's doctrinal vantage-point had changed, we do not know.

Whether or not you agree with Dale's theology, you must admit that it was a living reality to him and not a dead abstraction. What he believed, he sought to live, no matter what the cost. If his beliefs led him to the lecture platform to oppose the state church, or into the political arena to fight for better education, he willingly obeyed.

In 1877 Dale was invited to give the Yale Lectures on preaching, and there is every indication that he was quite a success. His series is published under the prosaic title *Nine Lectures on Preaching*. It is not an exciting book, but it is a helpful one. When he returned home, Dale tried to persuade Charles H. Spurgeon and Alexander Maclaren to accept the invitation to lecture at Yale, but both refused. Spurgeon's reply to the invitation was, "I sit on my own gate and whistle my own tunes and am quite content."

Dale was a man who loved the city, and the city of Birmingham in his day was hardly the Garden of Eden. Dale could have pastored a comfortable church in a quiet town, but he chose to minister in the city. This he felt was God's calling. While on a European holiday in 1863 he wrote to his wife: "The Lake of Lucerne . . . is before me—the noblest scenery, as some think, in all Europe; but I declare that there is nothing in this magnificent view which makes me feel half the thrill I have sometimes felt when I have looked down on the smoky streets of Birmingham from the railway, as I have returned to my work among you after a holiday. The thought of having to do, more or less directly, with all that mass of human thought and action, which is covered with the ceaseless smoke which hangs over us—the thought that you and I together may, with God's help, save multitudes—sends the blood through one's veins with an exultation and glow which the most magnificent aspects of the material universe cannot create." In this day when our great cities desperately need a steady evangelical witness, this kind of excitement is heartening. May his tribe increase!

In June 1893 Campbell Morgan began his ministry at the Westminster Road Congregational Church in Birmingham, England; a month later he visited Dr. and Mrs. Dale in their home. Since he was not a graduate of a recognized college or seminary, Morgan was concerned about his "inadequate qualifications" as a pastor in the great city of Birmingham. He shared his concern with Dale, and Dale solved the problem immediately. "Never say that you are untrained! God has many ways of training men. I pray that you will have much joy in His service."

Two years later, on 13 March 1895, Dr. R. W. Dale died, bringing to a close thirty-six years of ministry at Carr's Lane. An unfinished sermon lay on his study desk. The last sentence read: "—that, after our mortal years are spent, there is a larger, fuller, richer life in—." The sentence was broken, but the life was completed.

The biography of Dale written by his son, Sir A. W. W. Dale, was published in 1898 by Hodder and Stoughton in London. Be prepared to wade through 750 pages of material, some of which—particularly the sections dealing with British politics—is painfully dull. But Principal A. M. Fairbairn's appendix on "Dale as a Theologian" is probably the best analysis of Dale's doctrinal position you will find anywhere. I especially like the sentence "He ceased to be a Calvinist without becoming an Arminian."

Regardless of his theological classification, R. W. Dale is a man worth knowing, especially in this day when there is a tendency for us to divorce theology from ethics and from the practical ministries of the church. As Fairbairn put it, "It is not simply the heart, it is the whole man that makes the theologian." Perhaps we need this kind of wholeness today.

Bibliography

Dale, A. W. W. *The Life of R. W. Dale.* London: Hodder and Stoughton, 1898.

Dale, R. W. *The Atonement.* London: Hodder and Stoughton, 1875.

_____. *Christ and the Future Life.* London: Hodder and Stoughton, 1895.

_____. *Christian Doctrine.* New York: Armstrong, 1895.

_____. *The Living Christ and the Four Gospels.* New York: Armstrong, 1890.

_____. *Nine Lectures on Preaching.* New York: Barnes, 1878. Reprinted—New York: Doran, 1900(?).

5

Joseph Parker

(1830-1902)

If some homiletically inclined archangel were to permit me to select another time and place in which to live, I immediately would ask to be transported to Great Britain during the reign of Queen Victoria. What a paradise for preachers! On any given Lord's Day you could heard Charles H. Spurgeon at the Metropolitan Tabernacle or, at the other end of the spectrum, Canon Henry Liddon at St. Paul's. Pick the right year and D. L. Moody might be in London or any one of a dozen other cities in Great Britain; F. B. Meyer would be leading people into a closer walk with Christ; William Booth would be thundering against the sins of the city; and Alexander Maclaren in Manchester, R. W. Dale in Birmingham, and Alexander Whyte in Edinburgh each would be opening the Word to crowded congregations. But if I were in London on a Lord's Day and had already heard Spurgeon preach, I would hasten to the City Temple and there sit at the feet of Joseph Parker, whose congregations were second in size only to those of Spurgeon. That saintly friend of great preachers, W. Robertson Nicoll, said of Parker, "I have never heard him

preach without saying, 'I want to be a better man.' " The popular
evangelist John McNeill called Parker "Matthew Henry up to
date—the Gladstone of the pulpit." Without benefit of formal
training, this son of a Northumbrian stonemason ministered the
Word of God in power over fifty years, and his ministry continues
today in the books that he has left us.

Joseph Parker was born on 9 April 1830 at Hexham-on-Tyne,
Northumberland, and spent the first twenty-two years of his life in
that town. While just a lad, he was led to faith in Christ by his
father and his Sunday school teacher while the three of them were
walking home from church one summer Sunday night. He soon
began to teach a Sunday school class and to study the Bible
diligently. In fact, he used to get up at 6 A.M. each morning in
order to have time for reading, and he met with a local minister
who tutored him in Greek. One June afternoon in 1848, he
preached his first sermon. He stood at the sawpit on the village
green and (as he described it) "broke like a sudden thunderstorm
on that rural calm with the text: 'It shall be more tolerable for
Tyre and Sidon at the judgment, than for you' (Luke 10:14)."
The assembled saints had already heard two speakers, but Parker
was sure God wanted him to preach; so he borrowed a New Testament from the second speaker, opened his mouth, and preached!
"In accompanying my friends to the place of meeting," he wrote
that same year, "the idea of preaching did not occur to my mind. I
went out a hearer; I came back a preacher."[1]

In 1851 he married Ann Nesbitt, and the next year he went to
London as an assistant to John Campbell at Whitefield's Tabernacle. Campbell recognized Parker's gifts just as readily as he did
his limitations and determined to assist the young man in his
desire to preach the gospel. Nearly half a century later, Joseph
Parker would lay the cornerstone for the new Whitefield's Tabernacle, and he would be known as one of the preaching giants of his
day.

He remained at the tabernacle until 8 November 1853 when he
became pastor of the Banbury Congregational Church in Oxford-
shire. The place was run down, but before long it was throbbing
with activity and a new and larger sanctuary had to be built.
During his five years at Banbury, Parker took courses at the University College in London and also managed to publish four books
that met with moderate success. He also had seven invitations to
other churches, none of which he accepted. "All the Banbury days

---

1. *Studies in Texts,* 1:vi.

were happy so far as they could be made happy by friendship and love and sympathy," he wrote in *A Preacher's Life* (1899). "A very happy life is the life of a country pastor."

But he was not to remain a country pastor. In July 1858 he accepted a call to the Cavendish Street Congregational Church in Manchester. "I was never more coldly received in my life," he said, describing the first Sunday he preached as a guest minister. He preached two Sundays and then was asked to preach a third Sunday inasmuch as the next man, Samuel Martin of Westminister Chapel, had been forced to cancel. It was a wealthy church, and the coldness of the people in "their Gothic sepulchre" irritated Parker. "Every man seemed to be looking at me over the top of a money-bag!" But the Lord conquered, and Parker accepted the call. That same year Alexander Maclaren came to the Union Baptist Chapel in Manchester, and the two men were to become close friends. In 1862 Parker was granted an honorary doctor of divinity degree by the University of Chicago. He published four more books during his eleven years in Manchester and shared in the wider work of the Congregational Union.

"It never entered my mind that I could leave Manchester," he wrote. "What could any man desire more than some two thousand regular hearers, one of the finest buildings in Nonconformity, and one of the greatest cities in the country!" But on 22 October 1867 a deputation from the Poultry Chapel in London met with Parker and asked him to come and rescue their work. The church had an illustrious past. It had been founded in 1640 by that eminent divine Thomas Goodwin, meeting first in Anchor-Lane, Thames Street. It moved four times in the next two centuries, finally settling at Poultry in Cheapside. But the area was changing, and the ministry had to find a new location and get a new lease on life.

The church issued a formal call to Parker on 7 November 1867, and on 11 March 1868 he declined the call. But they renewed the call on 25 June, and Parker gave it serious consideration. The Poultry Chapel had been without a pastor for fifteen months, and the situation was desperate. Parker was very happy with his Manchester ministry and had no earthly reason to make a change. But there was a divine reason: the Head of the church wanted him to minister in London. On 19 September 1869 Joseph Parker began thirty-three phenomenal years as pastor of the City Temple. He preached for three years in the old Poultry Chapel, then sold it and built a new auditorium at the Holborn Viaduct in the City of London (London consists of twenty-eight boroughs, plus the City of London where the Lord Mayor and his council function). On

19 May 1874 the new City Temple was opened with Lindsay Alexander of Edinburgh bringing the message from John 1:16. From that pulpit Parker preached three times a week, twice on Sundays, and at noon every Thursday. His Sunday congregations filled the auditorium, which seated three thousand; and he would address a thousand or more at the noonday service.

What kind of a man was Joseph Parker? His close friend W. Robertson Nicoll warns us: "To estimate aright a personality so great, so complex, and so many-sided as that of Dr. Parker, is a task so difficult that I shrink from attempting it."[2] He then proceeds to give us the finest study on Parker that you will find anywhere!

Some called Parker an egotist. The famous theologian P. T. Forsythe remarked, "At one time I thought Dr. Parker was a good man touched with egotism; I have come to believe that he is an egotist touched with goodness." In his chapter on Parker in *The Best I Remember,* Arthur Porritt commented: "The judgment was harsh; but Dr. Parker always drew the lightning. Men either believed in him implicitly or voted him a poseur and a charlatan."[3]

To begin with, his was a strong personality. He was a law unto himself, and nobody inside or outside his church dared to annul that law. After the stewards took the collection, they handed it over to him. He managed all the financial affairs of the church—and gave an accounting to nobody. When they were designing his new church, the architects asked him what style of building he wanted, and he replied: "Any style! But build me such a church that when Queen Victoria drives into the city she will say, 'Why, what place is that?'—and she will be told, 'That is where Joseph Parker preaches!' "

An egotist? Perhaps not. A dramatist? In every fiber of his being! J. D. Jones put it this way in his delightful autobiography, *Three Score Years and Ten:* "He was boisterous, sometimes perhaps bombastic, but he had drama, he had passion, he had genius, he had great flashes of inspiration which made other preachers seem dull in comparison. When Parker died our greatest preacher passed. We never shall see his like again."[4]

His physical appearance immediately attracted attention. "His massive figure, and his leonine head, with its shaggy locks, would

---

2. *Princes of the Church,* p. 169.

3. P. 66.

4. (London: Hodder and Stoughton, 1940), p. 68.

have attracted attention anywhere," Alexander Gammie wrote in *Preachers I Have Heard.* "The gleaming eyes, the sweeping gestures, the constantly changing inflection of his wonderful voice, at one moment like a roar of thunder and the next soft as a whisper, held any audience spellbound. And there was always the element of the unexpected in what he said and how he said it."[5]

Yet, beneath Parker's rough exterior and dramatic pose was a feeling of inferiority that tortured him. He was not academically trained; he was a shy man who really had few close friends; he had a constant fear that the weather would rob him of his huge congregations; he feared criticism; and he lived in perpetual fear that he would say or do something wrong. He did not believe that people really loved him or appreciated his ministry, and he had to be told over and over again that his congregation's affections for him were real and lasting.

He lived for his wife, his preaching, and his writing, and nothing else really mattered. Perhaps Parker himself has given us the best picture of the man. When a smaller congregation invited him to become their pastor, he replied: "An eagle does not roost in a sparrow's nest!" That is what he was—an ecclesiastical eagle, living in solitude in the heights, surveying God's revelation, and descending to deliver his oracles. But is there anything wrong with eagles?

In 1889 A. C. Dixon was in London for the International Sunday School Convention, and he visited the notable churches. He sent this impression back home: "Joseph Parker, at the City Temple, is said by some to be the personification of pomposity. He did not so impress us. He has a stately manner, but his thoughts are stately. Both of the sermons we heard were thoroughly evangelical, and Christ was held forth with a pathos and a power that melted many hearts. We thanked God for Joseph Parker. The one criticism that we could make is that he puts too much condensed thought into one sermon. It made my head ache to follow him for one hour."[6] That criticism is not heard much today!

Joseph Parker was first and foremost a preacher, and he held the highest possible views of preaching. On Sunday evening, 28 September 1884, Parker announced to his congregation that he was planning to preach straight through the Bible and have the sermons stenographically recorded and then published in a twenty-

---

5. P. 40.

6. Helen C. A. Dixon, *A. C. Dixon: A Romance of Preaching* (New York: Putnam, 1931), pp. 106-7.

five–volume set to be called *The People's Bible* (not *The Speaker's Bible,* as stated in *20 Centuries of Great Preaching;*[7] *The Speaker's Bible* was edited by James and Edward Hastings). For the next seven years, three times a week he preached in this manner, with his publishers regularly issuing new volumes of the sermons. In May 1895 Parker wrote the final paragraphs for volume 25, completing what he considered to be his lifework. This set ought to be in the library of every serious preacher of the Word. It was recently reprinted by Baker Book House under the title *Preaching Through the Bible.*

This is a remarkable series of sermons. His stenographer—and one of his biographers—Albert Dawson, tells us that Parker did not like to read what he had preached, so it was left to his secretary to read the proofs. The prayers and sermons in *The People's Bible* are exactly what Parker spoke from his pulpit. "The language is the language of the moment," he wrote in that final volume.[8] "Every man can best follow his own method. I have followed mine." You will find as much spiritual food in Parker's prayers as in his sermons, so be sure to read them. In fact, reading a prayer daily, or a prayer at the beginning of each Lord's Day, might be a profitable exercise for the pastor.

How was he able to accomplish so much? He tells us in a chapter entitled "Retrospective" in *Studies in Texts:* "I have lived for my work. That is all. If I had talked all the week, I could not have preached on Sunday. That is all. If I had attended committee meetings, immersed myself in politics and undertaken the general care of the Empire, my strength would have been consumed. That is all. Mystery there is none. I have made my preaching work my delight, the very festival of my soul. That is all. Young brother, go thou and do likewise, and God bless thee!"[9] Parker was in his study every morning at 7:30. He would read the newspapers and answer correspondence and then devote himself to his studies or to writing. He would then take a long walk, usually on Hampstead Heath, during which he meditated on his texts, often talking to himself. He would put a few notes on paper and preach from that outline. Early in his ministry he wrote his sermons in full, but he later abandoned that practice. "When I stand up to preach," he

---

7. Clyde E. Fant, Jr., and William M. Pinson, eds., *20 Centuries of Great Preaching,* 13 vols. (Waco, Tex.: Word, 1971), 5:244.

8. P. 449.

9. 1:viii-lx.

confessed, "I hardly ever know the sentence I am going to utter. The subject itself I endeavor to know well."

His concern for young pastors led him to establish The Institute of Homiletics, which met Monday mornings at the City Temple, Parker presiding. Some of his Institute addresses, and evaluations of sermons, are found in the helpful set *Studies in Texts,* originally published in six volumes but recently reissued by Baker Book House in three volumes. While not as valuable as *The People's Bible,* the set is still a treasury of homiletical gems that the hard-working preacher can mine for himself. Most of Parker's other books (he wrote at least forty) have passed off the scene; but no matter. The valuable books that he left behind will establish him as one of history's greatest preachers.

As he grew older, Parker was concerned about the future of the City Temple. After all, "What can the man do that cometh after the king?" (Eccles. 2:12). It seems that Parker himself was confused: he told J. H. Jowett that he wanted him to be his successor, and apparently the City Temple officers agreed with this; but Parker also laid hands on R. J. Campbell, the popular pastor of Union Church in Brighton. Parker knew Campbell and felt the young man would carry on the kind of ministry to which Parker had given his life. But Parker was wrong.

Parker died on 28 November 1902, and Campbell was called. For the first two years Campbell's ministry was exciting and successful; but then Campbell began preaching his "new theology," and the bullets began to fly. (One theologian compared Campbell's "new theology" to a bad photograph—under-developed and over-exposed!) Along with his liberal views of the Bible, Campbell had socialistic convictions that did not impress his congregation, and ultimately he had to leave the church. In 1916 he was ordained in the Church of England, an act that would have stunned Parker. For when Parker had stood in the pulpit reading his wife's burial certificate, he burst into tears when he got to the part about her being buried in "unconsecrated ground." Parker had said during his ministry, "Should a time ever come when any message other than the pure Gospel of Christ should go forth from this pulpit, let 'Ichabod' be written across the portals!" During Campbell's ministry, some brave soul did actually paint "Ichabod" in living color against the grey stone facade of the church!

"In my judgment," wrote Parker seven years before he died, "the only preaching that can do profound and lasting good must be biblical. . . . Any pulpit that founds itself on personal invention, cleverness, ingenuity, audacity or affected originality will most surely cover itself with humiliation and pass into merited oblivion." In his autobiography, *A Preacher's Life,* he wrote, "I believe in the permanence of the institution of preaching." For this reason, today's preachers would do well to read Joseph Parker and get acquainted with preaching that not only meets the needs of the times but stands above the times because it is founded on the Word of God.

Bibliography

Gammie, Alexander. *Preachers I Have Heard.* London: Pickering and Inglis, 1945.

Nicoll, W. Robertson. *Princes of the Church.* London: Hodder and Stoughton, 1921.

Parker, Joseph. *The People's Bible.* 25 vols. London: Hazell and Watson, 1886ff. Reprinted—*Preaching Through the Bible.* 14 vols. Grand Rapids: Baker, 1971.

_____. *A Preacher's Life.* London: Hodder and Stoughton, 1899.

_____. *Studies in Texts.* 6 vols. New York: Funk and Wagnalls, 1898-1900. Reprinted—3 vols. Grand Rapids: Baker, 1973.

Porritt, Arthur. *The Best I Remember.* London: Cassell, 1922.

6

J. Hudson Taylor

(1832-1905)

A Presbyterian moderator in a Melbourne, Australia, church used all his eloquence to introduce the visiting missionary speaker, finally presenting him to the congregation as "our illustrious guest." He was not prepared for James Hudson Taylor's first sentence: "Dear friends, I am the little servant of an illustrious Master."

Nearly twenty years before, Hudson Taylor had written in an editorial: "All God's giants have been weak men, who did great things for God because they reckoned on His being with them." As he looked at himself, Hudson Taylor saw nothing but weakness; but as generations of Christians have studied Taylor's life, they have become acquainted with a man who dared to believe the Word of God and, by faith, carried the gospel to inland China—and saw God work wonders! "Want of trust is at the root of almost all our sins and all our weaknesses," he wrote in that same editorial, "and how shall we escape it but by looking to Him and observing His faithfulness. The man who holds God's faithfulness will not be fool-hardy or reckless, but he will be ready for every emergency."

How Hudson Taylor became a man of faith is a story that every Christian—and every Christian worker in particular—ought to know well; because in that story is the kind of spiritual encouragement that we need in these difficult days.

Begin by reading *Hudson Taylor's Spiritual Secret,* written by his son and daughter-in-law, Howard and Mary Taylor. It is available in several editions in paperback, although a cloth edition may still be available from the China Inland Mission, now known as the Overseas Missionary Fellowship. You may want to read the book twice—it is not long or difficult—and then secure the one-volume biography of Taylor by the same authors. The China Inland Mission published a beautiful centennial edition in 1965, but it is difficult to secure now. Fortunately, Moody Press has reprinted it in paperback with the title *God's Man in China.* This one-volume biography is a careful abridgement of a definitive two-volume work—*Hudson Taylor in Early Years* and *Hudson Taylor and the China Inland Mission.* The first volume is subtitled *The Growth of a Soul,* and the second, *The Growth of a Work of God.* If I were teaching a pastoral theology course in a seminary, I would require my students to read these two books to discover how God builds a man and then uses the man to build a work. It is unfortunate that this set is now out of print. The abridgement gives us all the important material we need, but the larger work includes sidelights and details that delight the reader who is interested in living history.

James Hudson Taylor was born on 21 May 1832, in Barnsley, Yorkshire, England. Taylor's parents were godly people who had dedicated their first-born to the Lord, for their heart's desire was that their son serve Christ. Even while still a child of four or five, Hudson Taylor showed a concern for the "heathen" in foreign lands. "When I am a man," he would tell visitors in the home, "I mean to be a missionary and go to China." His father was a chemist (American translation: druggist) by trade and was very active as a Methodist preacher in his district. Often the local pastors would gather at the Taylor table to discuss their work, and young Hudson would listen with keen interest. "I used to love to hear them talk," he recalled years later. "Theology, sermons, politics, the Lord's work at home and abroad, all were discussed with so much earnestness and intelligence. It made a great impression upon us as children."

He had just turned seventeen when he was converted, and a short time later he felt a call to Christian service. He had experienced most of the trials and temptations of youth, and the tuggings of the Holy Spirit on his heart; but for some reason he had resisted the call of God. The story of his conversion has often been told, but it is one that gets more wonderful with each telling. His mother had left him home alone while she visited a friend nearly a hundred miles away. Impressed by the Spirit to pray for her son, she left the table, went to her room, locked the door, and prayed for hours until she sensed in her heart that young Hudson had trusted Christ. Back at home, Hudson had found a tract in his father's library and was reading it primarily for the interesting stories that it might contain. While he was reading, he was struck by the phrase "the finished work of Christ." Immediately the words of Scripture leaped into his mind: "It is finished!" He said to himself, "If the whole work was finished and the whole debt paid, what is there left for me to do?" He fell to his knees and yielded himself to Christ; and when his mother returned home two weeks later, she told him she already knew!

Most people forget that Taylor was trained in medicine, and it was during his student days that he learned to trust God for every need. He realized that he could not leave England for some foreign land if he had not learned to prove God at home. How he trusted God for finances, not only for himself but also for others; how he was miraculously spared after being infected in the dissecting room; and how he grew in his exercise of faith—are all told in the biographies, and what exciting chapters they are! You feel as if you are revisiting the Book of Acts!

At this point Taylor's life takes on special interest for the Christian worker, for it is easy to see that Taylor permitted God to prepare him for the work He was calling him to do. It is for this reason that his biographers have devoted an entire volume of over five hundred pages to the first twenty-eight years of his life, the years of preparation. They say in the introduction to *Hudson Taylor in Early Years:* "At first sight it might appear to some that to devote not less than half of the biography of one who did a great deal of public work, to a description of his preparation for that work, evidences some lack of the sense of due proportion. The authors were fully alive to this aspect of the subject; but as they studied and pondered over the materials at their disposal, it was impressed upon them, with growing force, that the experience and the career of Mr. Taylor furnished a notable illustration of the truth that when God raises up a man for special service He first works in that man the principles which later on are, through his labors and influence, to be the means of widespread blessing to the Church and to the world."

We need this emphasis today. We have too many "celebrities" and not enough servants—"nine-day wonders" that may flash across the scene for a time and then disappear. Before God works *through* a man, He works *in* a man, because the work that we do is the outgrowth of the life that we live. Jesus spent thirty years preparing for three years of ministry! The statement may have become a cliche, but it is still true that "God prepares us for what He is preparing for us."

On 19 September 1853 Hudson Taylor sailed for China as a representative of the Chinese Evangelization Society; and even on the ship he had opportunity to witness for Christ and to trust God for miracles. At one stage of the voyage the ship lost its wind and began to drift toward a dangerous reef. Taylor and three other Christians on board prayed earnestly for God's help, and after a brief time of prayer, Taylor was convinced in his heart that God had answered. He went on deck and suggested to the first officer ("a godless man") that he let down the mainsail and make ready for the wind. The man cursed and refused to act. At that point the corner of the topmost sail began to tremble, and Taylor urged the man to move quickly. Before long, a strong wind began to blow and the ship was on its way!

From the very outset of his ministry in China, Hudson Taylor preferred to work independently. He had no particular denominational connections, yet was friendly with all who professed to know Christ. (His own convictions were Baptist.) He did medical work but was not a doctor; he did pastoral work but was not ordained. His life of discipline and sacrifice distinguished him among the missionaries. This does not mean that he rejected those who worked in the traditional ways. It was just that he preferred an independent ministry that left him free to follow God's leading without consulting the plans of men. It was this kind of devotion to Christ that led him to resign from the Chinese Evangelization Society in June 1857. Eight years later, on 27 June 1865, he officially founded the China Inland Mission.

On 20 January 1858 Hudson Taylor married Maria J. Dyer in China, and their romance is a love story that no fiction writer could concoct! For a detailed account read *Hudson Taylor and Maria* by John Pollock. Pollock claimed that the official biography errs in the order of events relating to Hudson's courting of Miss Dyer, suggesting that the missionary's memory failed him when he told his daughter-in-law the story years later.[1]

1. P. 101.

But the real bombshell in the Pollock book is his claim that in 1869, during the darkest hours of the mission, Hudson Taylor was so discouraged that he was tempted to end his own life! "Maria stood between Hudson and suicide," stated Pollock.[2] I once asked a veteran CIM missionary about this, and he claimed it was probably a misunderstanding. Pollock's source, he added, is "an unpublished note in the Taylor papers." Even if Hudson Taylor *did* express this kind of despair, two things are true: greater men than he have done the same (Moses and Elijah, for example); and he expressed it only *before* he experienced "the exchanged life." In fact, it was the valley experience of the Yanchow riots that prepared the way for his life-changing meeting with Christ.

There is no need for me to retell the story; you have it in *Hudson Taylor's Spiritual Secret.* On Saturday, 4 September 1869, Taylor read in a letter from missionary John McCarthy about the new freedom that had come into McCarthy's life. "Not a striving to have faith," McCarthy wrote, "but a looking off to the Faithful One seems all we need; a resting in the Loved One entirely, for time and for eternity." "As I read," said Taylor, "I saw it all. I looked to Jesus, and when I saw—oh, how joy flowed!" The "theology of the deeper life" is disturbing to some people, and for this reason they avoid it; but for Hudson Taylor "the exchanged life" was as simple and as real as salvation itself. His associates noticed the difference: he had a new power in ministry and a new poise in facing the problems of the mission. "He cast everything on God in a new way, and gave more time to prayer," wrote one colaborer. "Instead of working late at night, he began to go to bed earlier, rising at 5 A.M. to give time to Bible study and prayer. . . ." I cannot urge you enough to read the whole story for yourself and then take it to heart.

One of the by-products of reading Taylor's life is the introduction you receive to so many well-known Christians who in one way or another played a part in his life and ministry.

D. L. Moody was on the platform when, in 1872, Taylor gave the opening address at the "Mildmay" conference for the deeper life.

The Student Volunteer Movement that grew out of Moody's Northfield ministry attracted Taylor tremendously. When he came to America in 1888, Taylor spoke at Northfield and Moody had to arrange extra meetings to allow the students to get the most out of Taylor's ministry. Of course the story of "the Cambridge seven"

2. Pp. 202-3.

had reached North America, and it is possible that the dedication of these young men was one of the seeds that helped to bring the Student Volunteer Movement into fruition. There is little question that Moody's ministry in England assisted the progress of foreign missions in a tremendous way, and the China Inland Mission profited from this.

Moody and Taylor, of course, would disagree on the matter of financing the Lord's work. Both of them believed in prayer and trusting God, but Taylor refrained from asking anybody for support. "When our work becomes a begging work, it dies," said Taylor. Moody, on the other hand, was bold in asking Christians for financial support and raised huge sums for Christian enterprises both in the United States and Great Britain. While he greatly admired men like Hudson Taylor and George Muller, Moody felt that his own ministries operated by faith just as much as did theirs. He also felt that, sincere as they were, their emphasis on "making no appeals" was in itself an appeal. Thank God for the variety of men He uses, and thank God for men who can disagree without being disagreeable!

You also will meet other evangelical notables as you read the life of Hudson Taylor: F. B. Meyer (who was deeply moved by the Cambridge seven); H. Grattan Guinness, the British evangelist and Bible teacher (his daughter Mary Geraldine married Hudson Taylor's son, Howard, and helped him write the biography); Howard Kelly; W. J. Erdman; and many others. I was interested to discover that the founder of the Scandinavian Alliance Mission, Fredrik Franson, was greatly influenced by both Moody and Taylor. Taylor's pamphlet *To Every Creature* stirred this Swedish evangelist to form the China Alliance Mission.

Taylor's principles of ministry may not be agreeable to everybody, but they are certainly worth considering. He is the originator, as far as I know, of the oft-quoted statement "God's work done in God's way will never lack God's supplies."[3] "And what does going into debt really mean?" he asked. "It means that God has not supplied your need. . . . If we can only wait *right up to the time,* God cannot lie, God cannot forget: He is *pledged* to supply all our need."[4] It was also a principle of his to promote *missions* and not simply the work of his mission alone. "We do not need to

---

3. Quoted in Howard Taylor and Mary Taylor, *Hudson Taylor and the China Inland Mission*, p. 42.

4. Ibid., pp. 54-55.

say much about the C.I.M.," he wrote. "Let people see God working, let God be glorified, let believers be made holier, happier,
brought nearer to Him and they will not need to be asked to
help."[5] In this day when too many men and their ministries are
glorified and when some Christian enterprises have been fiscally
irresponsible, perhaps Hudson Taylor's counsel is appropriate. His
word about trials is also needed: "We might be lifted up, perhaps,
or lose spiritual life and power, if success were unaccompanied by
discipline."[6]

After you have become acquainted with James Hudson Taylor
through the books written *about* him, start reading the books
written *by* him. The Moody Colportage series used to carry *Union
and Communion,* Taylor's devotional commentary on the Song of
Solomon (written while he was courting Maria!); and *A Retrospect,* his personal recollections. In 1931 The China Inland Mission
published *Hudson Taylor's Legacy,* a series of devotional messages
taken from Taylor's various articles and editorials originally published in the mission's magazine. This book was edited by Marshall
Broomhall, whose ancestors were a part of the CIM ministry from
the beginning. The book is especially valuable in that it presents,
in his own words, Taylor's basic philosophy of missions and ministry. These three books are worth adding to your library.

One of Taylor's close associates, J. W. Stevenson, wrote of him,
"Oh, his was a life that stood looking into!" I suggest you do more
than "look into" his life. I suggest you get to know Hudson Taylor
intimately; for when you do, if you are open at all to God's truth,
the Holy Spirit will do something fresh and lasting in your heart.
For the Christian seeking faith for troubled times, for the servant
thirsting for fresh power, for the worker longing to know how to
build for God, the life of James Hudson Taylor can point the way
to Christ, who is the final answer to every need.

Taylor died on 3 June 1905 during his last visit to China, and he
was buried in that land whose people he loved so dearly. But
thanks to the printed page, "he being dead yet speaketh."

Bibliography

Pollock, John Charles. *Hudson Taylor and Maria.* New York: McGraw-Hill,
1962.

---

5. Ibid., p. 53.
6. Ibid., p. 461.

Taylor, Howard, and Taylor, Mary. *Hudson Taylor and the China Inland Mission: The Growth of a Work of God.* London: Morgan and Scott, 1918.

_____. *Hudson Taylor in Early Years: The Growth of a Soul.* London: Morgan and Scott, 1911.

_____. *Hudson Taylor's Spiritual Secret.* London: China Inland Mission, 1932. Reprinted—*J. Hudson Taylor: God's Man in China.* Chicago: Moody, 1971.

Taylor, J. Hudson. *Hudson Taylor's Legacy.* Edited by Marshall Broomhall. London: China Inland Mission, 1931.

_____. *A Retrospect.* London: Morgan, 1894.

_____. *Union and Communion.* London: Morgan and Scott, 1894. Reprinted—Minneapolis: Bethany Fellowship, 1971.

7

Charles H. Spurgeon

(1834-1892)

Perhaps one of the highest compliments anyone could pay a preacher would be to say that he preaches like Spurgeon. It would be very difficult to locate many people today who actually heard Charles H. Spurgeon preach (he died on 31 January 1892), but the compliment is valid just the same.

Spurgeon was a wonder in his own day, and he is still a wonder today. When the sermons of other men are covered with dust, Spurgeon's will still be read—and preached! But Spurgeon the man also needs to be discovered by each new generation of preachers and perhaps rediscovered by some of us who first met him years ago. "Sell all that you have . . . and buy Spurgeon!" wrote Helmut Thielicke in his *Encounter with Spurgeon,* and with this counsel we heartily agree.

Charles Haddon Spurgeon was a many-sided individual. You find his name appearing in almost every book that touches upon the religious scene in Victorian England. Just think of the years spanned by his ministry. In the year he was called to New Park

Street Chapel, the Crimean War began. The year he opened the great Metropolitan Tabernacle, the United States Civil War began. While he was ministering, Karl Marx wrote *The Communist Manifesto* and Charles Darwin his *Origin of Species.* He was contemporary with Phillips Brooks, Alexander Whyte, D. L. Moody, F. B. Meyer, Alexander Maclaren, R. W. Dale (whose liberal theology he criticized), and Joseph Parker. To get acquainted with Spurgeon is to become familiar with one of the greatest eras of preaching in the history of the church.

I suggest you begin with *C. H. Spurgeon* by W. Y. Fullerton. Published in 1920, this book has the value of having been written by one who was close to the great preacher. In fact, from 1879 to 1893 Fullerton served as one of Spurgeon's assistants at the tabernacle and often preached when the pastor was away. For several years Fullerton edited Spurgeon's sermons for publication each week and became so imbued with the great preacher's style that it is almost impossible to detect where Spurgeon leaves off and his assistant begins! While Fullerton naturally wrote with great admiration for Spurgeon, this did not prevent Fullerton from gently disagreeing with his hero. It is a delightful book, an informative book, even an inspiring book; it bears reading and rereading. His final paragraph is a masterpiece: "To me he is master and friend. I have neither known nor heard of any other, in my time, so many-sided, so commanding, so simple, so humble, so selfless, so entirely Christ's man. Proudly I stand at the salute!"

Now that you have the broad landscape of Spurgeon before you, you can obtain his autobiography, published by Banner of Truth in two volumes entitled *Spurgeon.* The original autobiography was published serially between 1897 and 1900 and was compiled from his letters and records by his wife and private secretary. These four volumes are not easy to secure, so we are grateful for this new edition. It is not identical to the original autobiography in that some extraneous material has been omitted—primarily sermon outlines, newspaper quotations, and unimportant letters. But in two respects the new edition is superior in that the editors have rearranged some sections to give greater continuity and added helpful footnotes. The beautiful thing about these two large volumes of over one thousand pages is this: you can read a chapter at a sitting and, before you know it, complete the book! They are perfect to keep on your bedside table or near your favorite easy chair. Spurgeon wrote just as he preached—in clear Anglo-Saxon English—and his latest editors have not tried to improve upon his style.

It may shock you to discover that Spurgeon was not only a preacher; he was a fighter! He boldly preached the truth as he saw it in Scripture, and if his sermons hurt some individual or groups, he did not apologize. "Some things are true and some things are false—I regard that as an axiom," he said in one of his famous lectures to his students. "But there are many persons who evidently do not believe it. . . . We have a fixed faith to preach, my brethren, and we are sent forth with a definite message from God." However, he warned his young students, "Don't go about the world with your fist doubled up for fighting, carrying a theological revolver in the leg of your trousers." He practiced what he preached, but when his preaching did lead to controversy, he was not one to retreat. The best study of this aspect of Spurgeon's ministry is *The Forgotten Spurgeon,* written by Iain Murray. In nine carefully documented chapters, the author takes us through Spurgeon's battles over baptismal regeneration, Arminianism, and liberalism in the Baptist Union.

Spurgeon preached no diluted gospel, and when he heard other men preach that way, he heard a call to arms. His first declaration of war came shortly after he began publishing his weekly sermons in 1855. His Calvinistic theology upset some of the brethren: he was not hyper- enough for one group and he was too Calvinistic for another. The controversy raged in the pages of religious publications, with some writers even questioning Spurgeon's conversion! "I am not very easily put down," Spurgeon wrote to a friend. "I go right on and care for no man on God's earth."

The second controversy grew out of the sermon against baptismal regeneration which was preached at the tabernacle on 5 June 1864.[1] His text was Mark 16:15-16. Spurgeon was sure the message would completely destroy the ministry of his printed sermons, but just the opposite occurred. His publishers sold over a quarter of a million copies! Fullerton stated that a "blizzard of pamphlets and sermons" swept down upon the churches as a result of this one message and that Spurgeon seemed to enjoy it!

"I hear you are in hot water," a friend said to him.

"Oh, no," Spurgeon replied. "It is the other fellows who are in hot water. I am the stoker, the man who makes the water boil."

Of course Spurgeon was aiming at something much larger than the doctrine of baptismal regeneration. He was concerned about the growing influence of Romanism in England, and he was bold to say so. This was the Puritan in Spurgeon, fighting for Biblical

---

1. In *The Metropolitan Tabernacle Pulpit,* 10:573ff.

truth and making any sacrifice necessary to defend the doctrines of God's grace.

Spurgeon's third controversy was perhaps the most painful for him because it touched the fellowship of the brethren in the Baptist Union. In 1887 he published, in his *Sword and Trowel* magazine, several articles dealing with growing heresy in the Baptist churches. The first two articles were called "The Down-Grade," and this led to the popular identification of the battle as the "down-grade controversy." "It now becomes a serious question," Spurgeon wrote, "how far those who abide by the faith once delivered to the saints should fraternize with those who have turned aside to another gospel. Christian love has its claims, and divisions are to be shunned as grievous evils; but how far are we justified in being in confederacy with those who are departing from the truth?" On 28 October 1887 (Fullerton said 8 October,[2] but this is an error) Spurgeon withdrew from the Baptist Union. "Fellowship with known and vital error is participation in sin," he wrote in the November *Sword and Trowel.* His decision was final, and it was public; the Baptist Union had to act. What they did and how they did it is beautifully recorded in Murray's book, and it stands (in my opinion) as a sorry indictment of a group of men who should have known better. Fullerton believed that Spurgeon himself should have come to the Baptist Union assembly, but since he had already resigned, this would have been impossible.

Alexander Maclaren was one of four pastors assigned to meet with Spurgeon, but he kept himself completely out of the matter. We wonder why. After Spurgeon's death the Baptist Union put in the entrance to its headquarters building an imposing statue of Spurgeon!

But, let's turn from these disappointing events and consider some other facets of this man's amazing life and ministry. It is well known that Spurgeon smoked, although it must be admitted that many famous British preachers smoked. (I have been told by one who ought to know that Campbell Morgan smoked as many as eight cigars a day! And R. W. Dale said that he could get along without food easier than without his tobacco.) Once Spurgeon was gently reprimanded for his smoking by a Methodist preacher. "If I ever find myself smoking to excess, I promise I shall quit entirely," Spurgeon said.

"What would you call smoking to excess?" the man asked.

"Why, smoking two cigars at the same time!" was the answer.

---

2. *C. H. Spurgeon*, p. 255.

In *Echoes and Memories,* Bramwell Booth's interesting book of reminiscences, the son of the founder of the Salvation Army mentioned Spurgeon's habit of smoking. Scheduled to preach at a Salvation Army meeting, Spurgeon arrived "in a fine carriage, smoking a cigar. His remark that he smoked to the honor and glory of God is one of those oft-quoted sayings which have done infinite harm to the world, putting into the mouth of many a youth not only a poisonous weed but a flippant and irreligious apology."[3]

Strange to say, while Spurgeon saw no harm in tobacco, he did oppose the theater. In fact, it was this (among other things) that precipitated his famous "open-letter" controversy with the famous Joseph Parker, eloquent pastor of the City Temple in London. Parker's congregation was second in size only to Spurgeon's, but his ecclesiastical circle was much wider and much more diversified. Spurgeon had been preaching in London for fifteen years when Parker came to Poultry Chapel (which later became the famous City Temple), and the men were on good terms. They exchanged pulpits and on occasion preached in support of various Christian enterprises in the city. On 23 February 1887 Parker invited Spurgeon to address an interdenominational gathering in defense of "the old evangelical faith." The next day Spurgeon wrote a letter of refusal, kindly pointing out that Parker's own ministry did not consistently defend the faith. The fuse had been lit. Parker immediately wanted to know if there was "aught against thy brother" and, if so, why Spurgeon had not told him sooner. Spurgeon replied, among other things: "The evangelical faith in which you and Mr. Beecher agree is not the faith which I hold; and the view of religion which takes you to the theater is so far off from mine that I cannot commune with you therein." Parker's reply was on a postcard: "Best thanks, and best regards—J. P."

The matter was forgotten until 25 April 1890 when Parker published an open letter to Spurgeon in the influential *British Weekly,* edited by W. Robertson Nicoll. Spurgeon's Pastor's College Conference was in session that week, making Parker's attack that much more devastating. Nicoll himself was a great admirer and defender of Spurgeon, and it is difficult to understand why he published the letter. It said in part: "Let me advise you to widen the circle of which you are the center. You are surrounded by offerers of incense. They flatter your weakness, they laugh at your jokes, they feed you with compliments. My dear Spurgeon,

---

3. P. 34.

you are too big a man for this. Take in more fresh air . . . scatter your ecclesiastical harem. I do not say destroy your circle: I simply say enlarge it. . . ."

Spurgeon ignored the letter and advised his staff and pastor friends to do the same. Parker should have known that Spurgeon's power lay in concentration, not diffusion. He functioned best within his own household of faith, although he was generous to evangelicals in other denominations. "I am quite sure that the best way to promote union is to promote truth," he said in a sermon. "It will not do for us to be all united together by yielding to one another's mistakes." There are men like Parker, Campbell Morgan, and D. L. Moody, who seem to belong to all believers, regardless of denominational affiliation; but there are also men like Spurgeon, Maclaren, and Truett, who helped the evangelical cause best by concentrating on their own denominational ministry. We need both kinds of preachers, and the one should not be quick to condemn the other.

You will want to read *Spurgeon: Heir of the Puritans* by Ernest W. Bacon, the best of the recent biographies; and also *A History of Spurgeon's Tabernacle* by Eric W. Hayden, who pastored the tabernacle for five years beginning in November 1956. The book is published in this country by Pilgrim Publications in Pasadena, Texas, and I urge you to secure it. It contains a wealth of information about the ministry of the tabernacle following Spurgeon's death, and the bibliographies of titles by and about Spurgeon are excellent.

But, above all else, read Spurgeon himself! Get a *complete* edition of his *Lectures to My Students* and read it carefully. Granted, some of the material is antiquated, but so much is relevant to our ministry. "The Minister's Fainting Fits" and "The Need of Decision for the Truth" ought to be required reading for all ministerial students.

I enjoy reading *An All-Round Ministry,* a collection of Spurgeon's presidential addresses to the students and alumni of the Pastor's College. I say "enjoy reading," but I must confess that these messages have more than once driven me to my knees in confession and prayer. Perhaps they will do the same for you.

Spurgeon was a lover of good books, with a library of some twelve thousand volumes, most of which are now housed at William Jewell College in Liberty, Missouri. His views on books are found in the delightful volume *Commenting and Commentaries,* first published in 1876 and reprinted by Banner of Truth in 1969 (the new edition includes a complete index to Spurgeon's sermons). If nothing else, simply enjoy reading his comments, many of which he must have written with a broad smile on his face. Naturally he favors the Puritans; but he had some kind words for writers of other schools—except the dispensationalists.

Of C.H.M.'s *Genesis* he wrote, "Precious and edifying reflections marred by peculiarities." Of *Exodus,* "Not free from Plymouth errors, yet remarkably suggestive." He warned that *Leviticus* "should be read cautiously." By the time he got to *Numbers,* he used both barrels: "Like the other notes of C.H.M., they need filtering. Good as they are, their *Darbyism* gives them an unpleasant and unhealthy savour." His comments about Darby's books are not flattering: "Too mystical for ordinary minds," he wrote about *Practical Reflections on the Psalms.* "If the author would write in plain English his readers would probably discover that there is nothing very valuable in his remarks." Of that other great Brethren writer, William Kelly, Spurgeon wrote: "Mr. Kelly's authoritative style has no weight with us. We do not call these lectures expounding, but confounding." Four decades later, C. I. Scofield would preach often in Spurgeon's pulpit during the pastorate of A. C. Dixon, who, by the way, had resigned from the Moody Church to go to London.

One could go on and on about Spurgeon, citing facts and recalling anecdotes; but this is something you need to experience yourself. Plunge right into his sermons, his autobiography, and his other writings, and revel in the grace of God that was so real to this mighty preacher. Like all of us, Spurgeon had his faults and weaknesses; but he magnified God's grace and glorified God's Son. We cannot all be Spurgeons, but we can all be faithful, as he was, in preaching the gospel of Jesus Christ.

Bibliography

Bacon, Ernest W. *Spurgeon: Heir of the Puritans.* Grand Rapids: Eerdmans, 1968.

Booth, Bramwell. *Echoes and Memories.* New York: Doran, 1925.

Fullerton, W. Y. *C. H. Spurgeon.* London: Williams and Norgate, 1920. Reprinted—Chicago: Moody, 1966.

Hayden, Eric W. *A History of Spurgeon's Tabernacle.* 2nd ed. Pasadena, Tex.: Pilgrim, 1971.

Murray, Iain. *The Forgotten Spurgeon.* 2nd ed. London: Banner of Truth, 1973.

Spurgeon, Charles H. *An All-Round Ministry.* London: Passmore and Alabaster, 1900. Reprinted—Pasadena, Tex.: Pilgrim.

_____. *Autobiography*. Edited by Susannah Spurgeon and Joseph Harrald. 4 vols. London: Passmore and Alabaster, 1897-1900. Reprinted— *Spurgeon*. 2 vols. Edinburgh: Banner of Truth, 1962-1973.

_____. *Commenting and Commentaries*. London: Passmore and Alabaster, 1876. Reprinted—London: Banner of Truth, 1969.

_____. *Lectures to My Students*. 3 vols. London: Passmore and Alabaster, 1875-1894. Reprinted—1 vol. London: Marshall, Morgan, and Scott, 1954.

_____. *The Metropolitan Tabernacle Pulpit*. 56 vols. London: Passmore and Alabaster, 1863ff. Reprinted—Pasadena, Tex.: Pilgrim.

Thielicke, Helmut. *Encounter with Spurgeon*. Philadelphia: Fortress, 1963. Reprinted—Grand Rapids: Baker, 1975.

8

Phillips Brooks

(1835-1893)

The year 1877 was a memorable one for Phillips Brooks, well-known rector of Trinity Episcopal Church in Boston. On 9 February a new church edifice was consecrated, five years after the old structure had burned down ("She burned majestically," Brooks wrote to a friend; "she died in dignity"). During the Lenten season Brooks participated in D. L. Moody's meetings in Boston at the six-thousand–seat tabernacle. One night, when Brooks led in prayer, Moody introduced him as "Phillip Brook" and shocked the proper Bostonians. On another occasion Brooks filled in for the evangelist and delivered a stirring sermon from Acts 26:17. But the event of 1877 that excited Brooks most was the privilege of delivering the annual Yale Lectures on preaching. His was the sixth in the series, but he was the fourth lecturer since Henry Ward Beecher had given the first three series. Phillips Brooks was forty-two years old and at the height of his ministry, exercising a powerful influence not only in America but also in Europe. Published as *Lectures on Preaching,* this series ranks with the finest homiletical literature ever produced by any preacher of any denomination.

Subsequent Yale lecturers have quoted Brooks and Beecher more than any other men, and since Beecher had three opportunities to deliver the lectures, this puts Brooks at the head of the list!

Brooks had been preaching for twenty years when he delivered the lectures. He was born on 13 December 1835, "the consummate flower of nine generations of cultured Puritan stock." (That was the opinion of Lewis O. Brastow, professor of practical theology at Yale at the turn of the century. His book, *Representative Modern Preachers,* is worth studying.) After graduating from the Boston Latin School at the age of sixteen, Brooks entered Harvard and graduated in 1855, thirteenth in a class of sixty-six. He returned to the Latin School to teach and, as long as he taught younger children, did quite well. But when he was given older pupils, he began to have discipline problems and the headmaster "released" him. This was a blow to the young man, and for nearly nine months he suffered, living under a cloud of defeat and discouragement. ("I have never known any man who fails in teaching to succeed in anything else," the headmaster had told him!)

He then talked with the president of Harvard and the pastor of his family's church, and both of them suggested he enter the ministry. Interestingly enough, the pastor, Dr. Vinton, told Brooks that conversion was a prerequisite to confirmation and the ministry—and Brooks confessed that he did not know what conversion is! The end result was entrance into the Episcopal Theological Seminary in Alexandria, Virginia, and three years of study. The faculty at that time was weak, so Brooks invested much of his time in wide reading. After graduation in 1859, he began his ministry at the Church of the Advent in Philadelphia, remaining almost three years. From 1861 to 1867 he pastored the Church of the Holy Trinity in that same city and then in 1869 began his phenomenal ministry at historic Trinity Church in Boston. He remained there for twenty-two years, resigning in 1891 when he was elected bishop. His untimely death on 23 January 1893 caught Boston by surprise and silenced a powerful voice.

Brooks never married; he was married to his pulpit. He was a big man—six feet, four inches tall—and at one time weighed nearly three hundred pounds. (The Harvard students who served as pallbearers at his funeral practiced by carrying a heavy casket with three hundred pounds of metal in it. In spite of this, one of the young men fell into the grave when the casket was lowered!) He walked rapidly, ate rapidly, and loved to drive fast horses. He was fond of antique furniture, books (especially biography), travel (his church sent him to Europe and once he sailed as far as Japan), sweets, and iced drinks. His cup of coffee began as a cup of sugar, then the coffee was poured in! In spite of his mother's pleas, Brooks continued to smoke; his ideal vacation was made up of "plenty of books and time and tobacco."

During his ministry Brooks published five volumes of sermons, and five more were published in the years following his death. They are often seen in used-book stores and, if the prices are not too high, they should be purchased. I suggest, however, that you read first the thirty-one sermons collected by William Scarlett and published in 1949 by E. P. Dutton under the title *Phillips Brooks: Selected Sermons.* This volume contains the best of Brooks's preaching, including his two famous sermons "The Candle of the Lord" and "The Fire and the Calf." If while reading these sermons you take a liking to Brooks, you can obtain the other volumes. Please do not expect expository sermons or messages vibrant with obvious evangelical doctrine and evangelistic warmth! Brooks considered himself evangelical and perhaps in some ways he was, but even in his own day his theology was suspect. The day he was consecrated bishop of Massachusetts, the procession into the church was delayed to allow two bishops to read a letter of protest! Of the fifty-two dioceses in the state, fifteen voted against him. Some of the furor was over his baptism: he had been baptized by a Unitarian and had refused to submit to the Episcopal rite. The brutal attacks in the religious press often kept him awake at night.

Basically, Brooks was a Christian humanist. He emphasized Christ's incarnation, not His death and atonement for sin. He felt that all men are children of God and that, once told this good news, their lives will change. He preached that all men are naturally religious and only need God's grace to reach their fulfillment in God. Yet, strange to say, the most moving of his Yale lectures is the last one, "The Value of the Human Soul." "If we could see how precious the human soul is as Christ saw it, our ministry would approach the effectiveness of Christ's," he stated. He then described the effects of "a concern for souls" on a man's ministry. He closed by saying: "May the souls of men always be more precious to you as you come always nearer to Christ and see them more perfectly as He does. I can ask no better blessing on your ministry than that."

His ministry attracted and helped people from all levels of society, and even some ardent evangelicals appreciated his work. On 3 December 1879 a pastor in Garrettsville, Ohio, wrote Brooks: "I would like here to acknowledge the debt I owe you for inspiration in my individual religious experience and in my public work. . . . Give us other works still." That pastor was R. A. Torrey, who later became president of Moody Bible Institute. One reason for this wide attraction, I think, is that Brooks did not deal with specifics. He preached on timeless themes and loved to use abstract words like *truth, goodness, humanity,* and (his favorite) *sympathy.* In fact he himself admitted to a pastor friend: "When I am interesting I am vague; when I am definite I am dull." The pastor who expounds the Scriptures or who explains a text finds it necessary to be specific—but this does not mean he has to be dull!

Phillips Brooks is an interesting man who (in spite of his bachelorhood) led an interesting life. If you wish to learn more about him, read the official biography by Alexander V. G. Allen. Avoid the original two-volume edition of 1900 and get the one-volume abridgement published in 1907. The book is as big as the man—nearly seven hundred pages of biography and of extracts from his many letters. If you do not feel up to that much reading, locate *Focus on Infinity* by Raymond W. Albright, published in 1961. This book is as scholarly as Allen's massive work, and it has the added advantage of the perspective of time. (For some reason, each book has an interesting typographical error. Allen wrote about "D. S. Moody" and Albright about "Charles W. Spurgeon"!)

Now for Brooks's *Lectures on Preaching,* a book every preacher ought to read once a year for five years, and then once every other year for the rest of his life. What makes these lectures so valuable is that they deal with basic principles, not with transient methods. The preacher who is looking for shortcuts will not find them here!

In the first lecture Brooks defined *preaching* as the communication of divine truth through human personality. The divine truth never changes, but the human personality does. This explains why two preachers can take the same text and develop two different sermons, or why the same preacher can preach often from the same Scripture passage and always discover something fresh. "The truth must come really through the person," said Brooks, "not merely over his lips, not merely into his understanding and out through his pen. It must come through his character, his affections, his whole intellectual and moral being." This means, of course, that the preparation for the ministry "is nothing less than the making of the man." The preacher of truth must be a man open to truth—*all* truth, no matter where it is found, because truth can come only from God. In his lectures on "The Influence of Jesus," Brooks described "the man of truth" as "a man into all whose life the truth has been pressed till he is full of it, till he has been given to it, and it has been given to him, he being always the complete being whose unity is in that total of moral, intellectual and spiritual life which makes what we call character." This leaves out in the cold the "busy preacher" who dives into his books for an outline or illustration, or, worse yet, who depends on "preachers' helps" for his messages week by week. It is not enough to write a sermon, said Brooks; we must have *a message,* "a message which we cannot transmit until it has entered into our own experience, and we can give our own testimony of its spiritual power."

The second lecture discusses "The Preacher Himself" and answers the question "What sort of man may be a minister?" God uses different kinds of men because each man's experience helps to interpret the truths of the Bible. But let each man be open to truth. Brooks abhorred narrow-minded bigotry that prevents a man from confronting truth from many sources. He emphasized too the importance of contact with humanity. "No man preaches well," he stated, "who has not a strong and deep appreciation of humanity." He advised us to "find the human side of every truth, the point at which every speculation touches humanity." He had some wise warnings in this lecture against some "dangers in the ministry."

"The Preacher in His Work" is the theme of the third lecture. "The powers of the pastor's success are truth and sympathy together. 'Speaking the truth in love' is the golden text. . . ." He emphasized the balance between *preaching* and *pastoring,* an emphasis sorely needed today. "The preacher needs to be pastor that he may preach to real men. The pastor must be preacher that he may keep the dignity of his work alive. The preacher who is not a pastor grows remote. The pastor who is not a preacher grows petty." He called for manliness in the ministry and deplored "the absence of the heroic element" in the churches.

Lectures 4 and 5 are on "The Idea of the Sermon" and "The Making of the Sermon," and they show how Brooks applied his philosophy of preaching to the practical problems of the work. "We hear a good deal about preaching over people's heads," he commented. "There is such a thing. But generally it is not the character of the ammunition, but the fault of the aim, that makes the missing shot." While Brooks did not have too good a word for expository preaching, he did say a great deal about the making of a message that will help even the most experienced preacher. I especially appreciate his reminder that no sermon should be considered alone. We are ministering to people week after week, and one message fortifies another. The harvest is not the end of the meeting; it is the end of the age.

"The Congregation" is the theme of the sixth lecture; and, as you might expect, Brooks discussed the different kinds of hearers that attend church. He saw four: the "pillars of the church," the skeptical, the habitual, and the sincere seekers after truth. I like the "three rules" that he gave early in the lecture: "First, have as few congregations as you can. Second, know your congregation as thoroughly as you can. Third, know your congregation so largely and deeply that in knowing it you shall know humanity."

If you are tired of hearing the words *relevant* and *contemporary*, then the seventh lecture, on "The Ministry of Our Age," will do you good. Listen to Brooks: "The man who belongs to the world but not to his time grows abstract and vague, and lays no strong grasp upon men's lives and the present causes of their actions. The man who belongs to his time but not to the world grows thin and superficial. . . . Truth and timeliness together make the full preacher." The era he was discussing was in many ways different from our era, but in many ways it was similar, simply because human nature is the same. He discussed several classes of people that exist in every age—the critics, the people who accept everything science says, the frightened—and he showed how the gospel meets their needs. As he ended this seventh lecture, Brooks said: "I must not close without begging you not to be ashamed or afraid of the age you live in, and least of all to talk of it in a tone of weak despair." It seems that every age has always been the worst and that every preacher has looked back and longed for "the good old days!"

I have already commented on the eighth lecture, "The Value of the Human Soul." It is this concept that empowers the ministry. "Without this power preaching is almost sure to become either a struggle of ambition or a burden of routine. With it, preaching is an ever fresh delight." He then explained the effects in a man's ministry of this supreme motivation: the doctrines of the faith become more meaningful; there is joy in seeing lives changed; there is a permanence to our ministry; and the preacher himself grows in courage and grace. "Go and try to save a soul and you will see how well it is worth saving, how capable it is of the most complete salvation. Not by pondering upon it, nor by talking of it, but by serving it you learn its preciousness."

After you have read *Lectures on Preaching*—and Baker Book House has an inexpensive paperback edition—look for a copy of Phillips Brooks's *Essays and Addresses,* edited by his brother John.

There is much that is good in this collection, but the most valuable piece is a lecture he delivered at the Yale Divinity School on 28 February 1878, one year after he gave the Yale Lectures. The address is entitled "The Teaching of Religion," and it ought to be included in all future editions of Brooks's *Lectures on Preaching.* In it Brooks comes to grips with the question, How can we communicate spiritual truth to men today? If his *Lectures on Preaching* is the dinner, then this address is the dessert! This address gave Brooks the opportunity to clarify and expand several of the important ideas in the original lectures, and for this reason it is important to the preacher who has benefited from that great series.

Permit me to close with a few quotations from Brooks that may help to whet your appetite:

"If your ministry is to be good for anything, it must be *your* ministry, and not a feeble echo of another man's."

"Let a man be a true preacher, really uttering the truth through his own personality, and it is strange how men will gather to listen to him."

"Fasten yourself to the center of your ministry, not to some point on its circumference."

"This surely is a good rule: whenever you see a fault in any other man, or any other church, look for it in yourself and in your own church."

"Let us rejoice with one another that in a world where there are a great many good and happy things for men to do, God has given us the best and happiest, and made us preachers of His Truth."

Amen and Amen!

Bibliography

Albright, Raymond W. *Focus on Infinity: A Life of Phillips Brooks.* New York: Macmillan, 1961.

Allen, Alexander V. G. *Life and Letters of Phillips Brooks.* 2 vols. New York: Dutton, 1900.

_____. *Phillips Brooks, 1835-1893: Memories of His Life.* New York: Dutton, 1907.

Brastow, Lewis O. *Representative Modern Preachers.* London: Hodder and Stoughton, 1904. Reprinted—Plainview, N.Y.: Books for Libraries, 1975.

Brooks, Phillips. *Essays and Addresses.* Edited by John Cotton Brooks. New York: Dutton, 1894.

_____. *Lectures on Preaching.* New York: Dutton, 1877. Reprinted—Grand Rapids: Baker, 1969.

_____. *Selected Sermons.* Edited by William Scarlett. New York: Dutton, 1949.

9

Alexander Whyte

(1836-1921)

When some future artist paints a series depicting great scenes in church history, I hope he includes a moving scene from an October day in Edinburgh in 1873. The great preacher and principal of New College, Robert S. Candlish, was dying. He summoned two men to his bedside: Robert Rainy and Alexander Whyte. Whyte told the story: "I had no sooner entered the room than the dying man put out his hand to me and said: 'Good-bye. I had hoped to be spared to help you a little longer'—he was always my helper, the humble soul [Whyte was Candlish's assistant at Free St. George's Church]—'but it is not to be. Good-bye.' And then he motioned to Dr. Rainy to kneel at his bedside. He threw his withered arms around Rainy's neck and kissed him and said: 'I leave the congregation to Whyte and I leave the New College and the Assembly to you.' It was a scene never to be forgotten. And it was a dedication and a sanctification to have seen it and shared in it."[1]

---

1. Quoted in G. F. Barbour, *The Life of Alexander Whyte*, pp. 160-61.

And so the mantle fell on Whyte, still in his thirties, to fill the pulpit of Edinburgh's leading church and one of Scotland's most important places of ministry. And he filled it—for over forty years Alexander Whyte preached solid Biblical messages that magnified the grace of God. "Never think of giving up preaching!" he wrote a Methodist pastor who had sought his counsel. "The angels around the throne envy you your great work!" Whyte's pulpit was his throne, and though he has laid down his scepter, his power is still felt wherever men read his sermons.

Whyte was born out of wedlock into great poverty on 13 January 1836 in Kirriemuir. His father, John Whyte, offered to marry Janet Thompson, but she refused. Whyte left town soon after Alexander was born, established a business in the United States, and became a useful citizen. He fought in the Civil War at the first battle of Bull Run, was captured, and spent many days in a Confederate prison camp. He later visited Scotland, met his son— then a student—and apparently established a warm relationship with him. John died in 1871. In the last letter to his son he had written: "Pray that all my former sins are forgiven and that I shall hereafter trust in Him, the Savior of the world."

Janet Thompson had raised her son in material poverty but spiritual plenty. Even at a young age Whyte had two passions: books and preaching. One day, when he was supposed to be caring for a neighbor's cows, he was dreaming about his future plans and the cows invaded a cornfield. The neighbor came running out, shouting, "I don't know what you're going to do or how in the whole world you'll ever earn an honest living!"

The lad replied, "What would you think if one day I was to wag my head in a pulpit?"

Another day he was trying to help his mother harvest in the fields, and she exclaimed: "Get out of my road, laddie! You may be good at your books, but you'll never make a shearer!"

He *was* good at his books, and his Sunday school teacher, James Kennedy, and two pastors, Daniel Cormick and David White, encouraged him (how soon we forget the men who helped make other men great!). When Whyte was seven years old, Robert Murray McCheyne visited Kirriemuir and gave the boy a tract.

In his early teens Whyte was apprenticed to a shoemaker, but he assured his mother that his final goal was the pulpit. Once when she was particularly discouraged, he said, "Don't cry, Mother; don't be afraid, for I will go and serve out my time—but mind you, I am going to be a minister!" During those difficult early years,

Whyte learned to use his time and discipline his will, achievements that helped make him a success later on.

From 1858 to 1866 Whyte was a student, first in Aberdeen and then in Edinburgh. The going was tough, but the boy was tougher. He sacrificed to purchase books, and he listened to the great preachers of that day. The call of the pulpit became stronger and stronger. During those student years he made several friendships that lasted his whole life. Upon graduation from New College, Edinburgh, he became an assistant at Free St. John's in Glasgow, and here he was ordained on 27 December 1856. He remained there until 1860 when he was called to Free St. George's in Edinburgh to work with the famous Robert S. Candlish (if you have not read Candlish's remarkable exposition of I John, by all means do—prayerfully). This was the beginning of forty-seven remarkable years of ministry in one church, first as assistant and then as pastor.

Above everything else, Whyte was a preacher. Preaching, to him, meant work. "I would have all lazy students drummed out of the college," he said, "and all lazy ministers out of the Assembly. I would have laziness held to be the one unpardonable sin in all our students and in all our ministers." A voracious reader and a diligent student, Whyte did not neglect his pastoral ministry or his family. In 1898, when Whyte was called to be moderator of the Assembly, he exhorted the pastors to concentrate on humility, prayer, and work. "We have plenty of time for all our work did we husband our time and hoard it up aright," he told them. "We cannot look seriously in one another's faces and say it is want of time. It is want of intention. It is want of determination. It is want of method. It is want of motive. It is want of conscience. It is want of heart. It is want of anything and everything but time."[2]

The sales manager of a successful Christian publishing house tells me that pastors are not buying books. "Most of the books sold in Christian bookstores are sold to and read by women," he said. If our pastors are not using their valuable time for study, what are they using it for? Perhaps Whyte had the answer: "We shroud our indolence under the pretext of a difficulty. The truth is, it is lack of real love for our work."

Alexander Whyte loved books, and he read them to his dying day. The Puritans in general and Thomas Goodwin in particular were his main diet. But he also thrived on the mystics and the princes of the Scottish church, such as Samuel Rutherford. Whyte

---

2. Ibid., pp. 284-85.

constantly ordered books for himself and his friends in the ministry. However, he cautioned young pastors against becoming book-buyers instead of book-readers. "Don't hunger for books," he wrote a minister friend. "Get a few of the very best, such as you already have, and read them and your own heart continually. . . ." Whyte often contrasted two kinds of reading—"reading on a sofa and reading with a pencil in hand." He urged students to keep notebooks and to make entries in an interleaved Bible for future reference. "No day without its line" was his motto. He wrote to Hubert Simpson: ". . . for more than forty years, I think I can say, never a week, scarcely a day, has passed, that I have not entered some note or notes into my Bible: and, then, I never read a book without taking notes for preservation one way or another."

In his preaching, Whyte magnified the vileness of sin and the graciousness of Christ. His sermons were (for lack of a better word) surgical. Alexander Gammie reported Whyte's criticism, expressed in conversation with a friend, of Henry Drummond: "The trouble with Hen-a-ry is that he doesna ken [know] onything aboot sin." Whyte certainly knew a thing or two about sin, and he was not afraid to preach what he knew. This was the Puritan in him, and he felt his sermon was not a success if he did not sting the conscience and expose the heart. Let me hasten to add that the preacher was more conscious of his own sins than those of others. In his study of sanctification, *The Pure in Heart,* William Sangster told of an evangelist who came to Edinburgh and criticized the ministers. A friend told Whyte, "The evangelist said last night that Dr. Hood Wilson was not a converted man." Whyte jumped from his chair. "The rascal!" he cried. "Dr. Wilson not a converted man!" Then the friend reported that the evangelist also said that Whyte was not converted. At that, Whyte stopped short, sat down, put his face in his hands, and was silent for a long time. Then he said to the visitor, "Leave me, friend, leave me! I must examine my heart!"

Another story illustrates the effect of Whyte's surgical sermons on his hearers. Two Highland miners, visiting Edinburgh, worshiped at St. George's. Whyte's sermon was one of his typically dramatic exposures of sin, and the two men left the church in deep silence. After a few blocks, one said: "Sandy, yon man must have been a *deevil* when he was a laddie!"

An incident in Whyte's childhood illustrates his theology of conviction. Whyte caught his arm in a threshing machine and everyone thought he would lose it—except a neighbor who was skilled in such matters in a homey way. She would not let them take the boy to the hospital for surgery. But the pain was severe, and Whyte's mother summoned the neighbor again. She looked over the situation and said: "I like the pain. I like the pain." She was right. The arm healed. The pain had been the first step toward recovery. When people complained that Whyte's sermons were too critical, he could well reply, "I like the pain—I like the pain."

Whyte was not only a great preacher and student but also a great pastor. In his *Bunyan Characters* he stated boldly: "For I am as sure as I am of anything connected with a minister's life, that a minister's own soul will prosper largely in the measure that the souls of his people prosper through his pastoral work. No preaching, even if it were as good preaching as the apostle's itself, can be left to make up for the neglect of pastoral visitation. . . ."[3] Even in the dismal winter days people would see Whyte walking the streets of Edinburgh to visit his people. His visits were not long, but they always brought a blessing. He was pastor not only to his people but also to a host of pastors who looked to him for encouragement and counsel.

Alexander Whyte was a great appreciator, almost to a fault. When George Morrison went to Edinburgh to be Whyte's assistant, a friend cautioned him, "Remember, all of Whyte's geese are swans!" Whyte loved nothing more than encouraging someone with a word of appreciation. He constantly sent postcards to friends thanking them for some article they had published or congratulating them for some achievement. Morrison had the same habit; he must have learned it from Whyte. Today, when so much ink is spilled criticizing God's servants, some of us need to start majoring more on encouragement. "Give, and it shall be given unto you."

Whyte was so much of an encourager that he forgot that Christians cannot accept every doctrine men preach, though the men may be fine people. As you read G. F. Barbour's magnificent biography of his uncle, you discover that Whyte was very ecumenical. He was a great admirer of Cardinal Newman (though he certainly disagreed with his theology) and even published an "appreciation" of him, to which he added selections from the cardinal's writings.

When Abdul Baha Abbas, leader of the Bahai movement, came to Edinburgh, Whyte received him warmly into his home and invited friends to come hear him. An action like that could be misinterpreted and could encourage a non-Christian movement.

Martyn Lloyd-Jones has told of a letter written by Whyte in

---

3. 1:263.

which the great preacher praised a book that was very liberal, saying "I wish I had written a book like this myself." We can well understand Whyte's desire to encourage, but surely he had to realize that his endorsement might lead somebody astray.

He defended Robertson Smith before the Assembly when it was likely that Smith's views of inspiration would only undermine the faith. "Fathers and brethren," Whyte cried, "the world of mind does not stand still! And the theological mind will stand still at its peril." True, but the theological mind must still depend on the inspired Word of God for truth and direction. Once we lose that anchor, we drift.

W. Robertson Nicoll stated Whyte's weakness perfectly: "He could not endure controversies with individuals." He would go to almost any length to build bridges, even if he had to build them on sinking sand.

But he was a great preacher and a great soul-winner, in spite of his charitable excesses. When D. L. Moody came to Edinburgh in 1874, Whyte shared in the meetings with great enthusiasm. He often spoke at meetings on behalf of Moody's work and was especially interested in the evangelist's work with the YMCA. When Chapman and Alexander came to Edinburgh in 1914, again Whyte threw himself into the work. A friend asked him how he could spare the time and strength (he was then seventy-eight years old), and Whyte replied, "I simply can't stay away."

Do not put off reading Whyte's sermons. His *Bible Characters* is a must for every preacher's library. How he can make Bible people live! *In Remembrance of Me* contains sermons given during communion seasons at St. George's. Of particular interest are Whyte's final messages, the last sermon he preached at St. George's and the last sermon he prepared but was unable to preach. *Lord, Teach Us to Pray* is probably the finest single book of sermons on prayer by any evangelical preacher. *With Mercy and Judgment* contains some great preaching, as does also *The Nature of Angels.* Baker Book House has published *The Treasury of Alexander Whyte,* edited by Ralph Turnbull. In it is John Kelman's "Memorial Address" on Alexander Whyte, which is certainly worth having. *The Spiritual Life* is Whyte's study of Thomas Goodwin, the Puritan preacher whose works were never out of Whyte's hands. Whyte urged young preachers to find one author who excited and helped them and to master his works. *The Walk, Conversation, and Character of Jesus Christ Our Lord* is a remarkable series of sermons on the life of Christ, flashing the kind of homiletical imagination for which Whyte was famous. He maintained that if a message is to have life and power, "it must be fused by the glow of personal experience and lit up by the flash of imagination."[4]

Alexander Whyte would not want any of us to imitate his style or approach to preaching—except for his study and hard work. When one of his assistants attempted to imitate his style, Whyte simply said, "Deliver your own message." That settled the matter. But I am sure all of us can benefit from Whyte's contribution to sermonic literature by pondering his messages, making them a part of our own spiritual experience, and then translating their truths into daily living and helpful preaching. No man could preach one of Whyte's sermons as his own and get away with it. And no man can read one of his sermons and easily get away from it.

"A congregation is awaiting you," Whyte said to some theological students one day, "to be made by you, after you are made by God." Here is a great preacher's philosophy of pastoral work: God makes a man; the man makes a ministry; the ministry makes a church. It worked in Edinburgh, and it will work today where you and I are ministering in the power of the Spirit.

Barbour's biography, *The Life of Alexander Whyte,* is one of the greatest biographies of an evangelical preacher ever written. It is a massive book of nearly seven hundred pages; and since it was published less than three years after Whyte's death, the author had to work diligently to release it so quickly. The best thing about the book is its emphasis on Whyte's inner life rather than on his activities and achievements alone. But I must warn you that the first three chapters are slow reading—to make it through them you must believe in the perseverence of the saints! After that the book becomes delightfully easy and entertaining—and edifying. I wish every seminary student were required to read chapters 16-18 to learn how this man studied, prepared sermons, and pastored his church.

While reading this biography, I was impressed with the amazing variety and number of friends who were woven into the fabric of Whyte's life. The book's index runs to seventeen pages, and most of it is devoted to the names of people Whyte knew and worked with as a pastor, preacher, denominational leader, author, and friend.

One of these is Dr. Joseph Bell, who, as you may know, was the original Sherlock Holmes. Dr. Bell was Whyte's friend and physician for nearly forty years. He was also a beloved elder at Free St. George's. Dr. Bell taught at the University of Edinburgh, and

---

4. Quoted in Barbour, *Alexander Whyte,* p. 299.

one of his students was a young man named Doyle. In fact, it was Doyle who often ushered in the patients during Dr. Bell's lectures, and the good doctor would proceed to reveal all manner of facts about them without asking them a single question! In his delightful book *The Life of Sir Arthur Conan Doyle,* John Dickson Carr described the amazing doctor as "very lean, with dexterous hands and a shock of dark hair standing up on his head like the bristles of a brush. . . ."[5]

Bell's uncanny faculty for observation enabled him to discern a man's occupation by observing his hands or the peculiar characteristics of his clothes. Diagnosing cases seemed like child's play to him. "The trained eye," he explained it. "A simple matter!" A few years after graduation Doyle used his old professor as the model for the world's most famous detective. "If he needed a model for his detective," wrote Carr, "he need look no further than a lean figure in Edinburgh, with long white dexterous hands and a humorous eye, whose deductions startled patients. . . ."[6] Thus, Sherlock Holmes was born. Even Whyte's biographer mentioned that Bell's "acuteness of observation was so striking that he was commonly believed to have suggested to Sir Arthur Conan Doyle, when a medical student in Edinburgh, the character of Sherlock Holmes."[7]

But the gifted doctor and the celebrated preacher did not always agree. Whyte was usually ready to throw his influence behind any cause that, to him, seemed right; and he also had a weakness for seeing good in projects that others considered dangerous. In 1887 when "the Irish question" was at its stormy height, Whyte found himself endorsing a controversial Irish leader named Dillon by inviting the man to speak to a private group of Presbyterian leaders at Whyte's home. Three weeks later, the pastor received a strong remonstrance signed by thirteen prominent members of the church, including eight elders; one of those elders was Dr. Joseph Bell. Whyte's physician agreed with his colleagues that their pastor was in danger of losing his influence in the pulpit by associating with those who, to the public, represented party politics. The letter cut Whyte deeply, particularly because it was signed by so many who were his friends. But Dr. Bell won his point. Whyte's oldest son, Fred, explained: "He

5. (New York: Harper, 1949), p. 23.

6. Ibid., p. 44.

7. Barbour, *Alexander Whyte,* p. 233.

[Whyte] showed no hesitation in his choice. His calling as a Minister had first claim on him then as always."[8]

In 1892 the church session accepted their pastor's request for an assistant. Dr. Bell had stood with his pastor and urged the officers to secure help as soon as possible. Whyte had been working tirelessly, and the pressures of the ministry were going to break him. For some unknown reason, the much-needed assistant was not called at that time; but we can be sure that Dr. Bell did not allow the matter to rest. Two years later, Dr. Hugh Black was called to Whyte's side.

But hard work took its toll. When he was seventy-three, Whyte accepted the principalship of New College in Edinburgh—in addition to his pastoral duties! The result was a breakdown in health at the end of 1909, a sudden heart attack that gave Dr. Bell cause for concern. He managed to get his illustrious patient through the winter, but a second heart attack followed a year later. Bell had often encouraged Dr. and Mrs. Whyte to take long holidays; once he had sent them to Italy for a much-needed rest. Perhaps it was Bell who inspired Whyte's "advice for a successful ministry": talk to no one after services, and always take long holidays! Alexander Whyte was a great preacher; but let us pause to give thanks to Dr. Joseph Bell, a faithful elder and friend, and a wonderful physician. Perhaps it was Bell's ministry that helped make Whyte the kind of man he was.

So much for doctors and detectives. As you peruse the list of names in the index to *The Life of Alexander Whyte,* you find D. L. Moody mentioned. I was encouraged to learn that it was Rev. John Kelman of Leith, among others, who had first invited Mr. Moody to preach in Edinburgh. Kelman's son, John, would become an assistant to Whyte in 1907 and in 1919 would succeed John Henry Jowett at New York's Fifth Avenue Presbyterian Church. Whyte's illustrious predecessor at Free St. George's, R. S. Candlish, died shortly before the Moody-Sankey meetings started, but he had predicted for Edinburgh "a great blessing which should not be despised though it come strangely." It was in Edinburgh that Sankey composed "The Ninety and Nine."

Whyte threw himself into the revival campaign and as a result saw an exceptionally large communicant's class the next year. He also saw his Tuesday night prayer meeting move from the church hall into the sanctuary itself. It would be interesting to discover

---

8. Quoted in ibid., p. 252.

the spiritual contributions Moody made to the life of that historic church.

I wonder what Alexander Whyte's attitude was toward fellow Presbyterian preacher John Kennedy of Dingwall. Kennedy was an opponent of the Moody-Sankey meetings and did not hesitate to express his opposition publicly. He was "rigidly conservative," said one biographer. He rejected hymns as "human inventions" and permitted only the singing of psalms in his services. He also opposed church organs. (He was not the only Scot who was horrified at Sankey's little organ, his "chest full of whistles." One dear lady in Edinburgh ran out of the meeting, shouting, "Let me oot! Let me oot! What would John Knox think of the like of ye?" She took refuge in the overflow meeting across the street, and when Sankey showed up there to sing, she repeated the same performance!) Known as the "Spurgeon of the Highlands," Kennedy was particularly opposed to Moody's theology, especially the use of the inquiry room. He wrote a strong pamphlet against the evangelist, something Whyte would not have done.

One of Alexander Whyte's best friends died over two hundred years before Whyte was born. I speak of Lancelot Andrewes, whose *Private Devotions* was one of Whyte's favorite books. In fact, Whyte named one of his sons *Lancelot* in honor of the Anglican divine who had lived from 1555 to 1626 (during the tense reign of King James I). It is unfortunate that Andrewes is almost forgotten today. The famous poet T. S. Eliot tried to stir up interest in Andrewes by publishing in 1926 his essay *For Lancelot Andrewes,* but he failed.

Andrewes was a scholar. Even when a student, he used his annual holiday to learn a new language; it was said that he mastered fifteen languages. In 1586 he was made a chaplain to Queen Elizabeth, and in 1601 dean of Westminster. He assisted in the coronation of King James on 25 July 1603 and was present in January 1604 at the Hampton Court Conference, at which the request was made for a new translation of the Bible. Andrewes was one of "fifty-four learned men" appointed to help translate the new Bible, serving as chairman of the group responsible for Genesis through II Kings. (If you wish to read a delightful account of the work of translating the King James Version, secure *The Learned Men* by Gustavus Swift Paine.[9] It may surprise you to discover the strange assortment of men that produced this masterpiece of English literature!)

---

9. New York: Crowell, 1959.

But it was not Lancelot Andrewes the translator that captivated Alexander Whyte; it was Lancelot Andrewes the man of prayer. You will want to secure Whyte's *Lancelot Andrewes and His "Private Devotions,"* one of the series of "Appreciation" volumes written by Whyte, because this is the best introduction to Andrewes. The learned bishop was not a great preacher, although many of his sermons are still available in old volumes. His *Sermons of the Nativity* are available in "The Ancient and Modern Library of Theological Literature," but you will find no exciting messages in these pages. Andrewes preached these seventeen sermons before King James; it was a standard procedure on Christmas Day that the bishop so address the court.

Andrewes was known even in his day as a great man of prayer, spending hours daily in his devotional exercises. Out of this came the book that so captured Whyte—*Private Devotions.* Andrewes did not write these devotions for publication. He gave his copy to his friend William Laud in 1626 (the year of Andrewes's death), and in 1675 Oxford Press published the first English translation (the original devotions had been written in Greek, Hebrew, and Latin). There have been several translations since then, but the book has never, to my knowledge, had wide distribution. After reading Whyte's *Appreciation,* you may want to secure a copy of *Private Devotions.* The best edition is the one edited by F. E. Brightman, published originally in 1903 but reprinted by Meridian Books in 1961. A second edition, edited by Thomas S. Kepler, was issued by World Publishing Company in 1956.

Andrewes's *Devotions* are not brief sermons or "helpful thoughts" based on Scripture. They are expressions of praise, penitence, faith, and intercession taken directly from the Bible and the church fathers. He included prayers for each day of the week, based, for example, on the week of creation described in Genesis 1. He had devotional exercises from Scripture for both the morning and the evening. "There is nothing in the whole range of devotional literature to be set beside Andrewes's incomparable *Devotions,*" wrote Whyte. I am sure that what captured Whyte's interest was Andrewes's emphasis on sin and repentance (Whyte was himself a master of surgical preaching on sin and confession), but perhaps we could use this emphasis today.

Not every believer will be set on fire by Andrewes, and if you are not, do not despair. But if you are, you will have acquired a source of spiritual help that will never fail you because it is grounded in the Word of God. It will take you time to master the bishop's approach. It will take concentration—spiritual concentration—to keep from merely reciting prayers in a routine fashion. But once you have leaped these obstacles, you will discover a new power and satisfaction in your personal devotional exercises. Using the *Private Devotions* will never make you another Alexander Whyte, but it can help to make you a better saint of God.

We have come a long way from Sherlock Holmes to the sainted Bishop Andrewes, and Alexander Whyte has been our guide for all the while. I encourage you to read Barbour's magnificent biography of his uncle. Who knows what interesting people you may meet in its pages, and Whyte himself will be the most interesting one of all!

Whyte died on 6 January 1921, and a few days later Nicoll wrote in the *British Weekly:* "What a gift he was to his Church, to his nation! How wide were the irradiations of faith and love and hope and repentance that came from his intense and prayerful life!"

Bibliography

Barbour, G. F. *The Life of Alexander Whyte.* London: Hodder and Stoughton, 1923.

Whyte, Alexander. *Bible Characters.* 6 vols. Edinburgh: Oliphant, Anderson, and Ferrier, 1898-1902.

_____. *Bunyan Characters.* 4 vols. Edinburgh: Oliphant, Anderson, and Ferrier, 1893-1908.

_____. *In Remembrance of Me.* Grand Rapids: Baker, 1970.

_____. *Lancelot Andrewes and His "Private Devotions."* Edinburgh: Oliphant, Anderson, and Ferrier, 1896.

_____. *Lord, Teach Us to Pray.* New York: Hodder and Stoughton, 1922.

_____. *The Nature of Angels.* London: Hodder and Stoughton, 1930. Reprinted—Grand Rapids: Baker, 1976.

_____. *The Spiritual Life: The Teaching of Thomas Goodwin.* London: Oliphant, 1918.

_____. *The Treasury of Alexander Whyte.* Edited by Ralph Turnbull. London: Oliphant, 1957. Reprinted—Grand Rapids: Baker, 1968.

_____. *The Walk, Conversation, and Character of Jesus Christ Our Lord.* Edinburgh: Oliphant, 1905. Reprinted—Grand Rapids: Baker, 1975.

_____. *With Mercy and Judgment.* London: Hodder and Stoughton, 1924.

10

W. Robertson Nicoll

(1851-1923)

He read an average of two books a day and edited a weekly journal, three monthly magazines, and a steady stream of scholarly books which included *The Expositor's Bible* (fifty volumes) and *The Expositor's Greek New Testament.* He was undoubtedly the most prolific and respected religious journalist in the English-speaking world from 1886 to his death in 1923. Not only was he the "unofficial literary agent" for such men as Marcus Dods, George Adam Smith, A. B. Bruce, and Alexander Maclaren (he persuaded Maclaren to publish his expositions), but he managed to write over forty books of his own, and compile, edit, or supervise the publication of over 250 more titles. Yet when he was knighted in 1909, William Robertson Nicoll wrote: "I had never contemplated a literary career. I had expected to go on as a minister, doing literary work in leisure times, but my fate was sealed for me. . . ."

His fate was "sealed" by ill health. Born at Lumsden, Aberdeenshire, on 10 October 1851, a son of the manse, Nicoll never was a "sturdy laddie." His father was a bookworm who preferred to pastor a small flock of about a hundred people and spend the rest of his time in his library. In spite of a meager income, the Rev. Harry Nicoll acquired a library of seventeen thousand volumes, probably the largest library belonging to any pastor in Scotland. In his charming little book *My Father,* Robertson Nicoll described this library and how his father used it.

Robertson's mother died when he was only eight years old. They called it "consumption" in those days, and it usually lingered with the family. Nicoll's weak lungs were to plague him for the rest of his life, ultimately (and providentially) taking him from behind the pulpit into the editor's chair. He often preached, but he could never have preached full time.

He graduated from Aberdeen University in 1870 and from the Free Church Divinity Hall in 1874. He was licensed to preach in 1872. From 1874 to 1877 he ministered at the Free Church in Dufftown, and from 1877 to 1885 at the Free Church in Kelso. Those were interesting years in Scotland: D. L. Moody was ministering there with great power; the Free Church was being torn asunder by Robertson Smith and his higher critical views; and new theological ideas were drifting over from the Continent.

Nicoll began his literary career while a student at the Divinity Hall. There were three weekly newspapers in Aberdeen at that time, and Nicoll was on the staff of the *Journal,* contributing reviews and literary notes and writing a weekly column, "Things in General." Reading and writing: these would be the hinges on which his long and influential life would turn. The long winter months in Scotland would make him a "prisoner" in his own house. "One had the absolution of the snow for any failure to discharge pastoral duties," he said. "I always look back with pleasure to my three months each winter there, when I was a prisoner alone with my cat and my books."

A year after he was inducted at Kelso, he married and settled down to the life of a pastor and a literary man. In 1884 he was made editor of *The Expositor,* a monthly theological journal published by Hodder and Stoughton and edited from its inception in 1875 by the famous Hebraist Samuel Cox (his volume *An Expositor's Note-Book* is worth adding to your library). Life was smiling upon the gifted young pastor, and then seeming tragedy struck. In 1885 Nicoll's younger brother died of tuberculosis, and while on a holiday in Norway, Nicoll himself was infected with typhoid and became dangerously ill. No sooner did he start to regain his health when pleurisy set in, and for a time it looked as though Nicoll would succumb to the same disease that had taken his mother, sister, and younger brother. The best doctors in Edinburgh agreed that he would have to resign the church, give up preaching for two or three years, and concentrate on regaining his health.

Nicoll and his wife went to the south of England, near Torquay. He continued his editing and admitted that he did not miss preaching—"I feel so unequal to it." What did he miss? "I feel rather lonely and depressed here away from my books." In 1886 the Nicolls moved to the Upper Norwood section of London and became neighbors to Charles Haddon Spurgeon. All his life, Nicoll admired and defended Spurgeon. This relationship began in 1874 when Nicoll was the "summer pastor" of a little church at Rayne, about twenty-five miles from Aberdeen. He discovered a complete set of Spurgeon's sermons and read it through! Soon after Spurgeon's death, Nicoll wrote a strong letter to Marcus Dods and reproached him for some unkind things he had written about the great preacher. "Your paragraph about Spurgeon really vexed me," he wrote, "and it is the only thing you have ever said, or written, or done, that did vex me or that I thought not worthy of your magnanimity." Then Nicoll confessed: "Every Sunday night I spend at least an hour reading him, and there is no devotional writing pleases me so well."

The key date in Nicoll's life is 5 November 1886, for it was on that date that the first issue of the *British Weekly* appeared, published by Hodder and Stoughton. It was intended to be a "high-class weekly journal for the advocacy of social and religious progress," and it lived up to its purpose. Nicoll was so sure the journal would succeed that he agreed to work for nothing until the profits started coming in; it was not long before the paper began to flourish and take its place as the leading nonconformist journal in Britain. Nicoll also had the genius for discovering and developing new writers. The by-lines in the *British Weekly* read like a *Who's Who* of literature: Marcus Dods, a regular contributor from the very beginning; James M. Barrie; R. W. Dale; Joseph Parker; Henry Drummond; and a host of other "worthies."

Not content with a weekly journal to edit (his deadlines must have been frightening!), Nicoll launched, on 1 October 1891, a monthly literary magazine called *The Bookman.* The entire first edition of ten thousand copies was sold within a few days, and it was followed by two additional printings! Two years later he started another monthly magazine, *The Woman at Home.* He was now editing the *British Weekly* and three monthly publications, *The Expositor, The Bookman,* and *The Woman at Home.*

However, it is not as a magazine editor that Robertson Nicoll touches the lives of Bible students and pastors today. It is as the author and editor of theological books, some of which are classics. It was the year after the *British Weekly* was born that Nicoll began to publish *The Expositor's Bible,* a work that is somewhat outdated today but still valuable to the serious student. The series was released in fifty volumes between 1888 and 1905. I believe that Alexander Maclaren's *Colossians* was the first volume released, and George Adam Smith's commentary on the minor prophets the last.

Evidently Nicoll was as hard on his writers as he was on himself, and some of them protested. His good friend Marcus Dods wrote, "Pharaoh might have taken lessons from you!" And Maclaren wrote, "I hope that *you* are not having any holiday this autumn! It would be some alleviation to think of you as stewing in Paternoster Row." But the editor had his problems, too. When he received the manuscript for George Adam Smith's *Isaiah* (for *The Expositor's Bible*), Nicoll wrote Marcus Dods: "I am wrestling with George Adam Smith's *Isaiah:* he has chopped up the prophet terribly."

Oddly enough, Nicoll did much of his work while in bed! His close friend and biographer, T. H. Darlow, wrote: "It was weird to watch him as he lay there, amid a medley of newspapers and books and pipes and cigarette ashes, and to know that his brain was busy absorbing knowledge and incubating ideas all the time." He kept a fire in his study almost all the year and claimed that fresh air was an invention of the devil! He had almost no interest in music or art, and unlike the traditional Scotsman, was not excited by sports. Why waste on games, time that could be invested profitably in books? His books and his cats and his publications were his life.

Like most extensive sets written by many writers, *The Expositor's Bible* is quite uneven in quality. Kellogg on Leviticus is a classic, as are Maclaren's three volumes on the Psalms and his exposition of Colossians. Unless you are wealthy and have a lot of empty shelves, do not purchase the fifty volumes separately. The entire set is available in a six-volume edition with large, double-column pages. I believe that this edition was originally published by Eerdmans. It may be out of print, but used sets are often available. *The Expositor's Greek New Testament* (also reprinted by Eerdmans) is still in print and is still considered a standard work for the careful student of the Greek New Testament, although some students prefer Dean Henry Alford's *Greek Testament,* published by Moody Press.

One of my favorite sets, edited by Nicoll, is one that is usually forgotten or is dismissed as unimportant. It is *The Sermon Bible,* published originally in twelve volumes and containing nearly five thousand outlines and precis of sermons actually delivered by famous preachers in the last half of the nineteenth century. It was republished by Baker Book House as *The Sermon-Outline Bible* and comprises the first six volumes of a fourteen-volume series called "The Preacher's Homiletic Library." I highly recommend this set, particularly to the pastor who is not too tired (or lazy) to dig again the homiletical wells of the past. (The other eight volumes of the set are *Homiletic Studies in the Gospels* by Harold F. J. Ellingsen, a rich mine of sermonic suggestion, and *Proclaiming the New Testament,* a book-by-book, chapter-by-chapter homiletic survey of the New Testament, edited by Ralph Turnbull.) This set gives the student the best of the old and the best of the new.

It may be that you have no interest in old sermons. If so, then *The Sermon-Outline Bible* will bore you. But before you consign it to the antique shop, let me suggest that you consider some of the men represented in these volumes: Joseph Parker, Henry Alford, Alexander Maclaren, Marcus Dods, Phillips Brooks, Adolph Saphir, R. W. Dale, Henry Ward Beecher, John Henry Newman, William Taylor, James Stalker, and J. J. Stuart Perowne, to name a few. Many of these men have written learned commentaries that are still available, but their sermons are difficult to come by. I do not know of any one set that offers so much historic material in such a convenient form.

But better still, the set contains sermons by relatively unknown preachers whose works are even less accessible today. For example, there are a number of sermons from Henry Melville, whom Spurgeon called "the Demosthenes of London." Coming from Spurgeon, that is quite a tribute! Henry Scott Holland is also represented in these pages. In his day (1847-1918) he was recognized as one of the leaders in applying the Christian faith to the needs of the common man. I was amazed to find dozens of sermons from Samuel Martin who pastored Westminster Chapel, London, from 1841 to 1878. Under his leadership the present church building was erected. (Interestingly enough, Samuel Martin was an architect before entering the ministry; yet the design of the Westminster Chapel does not seem to reflect it. When Jowett pastored there, he said he felt as if he were preaching in the

Charing Cross railway station. Martyn Lloyd-Jones has stated that the building helped to hasten the death of more than one pastor who preached there week after week.) Martin's sermons are probably available nowhere else today. Also represented in *The Sermon-Outline Bible* are Samuel Cox, Nicoll's predecessor at *The Expositor;* John Ker, who was George Morrison's favorite preacher; Horatius Bonar; Handley C. G. Moule; James Stalker; J. Oswald Dykes; and F. D. Maurice, who greatly influenced Phillips Brooks. These are not sermons that you will preach—their style and approach are not contemporary—but they are sermons you should read and study.

One of my favorite Nicoll books is *Princes of the Church,* a collection of thirty-four biographical essays on "notable figures in the Christian world." Spurgeon is here ("He has fallen like a tower, and his removal means for many a change in the whole landscape of life"), but so also are Henry Drummond, Robertson Smith, R. W. Dale, the great Roman Catholic preacher Cardinal Vaughan, George Matheson, Silvester Horne, Andrew Bonar, and Bishop Westcott. His essay on "The Centenary of Frederick Robertson" is one of the most perceptive I have ever read on this fascinating preacher from Brighton.

Nicoll's library contained twenty-five thousand volumes, including five thousand biographies! "I have for years read every biography I could lay my hands on, and not one has failed to teach me something," he wrote. His own biography, *William Robertson Nicoll: Life and Letters,* was written by Darlow and published in this country by the George H. Doran Company in 1925. Nicoll's long-time associate at the *British Weekly,* Jane T. Stoddart, wrote a brief biography, *W. Robertson Nicoll, LL.D., Editor and Preacher.* In a very real sense Nicoll was the father of modern religious journalism, but he was also a strong churchman and preacher. He died on 4 May 1923, and among his last words were "I believe everything that I have written about immortality!"

If you are a lover of good books and good men—and every pastor should be—then get acquainted with W. Robertson Nicoll and the rich literary heritage he has left us.

Bibliography

Darlow, T. H. *William Robertson Nicoll: Life and Letters.* London: Hodder and Stoughton, 1925.

Nicoll, W. Robertson, ed. *The Expositor's Bible.* 50 vols. London: Hodder and Stoughton, 1888-1905. Reprinted—6 vols. Grand Rapids: Eerdmans, 1943.

_____, ed. *The Expositor's Greek New Testament.* 5 vols. London: Hodder and Stoughton, 1897-1910. Reprinted—Grand Rapids: Eerdmans, 1956.

_____. *My Father.* London: Hodder and Stoughton, 1908.

_____. *Princes of the Church.* London: Hodder and Stoughton, 1921.

_____, ed. *The Sermon Bible.* 12 vols. London: Hodder and Stoughton, 1888-1893. Reprinted—*The Sermon-Outline Bible.* 6 vols. Grand Rapids: Baker, 1972.

Stoddart, Jane T. *W. Robertson Nicoll, LL.D., Editor and Preacher.* London: Partridge, 1903.

11

Charles E. Jefferson

(1860-1937)

"A shepherd cannot shine," wrote Charles E. Jefferson in his book *The Minister as Shepherd*. "He cannot cut a figure. His work must be done in obscurity. . . . His work calls for continuous self-effacement. It is a form of service which eats up a man's life. It makes a man old before his time. Every good shepherd lays down his life for the sheep." All of us know that *pastor* is the Latin word for "shepherd." The pastor of the local church is supposed to be a shepherd; but, alas, too often he is not. He may be a good preacher—and preaching is definitely important to pastoral work—and he may be a good organizer; but if he is not maintaining a personal interest in the flock, he is not fulfilling his divine calling. "It is the weaklings and not the giants, who neglect their people," Jefferson wrote. "It is the Pagan and not the Christian who shines in public and leaves undone the private duties which belong to him as an ordained steward of the Son of God."

The Minister as Shepherd has recently been reprinted by the Christian Literature Crusade in the series "Living Books for All," and I heartily recommend the book to you. It is one of four valuable books by Jefferson directed especially to the pastor, the other three being *The Minister as Prophet, Quiet Hints to Growing Preachers,* and his Yale lectures, *The Building of the Church.* The first two titles you will have to find in the used-book stores. His Yale lectures are available in a Baker Book House edition of 1969. I urge you to add these four volumes to your library, and I suggest you read and reread them; Jefferson's philosophy of the ministry is desperately needed today.

Charles E. Jefferson was born in 1860 and died in 1937. He started out not as a pastor but as a superintendent of schools in Worthington, Ohio. He also taught at Ohio Wesleyan and Ohio State. In 1884 he entered the Boston University Law School, and it was while he was in Boston that the challenge of the gospel ministry took hold of his heart. As he visited various churches, he became thoroughly disgusted with the preaching that he heard. Then he heard Phillips Brooks at Trinity Church, and everything changed. He enrolled in the theological course at Boston University and graduated in 1887. After brief pastorates in New Hampshire and Massachusetts, he accepted a call to the 34th-Street Tabernacle in Manhattan, where he was to labor for almost forty years. The tabernacle had a noble history; William M. Taylor was pastor there for twenty years (1871-1892). If you do not have Taylor's sermons on Christ's miracles and parables, by all means get them! And while you are looking, secure his great biographical series on Moses, Joseph, Ruth, Esther, David, Paul, and other Bible greats. What preaching!

When Jefferson accepted the call, he knew God was placing him into a difficult situation. After seven years the church relocated and built a new edifice at the corner of Broadway and 56th Street, changing its name to the Broadway Tabernacle Congregational Church. At that time, Broadway was known as "the great white way," and it was to this kind of à constituency that Jefferson ministered for almost forty years. Though the church was in one of the most difficult parts of the city, he managed to fill the building week after week and to minister, with great power and blessing, to a "needy parade." He witnessed the exodus of more than one church from the downtown area, yet he remained. What an example for us to follow!

He had a pastor's heart, and the combination of preacher-pastor was what made him an effective minister in that difficult downtown location. He believed in the local church, in *building* the church to the glory of God, and not simply *using* it as a tool to build his own career. "It is sad to see a man turning away from the ministry because he does not understand the church," Jefferson wrote in his Yale lectures, "but it is tragic to see one entering the ministry with a wrong attitude to the church. Young ministers sometimes look upon the church as a necessary evil, an inherited incumbrance, a sort of device by which preachers are handicapped in their movements and held back from largest usefulness. . . . They want to do things on a broad scale. To deal with so small and insignificant a body as a church seems parochial and belittling."[1] This is why he titled his lectures *The Building of the Church,* taking the "architectural idea" in the New Testament and applying it to the preaching of the Word and the pastoring of the people. "The crowning and crucial work of a minister is not conversion, but church building."[2]

His first lecture deals with "the church building concept in the New Testament." What does this have to do with preaching? "The sermon," said Jefferson, "comes not out of the preacher alone, but out of the church. . . . He is nourished by his environment— the family of Christ."[3] What a tremendous concept for the growing pastor to grasp! "The church is a growing organism and the preacher must know the stages of its development before he can feed it."[4] "A physician always looks at his patient before he goes to the medicine chest. A wise preacher begins, not with his books, but with his church."[5]

Recently a seminary president complained to me that some of his school's finest graduates "were not making it" in their churches. "Do you know what one of our boys did?" he asked. "He hadn't been in his first church three months before he started to revise the constitution! He didn't stay long." It is too bad that graduate had not read *The Building of the Church,* especially this passage: "Here again the preacher must begin by establishing right relations between himself and his church. . . . If a man has a contemptuous view of his church he is well-nigh certain to be afraid of it. But love casts out fear. If a man loves his church and proves his love by his life, he can say to it anything which is proper for a Christian teacher to say to his pupils, anything which is fitting for a Christian man to say to his friends. The preachers who get into

---

1. *The Building of the Church,* p. 11.
2. Ibid., p. 19.
3. Ibid., p. 5.
4. Ibid., p. 14.
5. Ibid., p. 15.

trouble by talking plainly to their people are as a rule preachers who do not love their churches."[6]

Of course the ministry of building demands time, and Jefferson pleaded for the longer pastorate. "He [the pastor] is a master-builder, and his task is not simply collecting material, but shaping it into a structure which shall become a shrine of the Eternal. . . . The highest place belongs to the man who, year after year, in the same parish, instructs men in the high and difficult art of living together, and trains them by long and patient processes in the work of bringing spiritual forces to bear upon the moral problems of the community."[7] "No matter how long he stays, there will be more work to do than there was in sight at the beginning. Men who engage in the building of the church know that the work is never done."[8] And yet some pastors are looking for new churches after two years of ministry!

In the remaining seven lectures Jefferson applied the building concept to various aspects of the ministry in the local church: building the brotherhood ("To create an ampler and a warmer fellowship inside the church of Jesus is the first work for which preachers are ordained. . . ."); building the individual ("Many a man is preaching to a dwindling congregation because his sermons have lost the personal note. He chills by his vague generalities, or enrages by his wholesale denunciations");[9] building moods and tempers ("A congregation possesses a disposition as pronounced and characteristic as that of any of its members");[10] building thrones ("The preacher who would make his church a power must begin by trusting common people");[11] building the worldwide church ("Every preacher should do his work in the radiance of the vision of the church universal");[12] building the plan ("It is not a waste of time to give hours and days to the work of pondering and maturing schedules for future operations");[13] and finally, building the builder ("The secret of an extended pastorate is a growing

---

6. Ibid., p. 17.

7. Ibid., p. 19.

8. Ibid., p. 21.

9. Ibid., p. 86.

10. Ibid., p. 119.

11. Ibid., p. 171.

12. Ibid., p. 193.

13. Ibid., p. 235.

man").[14] *The Building of the Church* is easily one of the finest books to come out of the Yale Lecture series, and its message is greatly needed today.

Jefferson's other three books are not quite so massive and detailed. *The Minister as Shepherd* contains five lectures that Jefferson gave in 1912, but they are amazingly contemporary. He began with "The Shepherd Idea in Scripture and History," proving that the shepherd has a key place in the plan of God. "When church leaders began to lose the vision of the Good Shepherd, they at the same time began to drift away from the New Testament ideal of ministerial service."[15] He then covered the shepherd's work, opportunity, temptations, and rewards, and he did so in a manner that convinces you that he himself possessed a shepherd's heart. He pointed out that the Eastern shepherd was a watchman, a guard, a guide, a savior, a provider, and a man who personally loved his sheep. I appreciate the way he explained the relationship between preaching and shepherding, and it is here that the influence of Phillips Brooks is most clearly seen. "The pastoral instinct is nowhere more sorely needed than in the work of preaching," he wrote. "No part of a minister's work is more strictly, genuinely pastoral than the work of preaching."[16]

In *The Minister as Prophet* Jefferson dealt particularly with preaching and the importance of proclaiming the truth of God. I am tempted to quote several passages, but I will settle for one: "A little man with narrow view can cause a world of trouble." I like his emphasis on patience in preaching and the importance he places on building the preacher as much as building the sermon. "I prepare my sermons by preparing myself," he told Edgar De Witt Jones. "Self-preparation is the most difficult work a preacher has to do. . . . A preacher who is spiritually anemic, or intellectually impoverished, or morally depleted, will wish often for a juniper tree."[17]

The fourth book, *Quiet Hints to Growing Preachers,* is somewhat of a pastoral fireside chat, twenty-six chapters on important ministerial matters that somehow have been omitted from the textbooks. "Many a man in the ministry fails, not because he is

14. Ibid., p. 298.

15. *The Minister as Shepherd,* p. 21.

16. Ibid., p. 61.

17. Quoted in Jones, *American Preachers of To-day,* p. 59.

bad, but because he has a genius for blundering."[18] "If a man expects to move men by his preaching he must first do a deal of living, and the sooner he begins to live the better."[19] "No man can long be interesting in the pulpit who does not think. No man can think wisely who does not study."[20] "Probably no other single sin works such havoc in the Christian church as the impatience of her ministers."[21] "Popularity is the most fearful of all tests."[22] This is the kind of book the pastor can keep on his desk and read a chapter a day—all chapters are brief—and remind himself of the things that too easily we forget.

Jefferson wrote not only for pastors but also for the church at large, including a number of books of sermons. His own preaching was doctrinal in emphasis but not theological in content. He used short, crisp sentences and sought to express the truth in the simplest manner. His *Cardinal Ideas of Isaiah* (1925) and *Cardinal Ideas of Jeremiah* (1928) are helpful to the pastor preaching on those books and prophets.

When you read Jefferson's ideas about preaching, you discover that he used several comparisons to make his point. In one place he compared the sermon to something you are cooking! "One never knows what is going to happen when he puts a truth to soak in the juices of the mind."[23] In another place he compared sermons to bullets. "How far they go does not depend upon the text or upon the structure of the sermon, but upon the texture of the manhood of the preacher."[24] But his favorite comparison was that of a sermon to a flower. "My sermons grow. They unfold. I never 'get up' a sermon. . . . A sermon of the right sort gets itself up. If I supply the soil and the seed and the sun and the rain, the sermon will come up of itself. My soul is a flower-garden. My business is raising sermons."[25]

I suppose the most helpful thing Charles E. Jefferson does for me is to remind me of the importance of the local church and the

---

18. *Quiet Hints to Growing Preachers,* p. 7.

19. Ibid., p. 19.

20. Ibid., p. 44.

21. Ibid., p. 59.

22. Ibid., p. 133.

23. *The Building of the Church,* p. 256.

24. Ibid., p. 277.

25. Quoted in Jones, *American Preachers of Today,* p. 60.

work the pastor must do if the church is to grow and glorify God. The pastor is a shepherd, a prophet, a builder. Jefferson himself was all three. Any man who can make a success of a city church in a difficult place is worth reading, and Jefferson is such a man. Get to know him soon!

Bibliography

Jefferson, Charles E. *The Building of the Church.* New York: Macmillan, 1910. Reprinted—Grand Rapids: Baker, 1969.

————. *Cardinal Ideas of Isaiah.* New York: Macmillan, 1925.

————. *Cardinal Ideas of Jeremiah.* New York: Macmillan, 1928.

————. *The Minister as Shepherd.* New York: Crowell, 1912. Reprinted— Grand Rapids: Zondervan, 1933.

————. *The Minister as Shepherd.* New York: Crowell, 1912. Reprinted— Fort Washington, Pa.: Christian Literature Crusade.

————. *Quiet Hints to Growing Preachers.* New York: Crowell, 1901.

Jones, Edgar De Witt. *American Preachers of To-day.* Indianapolis: Bobbs-Merrill, 1933. Reprinted—Freeport, N.Y.: Books for Libraries, 1971.

A. C. Gaebelein

12

A. C. Gaebelein (1861-1945) and
B. H. Carroll (1843-1914)

You could not find two more opposite men than Arno Clemens Gaebelein and Benajah Harvey Carroll. Gaebelein's ministry was, for the most part, an interdenominational one; Carroll was a devoted Southern Baptist and a strong denominational leader. Gaebelein held a dispensational view of Scripture; Carroll did not. Gaebelein was an itinerant Bible teacher; Carroll devoted most of his life to his church and to the seminary he helped to found. Why, then, bring these men together? For two reasons: both were self-made scholars with enviable reputations as teachers of the Word; and both have left behind sets of books dealing with the entire Bible. In Gaebelein's *The Annotated Bible* and Carroll's *An Interpretation of the English Bible* you have two different approaches to Scripture from men who were devoted servants of the Lord and able ministers of His Word.

Gaebelein was a remarkable man. Born in Germany in 1861 (the year Carroll joined the Texas Rangers), he was converted to Christ at the age of twelve and at the age of eighteen dedicated himself for Christian service. This dedication occurred on 31 October (the anniversary of Martin Luther's ninety-five theses), only a few months after he had arrived in America. "I had been reading my New Testament," Gaebelein wrote in his autobiography, *Half a Century,* "when suddenly a strong impulse came upon me to seek His presence and to tell Him that work for Him should be my life's work."

He identified with the German Methodists in Lawrence, Massachusetts, where he was living, and soon he found himself teaching classes and distributing tracts. A friend offered to send him to seminary, but Louis Wallon, the presiding elder of that district, advised against it. Gaebelein's training in Germany, which included Latin and Greek, actually put him ahead of some seminary graduates; and he was a tireless student on his own. Wallon loaned him theological books and encouraged him to study at home. Gaebelein was not critical of formal education, however; in later years he was to help found the Evangelical Theological College (out of which grew the Dallas Theological Seminary), and he delivered lectures at the school annually.

In 1881 he moved to New York City to assist Wallon in a German church. It was there that he was introduced to the premillennial position, but at first he rejected it. Later he became pastor of a German congregation in Baltimore, and there he began his study of Semitic languages. It was his habit to be at his studies at 4 A.M. each morning. He ministered in various German churches, and his knowledge of Hebrew and his love for the Jews gradually brought him into prominence as a missionary to the thousands of Jews pouring into New York City at that time. He had been converted to the premillennial position, and his addresses on prophecy attracted great crowds of both Jews and Gentiles. This ministry finally led to the establishing of the Hope of Israel Mission and a monthly publication in Hebrew for the Jewish people. A year later, in 1894, Gaebelein founded *Our Hope* magazine, one of the finest and most influential of the many publications of that era. He edited it for fifty-one years, until his death in 1945; it then merged with another publication and, unfortunately, ceased to exist. We could use today another Bible study monthly like *Our Hope.*

To read the life of A. C. Gaebelein is to come in contact with some of the great Bible teachers of that exciting era. The Niagara Bible Conference and other great conferences were in full swing during those years, and great crowds of believers gathered to study the Word in key centers across the country. In the pages of *Half a*

Century, you meet James H. Brookes, C. I. Scofield, F. C. Jennings (whose commentary on Isaiah is a classic), Lewis Sperry Chafer, George C. Needham, and a host of other gifted men who tirelessly traveled from city to city to teach the Scriptures. There were giants in the earth in those days.

However great these men might have been, the one man in this autobiography who deserves our appreciation is Samuel Goldstein, a Hebrew Christian who belonged to Gaebelein's congregation in Hoboken, New Jersey. One day Goldstein came into his pastor's library and was surprised to see so many volumes in Hebrew and other Semitic languages. "It is a shame that you do not make greater use of your knowledge," said Goldstein. "You should go and preach the Gospel to the Jews. I believe the Lord made you take up these studies because He wants you to go to my brethren, the Jews." That was the beginning of a remarkable ministry in New York City. Hundreds of Jewish people crowded into halls to hear Gaebelein expound their Old Testament Scriptures, and many found Christ as their Savior. For five years (1894-1899) Gaebelein superintended the Hope of Israel Mission, wrote books and tracts, edited two magazines, and sought to win both Jews and Gentiles to Christ. In 1889, because of denominational problems, he severed his relationship with the German Methodist Conference and embarked on the itinerant ministry that was to make him a tremendous blessing to multiplied thousands of people in the United States, Canada, and Europe. But as great as his public ministry was, it is the treasure of his written ministry that we want to consider.

His first book was *Studies in Zechariah,* and there is an interesting story connected with it. Gaebelein sent a free copy of the book to every rabbi in the New York City area and never received any acknowledgment from any of them. Some time later, however, a young Hebrew Christian began to attend one of Gaebelein's meetings regularly, and it turned out he had been secretary to a well-known rabbi. The rabbi had thrown *Studies in Zechariah* into the wastebasket, but the secretary had rescued it, read it, and trusted Christ! If you do not have Gaebelein's commentaries on John, Acts, and the Psalms in your library, by all means secure them. *The Jewish Question,* on Romans 11, is a classic study of this critical chapter. *The Prophet Daniel* was highly praised by Sir Robert Anderson.

The Annotated Bible was begun in 1912 and completed ten years later. It appeared originally in nine volumes, but you may purchase it today in a beautiful four-volume set published jointly

B. H. Carroll

by Moody and Loizeaux. This work includes an outline of each chapter in the Bible, an introduction to each book, and a discussion of the teachings of the Word. It is not a commentary; it is one man's "interpretation" of the total revelation of Scripture, a unified "overview" of the Word of God.

Since Gaebelein was one of the original consulting editors of *The Scofield Reference Bible,* you can expect these studies to reflect the premillennial, dispensational approach to Scripture. In fact, *The Annotated Bible* is really an expansion of the basic teachings found in the *Scofield Bible,* with very practical applications throughout. However, a student need not agree with the author to benefit from his insights into the Word of God. There is a devotional warmth to Gaebelein's writings that goes beyond any one system of interpretation.

People often asked Gaebelein how he was able to travel and speak so much, edit a magazine, and write so many books. His answer was always the same: "I never wasted time!" When asked why he did not play golf, he replied: "Not because it is wrong, but because I can use my time in a better way." He was a devoted student, a systematic worker, and a dedicated man; and we today are the happy heirs of the treasures God enabled him to mine for us out of the Word of God.

B. H. Carroll was another tireless worker and self-made scholar. He was born on 27 December 1843 in Carroll County, Mississippi, the seventh child in the family of Benajah and Mary Eliza Carroll. When he was seven years old, the family moved to Arkansas, and then in 1858 they relocated in Texas. It was in Texas that Carroll was to have his great ministry. It was B. H. Carroll who helped to "discover" George W. Truett and establish him in a ministry that is recognized today as one of the greatest in American church history (Andrew Blackwood called Truett "the mightiest pastoral evangelist since Charles H. Spurgeon"). It was B. H. Carroll who founded Southwestern Baptist Seminary and whose denominational leadership is remembered by Southern Baptists.

Strange as it seems, Carroll was a dedicated infidel until his conversion in 1865. From the first day he learned to read, Carroll had been a devoted student, reading whatever good books were available in that frontier region. He had an amazing memory and could recall at will material he had read years before, even to the point of giving the page locations! Eventually he was able to read three hundred pages a day without neglecting his regular responsibilities, and he even claimed to be able to read two lines at a time (actually, he was a forerunner of "speed-readers"; he read word groups instead of individual words, and he scanned pages). Even as an unbeliever, he read the Bible through several times, and few men dared to debate with him. He had a great mind and was a gifted orator. He also had a great, strong body; he stood six feet, four inches, and weighed two hundred pounds. His long beard, in later years, reached to his waist and gave him the semblance of an old prophet. One day, while boarding a train, he was asked by a stranger, "Where is your brother?"

"Which brother do you mean?" Carroll asked, since he had several brothers. "My brother Jimmie?"

"No!" said the stranger. "I mean your brother Aaron!"

Carroll enlisted in the Texas Rangers in 1861. Instead of carrying food in his saddlebags, he carried books! The next year, wanting something more exciting, he enlisted in the Texas Infantry and fought in the Civil War. He was seriously wounded at the Battle of Mansfield (Louisiana) and finally had to be sent home.

He was still a fanatical infidel and had even written a book on the subject; he had vowed never to enter a church again. But in 1865 he was persuaded to attend an old-fashioned camp-meeting. The preacher challenged the people to make a "practical, experimental test" of Christianity and to give Jesus Christ a fair trial. When he asked for those to come forward who were willing to make the test, Carroll went. His action amazed and delighted his Christian friends, but he was careful to explain that he was not converted yet; he was simply acknowledging that he would give the Christian faith a fair hearing. While riding home, he got down on his knees in the woods and fought the battle out—and Jesus Christ won. Carroll's life was transformed, and his great gifts were dedicated to Christ. In November 1866 he was ordained to preach, and four years later he was called to the First Baptist Church of Waco, Texas, where he carried on an exciting ministry for twenty-eight years. He was dean of the department of Bible at Baylor until he founded the new seminary and was named its first president.

An Interpretation of the English Bible grew out of Carroll's own teaching and preaching ministry. His lectures and sermons were stenographically recorded, and some of them were written out by Carroll himself. After his death, his assistant at the seminary, J. W. Crowder, was given the responsibility of editing and compiling Carroll's studies, and it is largely because of his persistence and faith that we have this magnificent set of books today. It was originally published in thirteen volumes in 1916 by Fleming H.

Revell, but that edition did not cover the entire Bible. In 1942 Broadman decided to bring out the set and commissioned Crowder to compile Carroll's material on the portions of Scripture not discussed in the first edition. This second edition went to seventeen volumes. It must be noted that J. B. Cranfill assisted in editing some of the volumes in the set. The completed edition was published in 1948. Baker Book House recently gave us a magnificent new edition in six large volumes, a set that ought to be in every pastor's library.

For one man to produce this much material is a feat in itself; and when you consider that Carroll was limited in his formal schooling, the feat becomes even more amazing. "His mind was not a sponge, absorbing the ideas of others, but rather a fertile soil into which every fact and truth dropped, germinated and bore fruit. He was not an assimilator of the information and illustrations of others, but rather a tireless investigator searching out for himself and arranging his material in his own forceful manner." So said George W. McDaniel in a memorial address at Houston on 16 May 1915. He added this word about *An Interpretation of the English Bible:* "As a commentary it is unique. Mark you, I don't rank it first; it is not himself at his best. For the average preacher, however, that commentary is a thesaurus of theology and a gold mine of homiletics." I have examined some of Carroll's other books, and quite frankly I believe that some of his *best* work is in this monumental set.

It is not actually a commentary; it is an "interpretation" on a broad scale. Sometimes Carroll pauses to preach a sermon; he may linger for pages on one verse, or he may skip over entire sections. I am glad the editors have not deleted his "asides," because they are sometimes the most interesting parts of a chapter! When Carroll reminisced about hearing some forgotten Baptist preacher, or when he lifted an experience out of his own exciting life, you find yourself suddenly paying close attention. This man was a giant of the faith, a great preacher, and a man who influenced men in a positive way toward faith in Jesus Christ. He is a man you ought to know.

Some students differ with Carroll's doctrine of the church or his views on prophecy, but these differences should not rob them of the values of this set of Biblical studies (I usually learn more from those I disagree with than from those I agree with!). If a young pastor started reading this set faithfully and read only fifty pages a week, he would complete the set in about two years and would have a knowledge of the Word of God from which he would profit for the rest of his ministry. If you only "consult" these books, you may be disappointed; but if you read them seriously, you will be enriched.

On 7 March 1933 Crowder, who edited all of Carroll's books, discussed Carroll's literary contribution in an address at Southwestern Baptist Seminary. I mention this because in this address Crowder made an interesting statement about D. L. Moody and the Moody Bible Institute. After rebuking another school in Chicago for departing from the faith, Crowder praised the institute for "holding rigidly to the purposes of its founding, having through the years supplemented, magnified, and multiplied the literary productions and spirit of its founder. This has proved to be a great bulwark to the Moody Bible Institute. . . . The tests of scholarship are its final issues, its fruits. It may be a tree of life or a tree of death. Scholarship, or no scholarship, the productions of B. H. Carroll, like the productions of Dwight L. Moody, are a tree of life." After warning the seminary family that their school, like others, could become modernistic, he suggested that Carroll's writings become the foundation, the fortification, against such doctrinal disintegration, even as Moody's writings had fortified the institute.

Carroll died on 11 November 1914, and the next day George W. Truett delivered the funeral message. "The pulpit was his throne," said Truett, "and he occupied it like a king." The king is gone, but some of the treasures of his reign are still with us. I encourage you to mine them; they will enrich your life and ministry.

Bibliography

Carroll, B. H. *An Interpretation of the English Bible.* Edited by J. B. Cranfill. 13 vols. New York: Revell, 1916. Reprinted—6 vols. Grand Rapids: Baker, 1973.

Carroll, J. M., et al. *Dr. B. H. Carroll: The Colossus of Baptist History.* Fort Worth: Crowder, 1946.

Gaebelein, A. C. *The Acts of the Apostles.* New York: Our Hope, 1912. Reprinted—Neptune, N.J.: Loizeaux, 1965.

_____. *The Annotated Bible.* 9 vols. New York: Our Hope, 1913-1924. Reprinted—4 vols. Chicago: Moody, 1970.

_____. *The Book of Psalms.* New York: Our Hope, 1939.

_____. *The Gospel of John.* New York: Our Hope, 1925. Reprinted—Neptune, N.J.: Loizeaux, 1965.

_____. *Half a Century: The Autobiography of a Servant.* New York: Our Hope, 1930.

_____. *The Jewish Question.* New York: Our Hope, 1912.

_____. *The Prophet Daniel.* New York: Our Hope, 1911. Reprinted—Grand Rapids: Kregel, 1955.

_____. *Studies in Zechariah.* New York: Fitch, 1905.

Scofield, C. I., ed. *The Scofield Reference Bible.* New York: Oxford University, 1909.

13

G. Campbell Morgan

(1863-1945)

D. L. Moody had a knack for finding men and helping them channel their gifts into the work of soul winning and building the church. One of his greatest "finds" was George Campbell Morgan—pastor, evangelist, Bible teacher extraordinary—the man who long before his death on 16 May 1945 was known throughout the English-speaking world as the "prince of expositors." Jill Morgan's life of her father-in-law, *A Man of the Word: Life of G. Campbell Morgan* (reprinted in 1972 by Baker Book House) ought to be read by every Christian who is serious about teaching and preaching the Word of God. I try to read it again each year; it always sends me away with a new zest for studying the Bible and sharing it with others.

Morgan's beginnings were as inauspicious as possible. He was born on 9 December 1863 in the little village of Tetbury, England. His father was an independent Baptist minister with Brethren leanings, and he believed in courageous preaching and living by faith. Somewhat frail as a child, Morgan received his early education at home. He had always "played at preaching" as a child, setting up his sister's dolls and preaching to them; so it was not a surprise when, at the age of thirteen, he asked to preach in a public meeting. He gave his first sermon in the Monmouth Methodist Chapel on 27 August 1876, and his theme was "salvation." Nobody in that little assembly that day realized that Campbell Morgan would be one of God's choicest instruments for spreading His Word in the years to come.

The family situation made it necessary for Morgan to find employment early, and he chose to become a teacher, a profession for which he was admirably gifted. But he took every opportunity to preach the Word, and God blessed his ministry. In the beginning he was quite aware of his gifts and was prone to display them. But one night a friend walked home with him from the meeting and gently pointed out his error; from that night on, Morgan preached to express the truth, not to impress the people.

Like many young men at that time, he went through an eclipse of his faith. In desperation, he locked all his books in a cupboard, secured a new Bible, and began to read it. "If it *be* the Word of God, and if I come to it with an unprejudiced and open mind, it will bring assurance to my soul of itself," he said. He canceled all his preaching engagements and devoted himself to the Bible. The result? "That Bible found me!" From that day on, Morgan never indulged in defending the Bible; he permitted the Bible to defend itself.

In 1886 Morgan was well known in his area as a Bible teacher, and he even conducted a follow-up mission for the hundreds who had been reached through Gipsy Smith's campaign in Hull. In his heart he felt a call to the ministry, but he knew he was unschooled. His first inclination was to join the Salvation Army, but both Gipsy Smith and Catherine Booth advised him, "Go on with the work you are doing." Morgan appeared at the Lichfield Road Church in Birmingham on 2 May 1888 to preach a "trial sermon" in consideration for entering the Methodist ministry. He had been accustomed to addressing many hundreds of people in his meetings—the Hull meetings drew two thousand—and on that day, in a church auditorium that seated over one thousand people, he faced an audience of only seventy-five. He failed miserably and was rejected from the Methodist ministry. He wired his father, "Rejected!" His father wired back: "Rejected on earth—accepted in heaven."

On 20 August 1888 Morgan married Annie Morgan, better known as "Nancy." He hesitated to propose to her because all he could offer was the life of an itinerant evangelist, but she knew that God's hand was upon him. "If I cannot start with you at the bottom of the ladder," she wrote, "I should be ashamed to meet you at the top." After a year of the itinerant ministry, the Morgans settled down in the little town of Stone in Staffordshire, where he became pastor of the Congregational church; and on 22 September 1890 he was ordained.

As it did the writer of Hebrews, "time would fail me" to relate the life and travels of this amazing teacher of the Word. One of his best friends, Samuel Chadwick, said that Morgan was a "nomad," and no doubt he was right. Except for twelve years at the famous Westminster Chapel in London, Morgan's ministry was made up of short pastorates punctuated by brief periods of itinerating.

He left the Stone church to go to nearby Rugeley in June 1891, staying there two years. In June 1893 he went to the Westminster Road Congregational Church in Birmingham, where he stayed until December 1896. He was recommended to this church, by the way, by J. Gregory Mantle, the Methodist preacher who had helped to "reject" him eight years before! From 1897 to 1901, Morgan pastored the New Court Church in North London; and from there he moved to the United States to direct the Northfield extension ministry for Will Moody.

Morgan ministered in the States until November 1903, when he sailed back to Britain and was contacted by the officers of Westminster Chapel, one of Congregationalism's greatest churches but at that time in desperate shape. In September 1904 he began what was to be his longest pastorate. He finally terminated it in 1917 and became interim pastor, for one year, of the Highbury Quadrant Church in London. Then he returned to the States for nearly seven years of ministry, living first at Winona Lake, Indiana, and then moving to Athens, Georgia. He tried five months as pastor of the Covenant–First Presbyterian Church in Cincinnati, but it just did not work out and he resigned. For one year he was on the faculty of Biola College in Los Angeles, resigning because he felt a fellow teacher had been wrongly judged by the board. For three years he pastored the Tabernacle Presbyterian Church in Philadelphia, resigning in 1933 for his son Howard to become pastor (all of Morgan's four sons became preachers).

Next Morgan did a remarkable thing: he returned to Westminister Chapel in London to become pastor again. He had pastored the church during World War I, and now he would pastor it again during World War II. From 1938 on, D. Martyn Lloyd-Jones was his associate in the work; and when Morgan resigned in August 1943, Lloyd-Jones became pastor and continued to lead that great church by means of the devoted exposition of the Word of God. Morgan died on 16 May 1945.

I have read Morgan's life many times; I have read his books, his sermons, and his expositions. And I still ask myself, "How do you explain a man like this?" He did not have the privilege of studying in a Bible school or seminary, yet he wrote books that are used in these schools (and by preachers around the world). He sat on the faculties of three schools and for three years was the president of a college. He never resorted to cheap tricks or oratory to get a crowd, yet wherever he went, people had to be turned away. Both as a pastor and as an itinerant Bible teacher, he was relatively isolated from the common people; yet his messages show his deep understanding of the needs of the common man. How do we explain him?

One answer, I think, is the providence of God. Morgan himself said something at a Moody Centenary service in Westminster Chapel in 1937 that, though he applied it to D. L. Moody, could just as easily be applied to Morgan. "In the history of the Church, times and a man have always seemed to come together. . . . And . . . God generally finds the man where men are not looking for him." Morgan's successor, Lloyd-Jones, pointed out that Morgan came on the scene in Britain just after the great Moody-Sankey meetings, when thousands of new converts needed to be taught the Word of God. Morgan met that need. In his early days Morgan was a successful evangelist, but gradually the gift of teaching the Word came to the forefront. He exercised it widely and with wonderful results.

God had to prepare His man for His work, and He did that during Morgan's early pastorates, when he was "buried" and alone. He himself has admitted that "all the spadework" for his Bible studies was done during his two years at Rugeley, when the winters were long and cold and he was confined to his study. Instead of wasting his time because his church was small, Morgan invested it in the concentrated study of the Word, and God prepared him for a wonderful ministry as a result.

High on the list of events that helped to widen Morgan's ministry was his association with D. L. Moody. The evangelist had never heard Morgan preach, but he invited him to speak at Northfield and at the institute in Chicago in 1896. Morgan was to cross the Atlantic fifty-four times during his lifetime. He returned to Northfield in 1897 and again in 1899, the year that Moody died. "He is one of the most remarkable men who ever came to Northfield," said Moody. "I believe him to be filled utterly with the Spirit of

God." After the evangelist's death Will Moody sailed to England to ask Morgan to come and assist in the Northfield ministry, and Morgan accepted. "It's a plain case of burglary!" declared Joseph Parker when he heard that Morgan was moving to the States, and most of Britain's religious leaders agreed. But what else was Morgan to do? "I have long felt that God was preparing me for a ministry to the churches, rather than to one particular church," Morgan explained. "Now the door stands open for such a work. It has not opened in my own country where I had hoped and thought it would." In a sense, America "discovered" Morgan before Britain really understood what she had. When Morgan returned to Britain three years later, he was given a king's welcome. The prophet was no longer without honor in his own country.

I think the real secret of Morgan's ministry (apart from his spiritual devotion) is found in one word—*work.* "Let me state in the briefest manner possible what I want to impress upon the mind of those who are contemplating Bible teaching, by declaring that the Bible never yields itself to indolence. Of all literature none demands more diligent application than that of the Divine Library."[1] When asked the secret of his success as an interpreter of the Word, he would say, "Work—hard work—and again, work!" He himself was in his study at 6 A.M., and he never permitted anyone to interrupt him before lunch. Some of us pastors may not be able to avoid some interruptions, but certainly we can make better use of our time. Morgan would read a Bible book forty or fifty times before attempting to preach on it or write about it. Jill Morgan correctly entitled her biography of her father-in-law, *A Man of the Word.*

Along with *The Study and Teaching of the English Bible,* you will want to secure two other books: *Preaching,* by Morgan; and *The Expository Method of G. Campbell Morgan,* by Don M. Wagner.[2] These three books are a good analysis of "the Morgan method." Of course they are no substitute for reading Morgan's expository works, which every preacher and teacher ought to do. You may also want to add *This Was His Faith,* a collection of excerpts from Morgan's letters, edited by Jill Morgan.[3] You will be surprised to discover in this book what Morgan believed about

1. *The Study and Teaching of the English Bible,* p. 74.
2. Westwood, N.J.: Revell, 1957.
3. Westwood, N.J.: Revell, 1952.

the condition of the heathen, Calvinism, speaking in tongues, falling from grace, and a host of other topics.

During his ministry Morgan was criticized in two areas: money and theology.

"You are an extravagant man!" someone said to Morgan one day.

He replied, "I am not an extravagant man, but I am an expensive man."

When other British preachers were trying to balance their budgets, Morgan was enjoying a "motor-car"—and being criticized for it. He received large honoraria for his ministry and, without question, earned every bit of it. In all fairness to Morgan, it should be stated that he did not make any of the arrangements for his meetings nor did he make any demands. This was usually done by his associate, Arthur Marsh, or by some other Christian leader. So to criticize Morgan would be completely wrong. Furthermore, he was lavishly generous toward others, even to the point of adopting entire families until they were able to make it on their own. No doubt Morgan's use of finances was more American than British.

As far as theology is concerned, Morgan was too liberal for the conservatives and too conservative for the liberals. He considered himself a preacher of the fundamentals of the faith, and certainly anyone who studies his books (especially *The Crises of the Christ*) will have to agree that he did. But he would not identify himself with any "theological camp" or carry the flag for any religious leader. He was his own man, and nothing would make him violate his conscience. He resigned from the Biola faculty because he thought his friend J. M. MacInnis was wronged. He even dedicated one of his books to MacInnis, describing him as "true as steel to the evangelical faith." He wrote: "I have long felt that, whereas I stand foursquare on the evangelical faith, I have no patience with those people whose supposed fundamentalism consists in watching for heresy and indulging in wicked self-satisfaction because they have an idea that they alone 'hold the truth'—hateful expression! Whereas in many ways I agree with their theological position I abominate their spirit." Especially during his latter years of ministry in the States, Morgan was attacked in the religious press. During a meeting in New York City, Morgan spoke openly in the pulpit about the cruel lies men had spread about him; and it so upset him that he actually fainted.

More than one writer has criticized Morgan for his "nomad ministry." Ernest H. Jeffs in *Princes of the Modern Pulpit* stated that Morgan might have been a better preacher had he stayed in one place and taken time to pastor a church. "A preacher who lives in a whirl of change and travel and ever-changing audiences loses touch to some extent with the daily problems of the ordinary man," Jeffs wrote.[4] No doubt this is true; but I cringe to think of what the world would have lost had Morgan wasted his time on committee meetings, in denominational gatherings, and (as he said once) "arguing over who would have the key to the back door." He had a gift; he developed and exercised it; and the Christian world is the richer for it. True, he did not make pastoral visits; but this does not mean that his messages were divorced from the needs of the people. If this is true, why did thousands come to hear him? Had Morgan adopted the life style of the typical pastor, we would have been robbed of a rich treasure.

There is one interesting thing about Morgan's preaching that I have never seen discussed anywhere—his seeming avoidance of the doctrinal epistles. He was basically a preacher of the four Gospels, but he never expounded, verse by verse, the great doctrinal epistles—Romans, Ephesians, Hebrews. "He left them for me," Lloyd-Jones told me one day, "and I'm glad he did!" I think one reason Morgan avoided these letters is that he was basically a devotional preacher, not a doctrinal preacher. This does not mean he avoided doctrine, but only that he did not emphasize it (Lloyd-Jones is a doctrinal preacher *par excellence!*). Morgan's ministry was to *all* the churches, and doctrinal controversies found no place in his system.

Perhaps we need a man like Morgan today, one who will minister the Word with clarity and power and make the Bible "come alive," one who will ride above the ripples and waves of denominational competition and theological controversy, one who is true to the doctrines of the faith but who also is able to share the Word in love with Christians of many denominational affiliations. Certainly H. A. Ironside was such a man, as was A. C. Gaebelein. But even they were identified with certain "branches" of evangelical faith and to some degree limited in their ministries. G. Campbell Morgan seemed to belong to all the churches and to Christians everywhere, not because he compromised, but because he majored on the great essentials of the faith and did not get detoured by the accidentals. He paid a price for this, to be sure; but we are the richer because of the price he paid.

Whenever you find a book by Morgan, buy it and study it. Read his life story and get acquainted with this unique teacher of the

---

4. P. 184.

Word. You do not have to agree with him to learn from him; he would be the first one to say that. "My work is wholly constructive," he wrote in 1923, "and I believe that that is the only kind that is really of value." We need more of this constructive ministry today.

Bibliography

Jeffs, Ernest H. *Princes of the Modern Pulpit.* London: Low, 1931.
Morgan, G. Campbell. *The Crises of the Christ.* New York: Revell, 1903.
_____. *Preaching.* New York: Revell, 1937. Reprinted—Grand Rapids: Baker, 1974.
_____. *The Study and Teaching of the English Bible.* New York: Revell, 1910.
_____. *This Was His Faith: The Expository Letters of G. Campbell Morgan.* Edited by Jill Morgan. Westwood, N.J.: Revell, 1952.
Morgan, Jill. *A Man of the Word: Life of G. Campbell Morgan.* London: Pickering and Inglis, 1951. Reprinted—Grand Rapids: Baker, 1972.
Wagner, Don M. *The Expository Method of G. Campbell Morgan.* Westwood, N.J.: Revell, 1957.

14

J. D. Jones

(1865-1942)

He could have been F. B. Meyer's successor at Christ Church in Westminster, or John Henry Jowett's successor when Jowett went to Fifth Avenue Presbyterian in New York City. In fact, Fifth Avenue Presbyterian approached him after Jowett had first turned them down. He was offered the principalship of Lancashire College and was even encouraged to run for office by members of Parliament. But none of these things moved him, and J. D. Jones remained for thirty-nine years as the beloved pastor of Richmond Hill Congregational Church in Bournemouth, retiring on 6 June 1937.

John Daniel Jones was almost "Lincoln Jones." When he was born in the little Welsh town of Ruthin on 13 April 1865, his father wanted to call him *Lincoln* in honor of the American president whom he greatly admired (interestingly enough, Lincoln was assassinated the next day). But one of the grandmothers was opposed to "such fancy names in the family," and so Joseph David Jones called his third son John Daniel and saved Lincoln for his fourth son born two years later. However, Grandmother may

have been right, because the name *Lincoln* created some compli-
cations in later years when J. D. was pastoring Newland Congregational Church in Lincoln. People were constantly confusing
"Lincoln Jones" with "Jones of Lincoln." But when J. D. Jones
began his long ministry at Richmond Hill on 5 June 1898, people
forgot about Lincoln and knew him simply as "Jones of Bournemouth."

Jones did his undergraduate work at Owens College, which he
entered in 1882, and his graduate work at Lancashire College,
receiving his degree in 1889. It was unusual for a new theological
graduate to go directly into the pulpit of an important church, but
that is just what happened. On 2 January 1889, before Jones
completed his work, the Newland Church in Lincoln called him to
be their pastor. In July of that same year, he was married. In his
delightful autobiography, *Three Score Years and Ten,* Jones said
this about his experiences as a young pastor in a leading church:
"Of course I blundered. At the very first Church meeting after my
settlement my Church Secretary brought in a resolution to em-
body a certain liturgical element in our worship, and I backed him
up. My Church—Puritan by tradition—would have none of it. It
was a bit of a rebuff for a young minister. I remember visiting an
old lady named Cropper shortly after and she said to me: 'Don't
take it too hard, laddie. We're a lot of stiffnecked 'uns down
here.' "

He remained almost ten years at Lincoln and then accepted the
call to Richmond Hill in Bournemouth. The church sanctuary held
over a thousand people and was ideally situated in the city. His
predecessor was a fiery Welshman named Ossian Davies, whose
intense personality had attracted great crowds; and Jones wondered if his own quiet preaching would really do the job. It did.
The people came and kept coming, and for thirty-nine years benefited from his simple presentation of the Word of God. Bournemouth is a popular resort and retirement city, and many well-to-
do people came to hear him preach; but J. D. Jones never tried to
build a "rich man's church." The common people heard him
gladly.

Peter Marshall once said that the first essential for success in the
ministry is to be born in Scotland. But others would prefer Wales,
that land of eloquent preachers and seers. Jones was a Welshman,
and according to Ernest H. Jeffs "he spoke as if words were notes
of music."[1] Oddly enough, he read his sermons from manuscript,

---

1. *Princes of the Modern Pulpit,* p. 127.

but his listeners could scarcely detect it. What they did detect was *witness:* here was a preacher whose life was controlled by the message he delivered. Jones himself once defined preaching as "a man—a real man—speaking real things out of a real experience." Even a manuscript could not stand between Jones and his hearers, for they always got the message.

He was a Biblical preacher, but he was not an expositor of the same type as Alexander Maclaren or, in our own day, the gifted Welshman, D. Martyn Lloyd-Jones. In the biography *J. D. Jones of Bournemouth,* Arthur Porritt remarked: "All his sermons were on a very high level. He was always on a plateau, but—as a friendly critic figuratively said—there were no mountains and no valleys—just a uniform level of excellence." He was not one to "preach to the times" and announce sensational topics about current events. There are men who can do this well, but if a man *cannot,* he had better know it! Jones liked to refer to a story about Archbishop Leighton. Criticized for not "preaching to the times," the archbishop said, "While so many are preaching to the times, may not one poor brother preach for eternity?"

His was a positive ministry, and a ministry of encouragement and comfort. He did not preach "easy Christianity," but he did identify with his people in their needs and try to make their pilgrim journey a bit more triumphant. In a remarkable sermon on "softness," with I Corinthians 6:9 as his text, Jones challenged his hearers to a courageous Christian faith. "All the calls of the Gospel are calls to hardship, to sacrifice, to battle," he stated. "Christ would have no man follow Him under the delusion that he was going to have an easy time of it." To him, the word *comfort* carried the original Latin meaning, "with strength," and he sought to comfort his people by showing them the strength that there is in Christ. Jones knew what it was to go through the valley himself. In July 1917, while he was preaching at Torquay, his wife became seriously ill and passed away before he had time to reach home. Six years later, his only son died in the Gold Coast of Africa, where he had been serving in the administration of a plantation. In September 1933 Jones remarried and had the joy of traveling and ministering with his wife and his daughter.

His very popular volume *If a Man Die* was published the same year his wife died, and this was followed in 1919 by *The Lord of Life and Death,* a volume of sermons based on John 11. This book was recently reissued by Baker Book House and should be on your shelf, particularly if you plan to preach from John 11. (Be sure to secure as well *Idylls of Bethany* by W. M. Clow and *Mary of*

Bethany by Marcus L. Loane.) While on the subject of books, let me suggest that you secure *Richmond Hill Sermons, The Way into the Kingdom* (on the beatitudes), *The Model Prayer, The Glorious Company of the Apostles* and *The Greatest of These* (on I Cor. 13). I wish some publisher would reprint Jones's commentary on the Gospel of Mark, which was originally written for the *Devotional Commentary*. When he first went to Bournemouth, Jones conducted a Tuesday morning ministry during the winter months, and his first series was on the Gospel of Mark. His commentary is homiletical rather than explanatory or doctrinal, but I still think it is one of the best.

J. D. Jones was a great denominational leader, although he tried not to let his outside ministry interfere with his pastoral duties. Congregational churches in his day were somewhat isolated from each other, and many of them were in deep financial straits. He accepted and defended the principle of local independence, but he was mature enough to see its dangers. He felt that among the free churches in general there was "a good deal of foolish rivalry, of needless competition and of consequent waste." Jeffs remarked, "Congregationalism was a good system for the strong man and the strong church. The price of the principle had to be paid by the weaker men and the little churches." But Jones did not use his position at Richmond Hill to build himself a kingdom: he used it to help others. He spearheaded programs that brought over two million dollars into the denominational coffers to increase the salaries of rural preachers and to provide for decent allotments at retirement. He and his people helped to establish thirty other churches, and he was always available to assist and encourage pastors in difficult places.

He was a great traveler, and often he was a representative to the Congregational International Council. In 1899 he first visited the United States, and on Sunday, 10 September, he heard D. L. Moody preach at the Plymouth Congregational Church in Brooklyn, where Henry Ward Beecher had ministered for almost forty years. Jones wrote that Moody looked "for all the world like a prosperous, countrified farmer." The evangelist spoke on the atonement and took the congregation literally from Genesis to Revelation, as only Moody could do. "He got down to the quick of things," wrote Jones, "and we felt the power of his speech." After the service, Jones and the other delegates met Moody in the vestry and enjoyed a pleasant talk about everything from Sunday newspapers to higher criticism! Moody told them that he felt that the bicycle, because of its popularity, was the greatest enemy of the Sabbath.

"I am glad, as I look back," wrote Jones, "that I had the chance of thus hearing and meeting D. L. Moody. I am glad I got a grip of his hand. Moody seemed to me a man of sterling common sense." Apparently Moody heard Jones speak at the Boston conference, because he invited him to speak at Northfield. Not until 1913 was Jones able to get to Northfield, and by that time Moody was dead and his son Will Moody was managing the schools and the conference. "I think Will Moody was dwarfed by the fact that he was D. L. Moody's son," Jones wrote in his autobiography. "Without doubt D. L. Moody was a very great man. W. R. Moody was not that . . . , but he was an able man. . . . He had great organizing and administrative abilities. . . ." Jones told how Will Moody kept "a firm hand upon all the Conference speakers. After an address by an English speaker who had let off a lot of 'hot air' but had not managed to say much that was worth saying, Will Moody said to me: 'We'll have no more of that. We have plenty of men on this side who can pour out that kind of stuff. I shall tell him he need not trouble to stay.' " Jones added, "It took me all my time to persuade Moody to let him finish. . . ."

It is worth noting that, while Jones had a keen interest in British politics, he did not get as carried away with it as did R. W. Dale. During the 1906 election Jones campaigned for several candidates of the Liberal Party, and every one of them lost in spite of the fact that the Liberals swept the country! When asked to run for office, Jones replied with the words of Nehemiah 6:3—"I am doing a great work, so that I cannot come down."

No doubt one of the secrets of his success was his concentration. Being a pastor was to him the highest calling possible, and it deserved the best that he had. When he rejected the principalship of Lancashire College, Jones received the following message from his friend W. Robertson Nicoll: "I have always held that the pastorate is the highest office open to a minister." The man who believes in the dignity of the pastorate and who has this sense of calling will accomplish far more in his ministry than the man who flits from ministry to ministry, always looking for some better opportunity.

Another strength of J. D. Jones was his faith in the preaching of the Word. No man could stay in one church nearly forty years if he were depending on his own resources. "When J. D. Jones took a text," wrote one religious editor, "it was the text that mattered, not the preacher's commentary upon it. The preacher's commentary had but one aim—to recall its hearers to the richness and wonder of the truth which the text enshrined. He never searched for excitingly unusual texts, nor did he strive to find startlingly unusual interpretations of his texts." The pastor who stops growing usually starts going. There is no substitute for a deepening knowledge of the Word of God.

A third factor in his ministry was his love for his people. His constant desire was to encourage them along the way. When you read *The Lord of Life and Death,* you will discover that these messages were written not from an ivory tower but from that difficult place "where cross the crowded ways of life." Because he knew and loved his people, he was able to make the Word meaningful to them from week to week.

We must not minimize the character of the man himself. When giving the "charge to the minister" at an ordination, Jones said: "The one indispensable condition of our usefulness and success in the work of the ministry is that we should be good men—men of pure and holy life—men of God. . . . We may be good ministers without being either learned or eloquent, but we cannot be good ministers without being good men. . . . The effect of our words on the Sabbath will really depend on our lives during the week, for it is always the man behind the speech which wields the power."

Finally, Jones realized that there was something more than the ministry of his own local church. He knew that he was a part of something much bigger than Richmond Hill, or even the Congregational Union. Without sacrificing his own convictions, he sought to build and encourage God's work everywhere. When the Episcopal and Free Church leaders met in their "conversations on reunion," Jones, giving the opening statement, made it quite clear that the Free Churches were not going to abandon their heritage. "There are certain principles—ecclesiastical and religious—which we hold dear. There are certain truths which—as we believe—have been committed to our trust. . . . We do not want our history and traditions to become a snare, but neither can we be expected lightly to flout and discard them." The largeness of his vision no doubt contributed to the greatness of his ministry.

Dr. and Mrs. Jones retired to Wales in 1937, although Dr. Jones was still quite active in his preaching ministry. His health remained good until August 1941, when anemia began to sap his strength. D. Martyn Lloyd-Jones visited him at Mrs. Jones's request to share the word that he could not get better, and Jones accepted the news with his usual poise and courage. On Sunday, 19 April 1942, he was called home. On his tombstone in the Bournemouth cemetery it says: "John Daniel Jones, Preacher of the Gospel. 'Simply to Thy cross I cling.' "

Bibliography

Jeffs, Ernest H. *Princes of the Modern Pulpit.* London: Low, 1931.

Jones, J. D. *The Glorious Company of the Apostles.* London: Clarke, 1904.

_____. *The Gospel According to St. Mark: A Devotional Commentary.* 4 vols. London: Religious Tract Society, n.d.

_____. *The Greatest of These: Addresses on I Corinthians 13.* London: Hodder and Stoughton, 1925.

_____. *If a Man Die.* London: Hodder and Stoughton, 1917.

_____. *The Lord of Life and Death.* London: Hodder and Stoughton, 1919. Reprinted–Grand Rapids: Baker, 1972.

_____. *The Model Prayer.* London: Clarke, n.d.

_____. *Richmond Hill Sermons.* London: Hodder and Stoughton, 1932.

_____. *Three Score Years and Ten: The Autobiography of J. D. Jones.* London: Hodder and Stoughton, 1940.

_____. *The Way into the Kingdom.* London: Religious Tract Society, 1900.

Porritt, Arthur. *J. D. Jones of Bournemouth.* London: Independent, 1942.

15

George H. Morrison

(1866-1928)

Whenever pastors get together and discuss their favorite preachers, they are sure to repeat such names as Charles Haddon Spurgeon, G. Campbell Morgan, Alexander Whyte, and J. H. Jowett, to name but a few. Rarely—only rarely—will you hear a pastor ask, "Have any of you read the sermons of George H. Morrison?" And the reply is usually, "George Morrison? Never heard of him! Who is he?" No alert pastor in Great Britain during the first quarter of this century would have asked that question! "Morrison of Wellington" was easily the most popular preacher in Scotland. And he was not only a popular preacher but also an effective pastor. His personal records reveal that he made over one thousand visits in an average year! When he died, he left a rich legacy of books of his messages that spoke meaningfully to hearts fifty years ago and still speak to hearts today.

Tragically, most of Morrison's writings are to be found only in secondhand bookstores, but Baker Book House has reprinted *The Wings of the Morning,* one of his matchless volumes. Like most of Morrison's books, this is a collection of Sunday evening sermons.

Morrison, like most Scottish pastors of his day, preached weighty expository sermons in the morning services, but his evening preaching was refreshingly different. He himself wrote: "It has been my habit at the morning service to handle the greater themes of the Christian revelation and then at the evening worship to allow myself a wider scope . . . to win the attention, in honorable ways, of some at least of that vast class of people who today sit so lightly to the Church."

And he succeeded! During the more than twenty-five years he pastored the Wellington United Free Church in Glasgow, great crowds would queue up in anticipation of the evening service, while at other churches the congregations were meager if not totally absent. It was not Morrison's fiery eloquence or oratory that drew and held his congregation. His voice was rather weak and his presentation anything but dramatic. Following one service, a lady turned to the famous A. J. Gossip and said, "Didn't Dr. Morrison preach a wonderful sermon?"

"Madam," Gossip replied, "I did not hear half of what he was saying."

"Neither did I," said the woman, "but wasn't it a wonderful sermon!"

Morrison's preaching strength lay in his knowledge of the Bible, his knowledge of his people and their needs, and his ability to put both together in an imaginative way that reached the heart.

In this day of "telling it like it is," Morrison's sermons and some of his sermon titles might be dismissed as sentimental and poetical. Such titles as "The Fault of Over-Prudence," "The Religious Use of Holidays," and "The Higher Ministries of Sleep" would not excite congregations today. But what about "Wasted Gains" (on Prov. 12:27—look it up!), "The Deceptions of God" (Jer. 20:7), "Unobserved Sins" (Exod. 2:12), and "The Intolerance of Jesus" (Matt. 12:30)?

His sermon on Isaiah 27:8 is a masterpiece. The text says, "He stayeth his rough wind in the day of the east wind." Morrison's points are: (1) our trials are timed; (2) our sufferings are measured; and (3) our lives are compensated. This sermon reveals both the pastor's heart and the scholar's mind. Or consider his message on Matthew 14:30—"Beginning to Sink." He brought out these lessons from Peter's experience: Peter began to sink in familiar waters; he began to sink after loyal discipleship; he began to sink on a permitted path; he began to sink when he began to fear; when he began to sink his Savior was not far away. That is preaching! Some of Morrison's sermons would give today's preachers ideas for a whole series of messages. "The Refusals of Christ" is one example; another is "The Lonely People of the Gospel" (Mary—the loneliness of love; Thomas—the loneliness of doubt; Judas—the loneliness of sin; etc.).

As you read Morrison's sermons, you discover a man acquainted with the Bible, alert to the news and problems of the day, sympathetic with suffering (he lost his wife while pastoring in Dundee and he lost a son in the war), and able to say the most profound truths in a remarkably simple way. In fact, the simplicity of his preaching is utterly disarming. He never used too many words but always seemed to use the right words, making truth glow in an imaginative way. For example: "One of the saddest stories ever written is just the story of our mismanaged triumphs." Or, "Faith is expectant, eager, childlike, buoyant. Its opposite is not doubt, but death." Or, "Christ will have nothing of the culture of the brain, at the expense of the culture of the character."

George Herbert Morrison was born in Glasgow, Scotland, on 2 October 1866. After completing his university studies, he was not sure of his vocation. He became an assistant to Sir James Murray at Oxford, helping with the *New English Dictionary* while trying to "find himself." No doubt this experience helped to make him such an accurate writer and to give him love for words. It is worth noting that G. Campbell Morgan, J. H. Jowett, and Alexander Whyte were, like Morrison, great students of words and readers of dictionaries.

While working at Oxford, Morrison felt the call to preach. He entered the Free Church College in Glasgow and graduated in 1893. At that time a second providential event occurred in his training: he was chosen to assist the famous Alexander Whyte at Free St. George's in Edinburgh. Morrison's responsibility was to conduct the then-new evening service, a challenge he accepted with confidence. He remained with Whyte only a year, but that one year with the gifted preacher gave him spiritual values which controlled his ministry for the rest of his life. His diligent study, his concern for his people, his sanctified imagination, his love of books (he had a library of over six thousand volumes)—all were strengthened and stimulated during that year at Edinburgh. We wonder what would happen to younger preachers today if they spent a year as understudy to some successful pastor? We might have fewer ministerial dropouts.

Morrison pastored at Thurso in northern Scotland and after four years moved to Dundee. Later he accepted the call to the Wellington United Free Church in Glasgow and became known as

"Morrison of Wellington." Until his unexpected death in 1928, Morrison gave his best to his people, both as pastor and preacher. With clock-like regularity he spent his mornings in the study, his afternoons with his people in their homes, and his evenings either at church meetings or at home studying and writing. Like Whyte, he took long holidays, using the summer months for additional study, meditation, and rest. "The only piece of advice Whyte gave me when I was with him," said Morrison, "was to take long holidays!" To this Whyte later replied, "And did you or your people ever regret it?" Although today's overworked pastors might not be able to take off two months each summer, an occasional interruption for incubation would no doubt improve the man and his ministry.

Morrison did not wrestle with Biblical criticism or seek to explain the great questions of his day, even though he was a scholar and a voracious reader. Morrison felt his responsibility was to encourage his people with the truths of Christ which he had proved in his own life, not to discourage them with academic questions. He faced and solved these important questions in his study, but he stepped into the pulpit with exclamation points, not question marks.

Preaching in a church located directly across from the university, Morrison had a special concern for the youth. He kept up with the honor list and always sent a personal note to students who made it. He did not preach what we would call youth messages, but the students flocked to hear him. He organized "The Round Table" and met with the students following the evening service to discuss the questions that troubled them. At the open forum the pastor did not permit himself pulpit privileges. It was Morrison unfrocked that won their hearts and helped direct their lives. This personal interchange helped to make them better Christians and him a better preacher and pastor.

The preacher who reads *The Wings of the Morning* probably will not be satisfied until he secures everything else Morrison wrote. He will want to get *The Wind on the Heath, The Ever Open Door, The Afterglow of God, Flood-Tide, The Unlighted Lustre, The Weaving of Glory, The Footsteps of the Flock* (a remarkable devotional book for each Sunday of the year, taking the reader through the key passages of the Bible—a gold mine of sermonic material!), *The World-wide Gospel, The Return of the Angels, Sun-Rise,* and others. The wise preacher will index these great sermons. If he is wiser still, he will read each message carefully, first for his own heart and then to improve his ministry. Morrison himself read one sermon a day from a different preacher. Morrison's sermons would be a good place for us to start today!

As he lay dying, Morrison's final words were: "It's an ever open door, never closed to anyone. It's open for me now and I'm going through!" By means of his reprinted sermons (and, we trust, additional volumes will follow), Morrison helps today's preachers point others to that "ever open door" which is Jesus Christ.

Bibliography

Gammie, Alexander. *Dr. George H. Morrison: The Man and His Work.* London: Clarke, 1928.

Morrison, Christine M. *Morrison of Wellington.* London: Hodder and Stoughton, 1930.

Morrison, George H. *The Afterglow of God.* New York: Hodder and Stoughton, 1912.

_____. *The Ever Open Door.* London: Hodder and Stoughton, 1929.

_____. *Flood-Tide.* London: Hodder and Stoughton, 1901. Reprinted—Grand Rapids: Baker, 1971.

_____. *The Footsteps of the Flock.* London: Hodder and Stoughton, 1904.

_____. *The Return of the Angels.* London: Hodder and Stoughton, 1909.

_____. *Sun-Rise.* London: Hodder and Stoughton, 1903. Reprinted—Grand Rapids: Baker, 1971.

_____. *The Unlighted Lustre.* London: Hodder and Stoughton, 1905. Reprinted—Grand Rapids: Baker, 1971.

_____. *The Weaving of Glory.* London: Hodder and Stoughton, 1913.

_____. *The Wind on the Heath.* London: Hodder and Stoughton, 1915. Reprinted—Grand Rapids: Baker, 1971.

_____. *The Wings of the Morning.* London: Hodder and Stoughton, 1907. Reprinted—Grand Rapids: Baker, 1970.

_____. *The World-wide Gospel.* London: Hodder and Stoughton, 1933.

16

Frank W. Boreham

(1871?-1959)

It amazes me that my favorite biographical handbook, *Who Was Who in Church History,* mentions Caesar Borgia and William Briconnet but contains not one line about Frank W. Boreham. I can easily conceive of a preacher getting along in his ministry knowing nothing about Borgia's sensuous intrigues or Briconnet's cowardly defections; but how he can get along knowing nothing about Boreham's *A Bunch of Everlastings* or his beloved flock at Mosgiel in New Zealand or his hundreds of delightful essays is really more than I can understand. I trust that a generation has not arisen that knows not Frank W. Boreham. If this be the case, let me remedy it immediately by devoting a chapter to this world-famous British preacher and essayist. The moderator of the Church of Scotland once introduced Boreham as "the man whose name is on all our lips, whose books are on all our shelves and whose illustrations are in all our sermons." Fortunate is the pastor who gets to know and love the writings of Boreham.

"Salvoes of artillery and peals of bells echoed across Europe on the morning of my birth," wrote Boreham in the first paragraph of his delightful autobiography, *My Pilgrimage.* It was Friday, 3 March 1871, the day the Franco-Prussian War ended. When he was four months old, he was on an outing with his nurse when a gypsy caravan passed by and an old gypsy woman, noticing the child, came over to them. She looked at the little boy's hand and said to the nurse, "Tell his mother to put a pen in his hand and he'll never want for a living." The prophecy proved true: Boreham became one of the world's most prolific religious writers, with more than fifty books to his credit, not to speak of hundreds of newspaper and magazine articles and essays.

As the boy grew up, he was introduced to both the things of the Spirit and the things of the mind. Faithful Christian parents saw to it that he was trained in the Word of God and also that he learned to appreciate good reading (children learn to appreciate good books by contagion, not compulsion). Frank's father, noticing that Frank was reading some shallow novels, introduced him to the vast treasures of biography, and the boy was "hooked for life." At sixteen Frank decided to go to London and get a job; this proved to be the first of several turning points in his life. He had trained himself in shorthand, at which he was very competent, and he had a beautiful copperplate script, so landing a job was no great problem. After a short stay with a real estate firm, he worked for a London railroad.

London in 1887 was an exciting place. Charles H. Spurgeon was preaching (when not incapacitated by gout) at the Metropolitan Tabernacle; Joseph Parker was electrifying congregations at the City Temple; J. Hudson Taylor was challenging Christians with the needs of China; and F. B. Meyer was teaching believers the joys and victories of the Christian life.

"Honesty compels me to confess," Boreham wrote, "not without shame, that Mr. Spurgeon never really appealed to me. It was, of course, my fault. . . . I enjoyed every sermon that I heard Mr. Spurgeon preach: I marvelled at his power to attract the multitudes: I was thankful for his enormous influence. But he never gripped me as some other preachers did." The great preacher's poor health those closing years may help to explain Boreham's evaluation. It was F. B. Meyer who attracted and held the young man from Tunbridge Wells. Boreham attended Meyer's church in Regent's Park and also the famous Saturday afternoon Bible classes at Aldersgate Street, directed especially to the young men of the city. "I really think that we lived for those Saturday afternoons," Boreham said in his autobiography. "We counted the hours till they came; and, when they came, they never failed to minister to us such hope and faith and courage as sent us back to our tasks with higher spirits and with braver hearts."

There is no doubt that Meyer's positive ministry of encouragement helped to mold Boreham's own ministry, for, like Barnabas, Frank Boreham was "a son of encouragement" (Acts 4:36). Meyer was a Baptist and Boreham had been raised an Anglican, but Boreham's own study of the Bible had convinced him that he should be immersed. So on Easter Tuesday evening in 1890, he was immersed at the Stockwell Old Baptist Church. Little did he realize that his Baptist associations would play an important role in his life and ministry.

In 1891 he united with the Kenyon Baptist Church in Brixton, of which the pastor, James Douglas, was a good friend of Spurgeon. When the pastor discovered that Boreham was considering the ministry, he naturally urged him to apply to Spurgeon's Pastor's College. Boreham did, and he was the last student that Spurgeon personally selected before his lamented death on 31 January 1892. The Spurgeon family would be used of God to direct Boreham's ministry in ways that he never dreamed of, but all of which were part of God's plan.

In 1894 Thomas Spurgeon returned to London after ministering in New Zealand, and he brought with him a request for a pastor from a new church at Mosgiel. Founded by Scottish immigrants, the Mosgiel church was ten years old and gave promise of being an effective work for the Lord. The college staff decided that Boreham was their man. After a conference with Thomas Spurgeon and with Boreham's parents, the student (who still had one year's training before him) decided it was the Lord's will that he terminate his work at the college and sail for New Zealand. At the farewell service, held at the tabernacle, Boreham made a prophecy of his own that, in the providence of God, came true: "And it is my hope that in the course of my ministry I shall hold three pastorates, and then be free to travel in many lands preaching the everlasting gospel among all denominations."

He served in Mosgiel, New Zealand; Hobart, Tasmania; and Armadale, Australia; and then he traveled to many lands and preached to vast congregations. Where he was unable to travel personally, his books carried his messages; and it is these that I want to discuss. If you are interested in the story of his life—and you ought to be—then secure *My Pilgrimage,* published in the United States by Judson Press; and also *The Story of F. W. Boreham,* written by T. Howard Crago.

Boreham had begun writing while a youth in London, but his

newspaper articles, plus a devotional booklet, had caused little stir. He knew the gift was there; it would simply take time to develop and discipline it. His first love was preaching, but there was no reason why he could not also write. After all, his spiritual mentor, F. B. Meyer, was the author of dozens of books; and even Spurgeon made good use of his pen.

After settling down in Mosgiel, Boreham hit upon the idea of publishing a sermon each week in the local newspaper, an idea that the editor approved with enthusiasm. Many readers were unable to travel to church every Sunday, and the printed sermon would meet their needs. At the beginning, Boreham solicited sermons from other pastors; but their contributions gradually fell off, leaving it to Boreham to fill up the two columns each week. He enjoyed the discipline of writing out a message, and the publication of his messages in the newspaper helped to fill his church. In time other newspapers "down under" were reprinting his material, and several editors asked him for original material for their publications. In the years to come, most of his essays would be shared by several periodicals and then would be published in book form.

His first book, *The Luggage of Life,* was turned down by Hodder and Stoughton, but Epworth Press[1] accepted it and launched him into his phenomenal literary career. At one time during his ministry, Boreham was publishing two books a year, with no diminishing of the sales. Needless to say, Hodder and Stoughton was embarrassed at the loss of such a successful writer; in later years it tried to capture him for its list, but without success.

I think the best of Boreham's to read first is the first volume of his "Texts That Made History" series (which was reprinted by Judson Press), *A Bunch of Everlastings.* The story behind this unique, five-volume series is this: Boreham was about to begin a Sunday evening series on "The Specters of the Mind" when it dawned upon him that a series on alternate Sunday evenings would encourage the congregation to return week after week. As if by inspiration, it came to him to preach on "Texts That Made History"; and thus he announced that the next Sunday evening he would preach on "Martin Luther's Text." Subsequent sermons were "John Bunyan's Text," "Oliver Cromwell's Text," "John

---

1. The publishing arm of the Wesleyan Conference did not, however, adopt the name "Epworth Press" until 1918, six years after *The Luggage of Life* had appeared. Before that, books published by the Conference were imprinted with the name of Conference Book Steward C. H. Kelly.

Wesley's Text," etc.—this series put to practical use Boreham's interest in biography. Little did he realize that these sermons would continue for 125 Sunday evenings and attract more interest and win more people to Christ than any other series he ever preached.

Every preacher ought to secure these five volumes, read them, and index them—and beware of stealing Boreham's sermons! Following *A Bunch of Everlastings,* look for *A Handful of Stars, A Temple of Topaz, A Casket of Cameos,* and *A Faggot of Torches.* Turn next to his essays; you have over forty volumes to choose from! By all means secure the first book he published, *The Luggage of Life,* and I would also suggest *The Other Side of the Hill and Home Again, The Silver Shadow, The Last Milestone* (which contains many of his pithy biographical essays on famous people and events), *The Passing of John Broadbanks,* and *Mushrooms on the Moor.* But selecting a Boreham book is like choosing a beautiful rose from a large bouquet or selecting a dessert from a tray of French pastries—you can never make a mistake.

To be sure, the essays in each book are of uneven quality and some will strike your fancy more than others, but all of them will do you good. I personally prefer his autobiographical essays dealing with the church at Mosgiel or with his good friend "John Broadbanks." Once you have met "Tammas" and "Wullie" and "Gavin," you will fall in love with them and no doubt identify them with people you have met in your own church. And it will not take you long to discover who "John Broadbanks" really is. It does my soul good to reach across the miles and the years to "fellowship" with the Mosgiel congregation and to share their joys and sorrows, their disagreements, and their "love affair" with their pastor.

Let me warn you: Frank Boreham will not tell you how to double attendance at the evening service, increase the budget, or expand the youth ministry. But he will put you in touch with the essentials of life.

Everything he saw, heard, and experienced became a part of his treasury from which, in later years, he brought out "things new and old." Can you imagine writing an essay on "The Man in the Moon" or "Maxims of the Mud" or "Wet Paint"? It is this kind of imaginative writing that can teach and encourage the preacher to be alert to life and to make sure that his messages lay hold of reality. Boreham said: "We shall never attract or arrest our hearers by an elaborate display of theology. . . . Theology is to a sermon what the skeleton is to the body: it gives shape and support to the preacher's utterance without itself being visible." Boreham was not an expositor of the Scriptures in the manner of Spurgeon or Maclaren, but he was a Biblical preacher and writer who reached many people who perhaps would have turned away from the conventional sermonic approach. I am not suggesting that you imitate his style; I am suggesting that you get excited about the potential in the common things around you.

Boreham was a disciplined reader. Early in his ministry he determined to read at least one book a week, and often he exceeded his quota. While he especially enjoyed biography and autobiography, he did not limit himself. Whenever he had an idea for an essay or a sermon, he immediately wrote it down and filed it away. (Whenever he went on vacation, he buried his precious notes and manuscripts in the back yard lest the house burn down and they be lost.) By constantly adding to his treasury, he was never at a loss for new ideas; not until late in his life was the treasury exhausted. After he had retired from the pastoral ministry, he was still getting literary dividends from ideas he had noted years before. "Write it down!" was a basic rule of life, and he even kept pen and paper next to his bed in case a night visitor should come and be lost by morning. By the way, I should mention that Boreham wrote all his material by hand. At one stage he tried using a typewriter, but his muse was not mechanical.

Pastors will be interested in three convictions that Boreham held. First, he was sure that nobody wanted to be visited immediately after the noon meal; so he went to bed every afternoon and slept for one hour. This helps to explain why he lived such a long life—eighty-eight years (he died on 18 May 1959). Second, he was always punctual and was unhappy with anybody who was not. While never in a hurry, he was always busy. He disciplined himself to do the important things and wasted no time on the trivial. Third, he was convinced that no pastor could preach two entirely new sermons each Lord's Day and do his best; so he always revised an old sermon for one of the Sunday services. He did not simply repreach it. He revised it and tried to give it a fresh approach based on experience gained since the first time it was preached. He wrote: "Dr. Parker taught me—as also did Dr. Meyer—the high art of repeating myself. I heard Dr. Meyer say identically the same thing on half a dozen different occasions. But he displayed such craftsmanship in his repetition that, unless you had previously heard him say it, you would never have suspected him of having said the same thing before." Alas, many pastors do not work at revising their messages. They find it easier to change churches and use the same material over again.

One of the penalties of effectiveness in writing and preaching is plagiarism, and Frank Boreham was plagiarized much of his life. One American preacher told an Australian friend that he would hate to meet Boreham: "I've plagiarized so many of his sermons, I couldn't bear to look him in the eye!" One London preacher even dared to preach one of Boreham's sermons over the BBC. Unfortunately for him, Boreham's father was listening, recognized the sermon, identified it in one of his son's books, and wrote the preacher a rather pointed letter. The man sent his apology and even wrote Dr. Boreham; but sad to say, he felt that since the sermon was already in print, it was worth sharing with others. (This brings to mind the fact that G. Campbell Morgan was often plagiarized. When it was announced that he was to preach in various places, he would often receive anonymous letters begging him not to preach certain sermons because they had already been preached there—by others!) I wonder at the effectiveness, not to speak of the character, of a man who must steal material in order to minister. If we do borrow, at least we should give credit.

If at first Boreham does not excite you, give him time. He grows on you. He has a way of touching the nerve centers of life and getting to that level of reality that too often we miss. Some may consider him sentimental; others may feel he is a relic of a vanished era. They are welcome to their opinions. But before you pass judgment, read him for yourself and read enough to give him a fair trial. If you are preaching from Luke 15, read *The Prodigal* and marvel at Boreham's new insights into this old story. *The Heavenly Octave* deals with the beatitudes. There is something for everybody in a Boreham book because his writing touches on the unchanging essentials of life, not the passing accidentals; we need this emphasis today.

Bibliography

Boreham, Frank W. *A Bunch of Everlastings.* London: Epworth, 1920. Reprinted—Philadelphia: Judson, 1942.

_____. *A Casket of Cameos.* London: Epworth, 1924. Reprinted—Philadelphia: Judson, 1950.

_____. *A Faggot of Torches.* London: Epworth, 1926. Reprinted—Philadelphia: Judson, 1951.

_____. *A Handful of Stars.* London: Epworth, 1922. Reprinted—Philadelphia: Judson, 1950.

_____. *The Heavenly Octave: A Study of the Beatitudes.* London: Epworth, 1935. Reprinted—Grand Rapids: Baker, 1968.

_____. *The Last Milestone.* London: Epworth, 1961.

_____. *The Luggage of Life.* London: Kelly, 1912.

_____. *Mushrooms on the Moor.* London: Kelly, 1915.

_____. *My Pilgrimage: An Autobiography.* London: Epworth, 1940.

_____. *The Other Side of the Hill and Home Again.* London: Kelly, 1917.

_____. *The Passing of John Broadbanks.* London: Epworth, 1936.

_____. *The Prodigal.* London: Epworth, 1941.

_____. *The Silver Shadow and Other Day-Dreams.* London: Kelly, 1918.

_____. *A Temple of Topaz.* London: Epworth, 1928. Reprinted—Philadelphia: Judson, 1951.

Crago, T. Howard. *The Story of F. W. Boreham.* London: Marshall, Morgan, and Scott, 1961.

17

A. W. Tozer

(1897-1963)

From 1928 to 1959, A. W. Tozer pastored the Southside Alliance Church in Chicago and functioned as the conscience of evangelicalism at large. I heard him preach many times—always with profit—and waited for his books to be published as impatiently as a detective-story addict waits for the next installment of the current serial. I still reread his books regularly and always find in them something new to think about. This does not mean I always agreed with Tozer. There were times when I felt he was leading a parade of one down a dead-end street, such as when he vigorously opposed Christian movies. His sometimes acid criticisms of new Bible translations and of churches that "majored in counting noses" were but small defects in an otherwise straight and sturdy wall. There was an intensity about his preaching, as there is about his writing. Tozer walked with God and knew Him intimately. To listen to Tozer preach was as safe as opening the door of a blast furnace!

To prevent a generation arising that knows not Tozer, I want to devote the first half of this chapter to the man and his books; then I want to consider some other Christian mystics.

The official biography of Tozer is written by David J. Fant, Jr., and is entitled *A. W. Tozer: A Twentieth-Century Prophet.* Unfortunately, the book does not tell too much about the man, and what it does tell might have been written for a press release or for page 1 of an appreciation booklet. The first chapter takes us from his birth (21 April 1897) to his death (12 May 1963), and the remaining eleven chapters concentrate on Tozer's writings, summarizing what he believed and why he believed it. If I understand Tozer's philosophy of books and writing, he would disagree with Fant's approach. "Read the man himself!" he would say. "Don't read *about* the man, or what some writer says about the man. Read the man himself!" While I appreciate the excellent quotations Fant selected and agree with his analysis of Tozer's thinking, I still feel that getting acquainted with this vibrant writer via a biographer is like going to a flower show over a telephone. I suggest you read Tozer's books first, then read Fant's biography.

Begin with *The Pursuit of God,* one of the best devotional books ever written by an American pastor. As your grandmother used to say about her home medicines, "It's good for what ails you!" *The Pursuit of God* polishes the lenses of my soul and helps me see better. It cures the fever that often makes a man mistake activity for ministry. It rebukes my lack of worship. For these reasons (and many more), I try to read the book at least once a year. Follow with *The Divine Conquest,* then with *The Knowledge of the Holy,* a book that, to me, is the finest modern devotional treatment of the attributes of God. Once you have read these three volumes, you will have a grasp of the essentials of Tozer's thinking about God, Christ, the Holy Spirit, the church, the Bible, and the responsibility of the believer in today's world. You are then prepared to launch into his books of spiritual essays, such as *The Root of the Righteous, Born After Midnight, Of God and Men, That Incredible Christian, Man: The Dwelling Place of God,* and (if you enjoy poetry and hymnody) *The Christian Book of Mystical Verse.* All of his books are published by Christian Publications, with the exception of *The Knowledge of the Holy,* which is published by Harper. Nearly all these essays originally appeared as editorials in *The Alliance Witness,* which Tozer edited for many years and which was perhaps the only evangelical publication people read primarily for the editorials!

Let me suggest that you *not* read these books the way you read other books, attempting to finish them quickly, perhaps at one sitting (a phrase Tozer despised). Read Tozer leisurely, meditatively, almost as a worship experience. Read each essay slowly, as though the writer were chatting with you personally in front of a friendly fireplace in his living room. Read with your heart; keep your ear tuned to that "other Voice" that will surely speak to you and remind you of the truths of God's Word. My experience has been that, when reading a book by Tozer, some passage will cause me to put down the book, pick up my Bible, and then start thinking about some truth on my own. And this is exactly what Tozer would want! "The best book is not one that informs merely," he wrote in "Some Thoughts on Books and Reading," "but one that stirs the reader up to inform himself."[1] I try to keep a notebook at hand when I read any book, but especially when I read Tozer.

After becoming acquainted with his devotional essays, read the two biographies he wrote: *Wingspread,* the life of A. B. Simpson, founder of the Christian and Missionary Alliance; and *Let My People Go!* the life of missionary Robert A. Jaffray. Then investigate the volumes of sermons that have recently appeared, edited by Gerald B. Smith. Frankly, this series does not excite me. I can hear Tozer *in* these messages, but I believe he would have edited this material differently. I fear this may be prejudice on my part, but I prefer the incisiveness of the essays to the expansiveness of the sermons. But, since they are "genuine Tozer," I have them on my shelf and I read them.

Aiden Wilson Tozer (he preferred his initials, and who can blame him) considered himself an "evangelical mystic." Unfortunately the word *mystic* has never been a popular word in the evangelical vocabulary, especially in this day of activism and statistics. To most evangelicals, a mystic is an odd person who sees visions and hears voices and is about as useful to the church as a spare tire on a bobsled. If that were what mysticism is, I would want no part of it. But that is *not* mysticism; it is only a caricature of it. A mystic is simply a person who: (1) sees a real spiritual world beyond the world of sense; (2) seeks to please God rather than the crowd; (3) cultivates a close fellowship with God, sensing His presence everywhere; and (4) relates his experience to the practical things of life.

In his preface to *The Christian Book of Mystical Verse,* Tozer put it this way: "I refer to the evangelical mystic who has been brought by the gospel into intimate fellowship with the Godhead.

---

1. In *Man: The Dwelling Place of God,* p. 149.

His theology is no less and no more than is taught in the Christian Scriptures. . . . He differs from the ordinary orthodox Christian only because he experiences his faith down in the depths of his sentient being while the other does not. He exists in a world of spiritual reality. He is quietly, deeply and sometimes almost ecstatically aware of the presence of God in his own nature and in the world around him. His religious experience is something elemental, as old as time and the creation. It is immediate acquaintance with God by union with the eternal son."[2] Tozer's essay "Bible Taught or Spirit Taught?" is a good summary of his views on practical mysticism: "It is altogether possible to be instructed in the rudiments of the faith and still have no real understanding of the whole thing," he wrote. "And it is possible to go on to become expert in Bible doctrine and not have spiritual illumination, with the result that a veil remains over the mind, preventing it from apprehending the truth in its spiritual essence."[3] Tozer's sermons often confront us with these questions: Is God *real* to you? Is your Christian experience a set of definitions, a list of orthodox doctrines, or a living relationship with God? Do you have a firsthand experience with Him, or a secondhand experience through others? Is your heart hungering and thirsting after personal holiness? These questions are applicable today, perhaps more than we dare to admit.

Fant, at the end of his biography of Tozer, listed the books and authors that most influenced Tozer, and this list is something of a basic bibliography on the mystics. I am sure that many evangelical pastors today have either never been exposed to this wealth of devotional writing or have purposely avoided it, so I recommend the list to you. However, before you spend your book budget in securing these volumes, I suggest that you sample them in a manner that is quite easy and (best of all) inexpensive. The Upper Room (Nashville, Tennessee) publishes a series of attractive pocket-size booklets called "The Great Devotional Classics." I believe there are thirty titles in the series, ranging from William Law (who strongly influenced the Wesleys) to William Temple (archbishop of Canterbury until his death in 1944). I suggest you carry one of these booklets with you to read in spare minutes. Each booklet contains from thirty to forty pages; there is a biographical introduction and a brief discussion of the influence of the writer (or the book) in church history. The thirty or more writers (or

---

2. P. vi.

3. In *The Root of the Righteous,* pp. 34-37.

titles, where the writers are anonymous) cover a wide spectrum of theological and ecclesiastical groups.

You will find John Knox, prophet of the Reformation in Scotland; Francois Fenelon, close friend to Madame Guyon; George Fox, founder of the Quakers; John Wesley and Francis Asbury, the great Methodist leaders; Henry Scougal, whose *Life of God in the Soul of Man* is easily the greatest devotional work to come out of Scotland; Soren Kierkegaard, the melancholy Danish philosopher; Dietrich Bonhoeffer, the German theologian; and even Thomas Kelly, the young Quaker writer whose untimely death halted an exciting career. There are selections from anonymous works: *Theologia Germanica,* which Luther put alongside the Bible and Augustine's writings; and *Cloud of Unknowing,* which Tozer loved to quote.

If you profit from this excursion into the land of Christian mysticism, then search for another volume that must be on your devotional shelf. Unfortunately, like many fine books, it is out of print. Abingdon Press ought to reissue this book and make it available to this generation of preachers. I refer to *The Fellowship of the Saints,* an anthology of devotional writings edited by Thomas S. Kepler, for many years professor at Oberlin College. Kepler was an ardent student of the mystics, and in this large (800-page) volume he gives the best of their writings in a chronological sequence that enables the reader to trace the influence of one writer on the next. He started with Clement of Rome and ended with selections from twentieth-century writers. To be sure, there is some chaff here; but there is so much fine wheat that the chaff does not upset me. Look for a copy in used-book stores; I hope you find one!

Kepler compiled another anthology that you may want to secure: *The Evelyn Underhill Reader.* Evelyn Underhill was a well-known British mystic who died in 1941. Her books, *Mysticism, Practical Mysticism,* and *Worship,* are almost standard texts on these subjects. Unfortunately she was never quite sure of her theology, and it is here she parts company with Tozer. She confessed to being "a modernist on many points." But some of her personal insights are helpful, and therefore she should be read. Like poison, these matters should be "handled" but not permitted into one's system!

Harper and Row has published two basic books that should be in your library: *Christian Perfection,* written by Francois Fenelon and published in 1947; and *Treatises and Sermons of Meister Eckhart,* published in 1958. Fenelon's book is priceless for devotional reading, a chapter a day. Here is a man who conducted "spiritual conferences" in the court of Louis XIV! Chapter 1 is "On the Use of Time" and is one of the finest treatments of this elusive subject, from a spiritual point of view, that you will find anywhere. Chapter 2 deals with "Recreation." Chapter 8 considers "Fidelity in Little Things." Every pastor will want to read chapter 14: "Dryness and Distraction." These chapters are not long, but they are deep and profoundly practical. I cannot recommend this book too highly. Eckhart was a German mystic (1260-1327) whose purity of life gave great power to his preaching. Selections from his many writings are available in different editions, the most popular of which is probably *After Supper in the Refectory: A Series of Instructions,* published in 1917. Tozer recommended this book. The volume referred to above contains selections from *Talks of Instruction* as well as material from other writings.

If you wish to purchase a copy of *Cloud of Unknowing,* the edition edited by Evelyn Underhill is perhaps the best. The introduction by the editor and the glossary of terms are both very helpful to those not conversant with mystical writings. However, I must confess that, so far, this book has failed to reach me, although here and there some statements have struck fire. The repeated phrase "O Ghostly friend in God" still makes me chuckle. Out of respect for the anonymous author, I try to chuckle in a mystical way, but I fear I do not always succeed. As I grow spiritually, I am sure I will better appreciate this book.

The mystics wrote to cultivate the inner man, and certainly this is a neglected activity in our churches today. We have more Marthas than Marys! But, in the long run, the ideal Christian will not be one or the other: he will be a balance of both. Worship and work will not compete; they will cooperate. This is the contribution the evangelical mystics can make to our lives, and I trust you will sincerely give them the opportunity.

Martyn Lloyd-Jones and I were discussing the mystics over dinner one evening, and he related an interesting experience. With his permission I repeat it here.

"Dr. Tozer and I shared a conference years ago," he said, "and I appreciated his ministry and his fellowship very much. One day he said to me, 'Lloyd-Jones, you and I hold just about the same position on spiritual matters, but we have come to this position by different routes.'

" 'How do you mean?' I asked.

" 'Well,' Tozer replied, 'you came by way of the Puritans and I came by way of the mystics.' And, you know, he was right!"

Which perhaps goes to prove that doctrine and devotion have been joined together by God and that no man dare put them asunder. Our understanding of doctrine ought to lead us into greater devotion to Christ, and our deeper devotion ought to make us better servants and soul-winners. Jesus beautifully joined both together when He said: "Abide in me and I in you . . . for without me, ye can do nothing." This is the message of the evangelical mystics, a message we desperately need to hear today.

Bibliography

Cloud of Unknowing: A Book of Contemplation. Edited by Evelyn Underhill. London: Watkins, 1970.

Eckhart, Meister. *After Supper in the Refectory: A Series of Instructions . . .* Translated by N. Leeson. London: Mowbray, 1917.

_____. *Treatises and Sermons.* Edited and translated by James M. Clark and John V. Skinner. New York: Harper, 1958.

Fant, David J., Jr. *A. W. Tozer: A Twentieth-Century Prophet.* Harrisburg, Pa.: Christian Publications, 1964.

Fenelon, Francois. *Christian Perfection.* Edited by Charles F. Whiston. Translated by Mildred Whitney Stillman. New York: Harper, 1947.

Kepler, Thomas S., ed. *The Fellowship of the Saints.* New York: Abingdon, 1948.

Tozer, A. W. *Born After Midnight.* Harrisburg, Pa.: Christian Publications, 1964.

_____, ed. *The Christian Book of Mystical Verse.* Harrisburg, Pa.: Christian Publications, 1963.

_____. *The Divine Conquest.* Harrisburg, Pa.: Christian Publications, 1950.

_____. *The Knowledge of the Holy: The Attributes of God.* New York: Harper, 1961.

_____. *Let My People Go! The Life of Robert A. Jaffray.* Harrisburg, Pa.: Christian Publications, 1947.

_____. *Man: The Dwelling Place of God.* Harrisburg, Pa.: Christian Publications, 1966.

_____. *Of God and Men.* Harrisburg, Pa.: Christian Publications, 1960.

_____. *The Pursuit of God.* Harrisburg, Pa.: Christian Publications, 1948.

_____. *The Root of the Righteous.* Harrisburg, Pa.: Christian Publications, 1955.

_____. *That Incredible Christian.* Harrisburg, Pa.: Christian Publications, 1964.

_____. *The Tozer Pulpit.* Edited by Gerald B. Smith. Harrisburg, Pa.: Christian Publications, 1967.

_____. *Wingspread: Albert B. Simpson.* Harrisburg, Pa.: Christian Publications, 1943.

Underhill, Evelyn. *The Evelyn Underhill Reader.* Edited by Thomas S. Kepler. New York: Abingdon, 1962.

18

W. E. Sangster

(1900-1960)

When you visit Westminster Abbey in London, be sure to visit as well the nearby Methodist house of worship known as Westminster Central Hall. For sixteen years, from 1939 to 1955, William Edwin Sangster pastored the flock that met in that house of worship, and he not only pastored the flock but, during World War II, managed an airraid shelter in the basement of the building. For 1,688 nights he ministered to the physical, emotional, and spiritual needs of all kinds of people, and at the same time he wrote and preached exciting sermons, earned a Ph.D., led hundreds of people to faith in Christ, and established himself as a worthy successor to John Wesley as one of Methodism's great leaders.

Sangster was born in London on 5 June 1900, and when he was nine years old identified himself with the Radnor Street Mission in his neighborhood, one of the branch ministries of the Wesley Chapel on City Road. In October 1913 the superintendent of the mission, Frank Wimpory, led Sangster to the Lord, and in a short time the lad became active in soul-winning activities. But the

Radnor Street Mission was not only the scene of Sangster's conversion but also the place where he met Margaret Conway and fell in love with her in 1916. Ten years later they were married. He preached his first sermon at the mission on 11 February 1917. His father wanted him to become an accountant, but his Sunday school teacher, Robert Flenly, urged him to consider the ministry. He did. God called him, and he surrendered.

After spending time in the army, he entered college and worked hard to prepare himself for the ministry. One of his problems was his accent, which smacked of his London upbringing. He took private lessons in elocution and often spent hours reading sermons aloud or practicing recitations. In his fine biography of his father, *Doctor Sangster,* Paul E. Sangster related that these elocution lessons were very trying to students in adjacent rooms. One day, when Sangster had repeated for the tenth time "Who shall deliver me from the body of this death?" a student knocked at the door and asked, "Will *I* do?" But the practice paid dividends, and Sangster mastered the art of public speaking.

He was probationary minister in the Bognor Circuit from 1923 to 1926, ministering in several Methodist churches. On 27 July 1926, he was ordained at the Wesley Chapel in York; two weeks later he married his childhood sweetheart. He made it very clear to her that he would not be a handyman around the house (he was very unhandy!) or a gardener or a dishwasher, but that he would love her and make her happy—and he kept his word. His book *He Is Able* he dedicated "to Margaret, my wife, with whom it is as easy to keep in love as to fall in love." But his growing ministry often took him away from home, and it is probable that his death on 24 May 1960 was brought on partly by overwork. "I just can't do enough!" was the motto of his life. Yet, on his 1957 Christmas greeting he wrote, "Slow me down, Lord!" Alexander Whyte always advised pastors to "take long holidays," but Sangster was not made in that mold.

His first official charge after ordination was at Conway in North Wales. I have visited this beautiful town on Colwyn Bay, walked across its famous suspension bridge, and investigated the ruins of its historic Conway Castle. What a place for a young man to begin his ministry! He pastored two Methodist churches there, yet he said that he felt as if he were "perpetually on a holiday." Before long the congregations were filling the churches and his reputation as a preacher was growing. His sanctified sense of humor at first upset some of the Welsh saints, but in time they grew to love him and to appreciate his balanced approach to Christian living. In

1929 he moved to Liverpool where again he pastored two churches, and again the churches were filled. It was at Liverpool that Sangster went through a deep spiritual crisis, the details of which are unknown. "Not even my mother knew exactly what was wrong," his son wrote. "She only knew something *was* wrong."[1]

After his father's death, Paul found a handwritten "spiritual analysis" buried in the bottom drawer of the desk. It was dated "18.9.30" and was clearly the record of the spiritual conflict that Sangster had gone through at that time—in spite of large congregations and obvious success in his ministry. It begins, "I am a minister of God and yet my private life is a failure in these ways. . . ." Then he listed eight areas of defeat. He concluded: "I have lost peace. . . . I have lost joy. . . . I have lost taste for my work. . . . I feel a failure." What was the answer? "Pray. Pray. Pray. Strive after holiness like an athlete prepares for a race. The secret is in prayer." He ultimately found victory, although at times his depression was so acute that he considered resigning from the ministry. No doubt this valley experience helped him in later years, especially during the war when he had to encourage so many brokenhearted people.

In 1932 the Sangsters moved to Scarborough, and at first the decision seemed to be a mistake. The church was "run" by four powerful men, three of whom were very wealthy, and they handed down their decisions as the will of God. One of their decisions was that "famous guest preachers" occupy the pulpit ten Sundays during the year, but they soon discovered that the "big names" drew smaller congregations than did their own pastor! The four generals, realizing their error, then offered Sangster a bonus for preaching in his own pulpit! In the end, pastoral leadership prevailed, but there were several skirmishes and not a few battles.

I cannot help but pass along a story about one of the members of the Queen Street Church in Scarborough who happened to be a bit "backward," because almost every church has its eccentric member, someone who is both loved and laughed at, scolded and sheltered. The man in Queen Street was a barber who felt it was his duty to witness to his customers, but often he was not careful in his approach. After lathering a man for a shave, the concerned barber picked up his razor and said, "Sir, are you prepared to meet your God?" Needless to say, the customer fled with the lather still on his face. This same brother was as eccentric in his praying as he was in his witnessing. Once he opened his prayer with "O Lord,

---

1. Paul E. Sangster, *Doctor Sangster*, p. 89.

Thou wilt have noticed in the evening paper. . . ." I can just see Sangster chuckling to himself and praying for his odd friend.

In 1936 Sangster was asked to take the Brunswick Church in Leeds and thus to follow the well-known preacher and psychologist, Leslie Weatherhead. Every pastor ought to read Sangster's soul-searching analysis of this call.[2] It begins: "A ferment of thought in my mind in these days—a shrinking from the task." What faithful minister of the Word has not felt that way at one time or another! But it was during this time of soul-searching that Sangster felt his call to summon Methodism back to evangelism and revival. "Something else has come too," he wrote. "A sense of certainty that God does not want me only for a preacher. He wants me also for a leader—a leader in Methodism." And a leader he did become, not only during his three years in Leeds but more during those sixteen remarkable years at Westminster Central Hall in London.

On 3 September 1939 William Sangster began his ministry at Westminster, and one of his first tasks during that morning worship service was to announce that Britain and Germany were officially at war. A year later the devastating air raids began, and Sangster turned the church basement into a shelter; night after night he lived with the people, encouraged them, and ultimately led many of them to Christ. The Sunday services were continued, and the sanctuary was usually full. One Easter Sunday a lady visitor arrived too late to get a seat and was offered by the steward a seat on one of the stone steps in the choir. Of course this was an insult, and she stalked away, muttering, "If that's the way you treat visitors, no wonder the churches are empty!"

So successful was Sangster as a preacher-evangelist that in 1955 he was appointed general secretary of the Home Mission Department, and under his leadership personal evangelism, prayer, and personal holiness became important matters in Methodist churches across the country. His sermons, books, articles, and personal contacts were used of God to awaken not only his own denomination, but other groups, to the importance of winning the lost to Christ. He conducted preaching seminars, evangelism clinics, and other meetings in scores of cities, always hoping to rekindle in the hearts of Methodist preachers and lay leaders the fire that had burned in Wesley's heart. But in 1957 physical problems definitely slowed him down, and in 1958 the diagnosis was made: progressive muscular atrophy—cause, unknown; cure, unknown.

---

2. Ibid., pp. 109-10.

When Sangster found out he was slowly dying, he made four resolutions: "I will never complain. I will keep the home bright. I will count my blessings. I will try to turn it to gain." Later he wrote: "There have been great gains already from my sickness. I live in the present. I am grateful for little things. I have more time—and use it—for prayer." For the next thirty months he experienced the slow paralysis of his muscles, finally being able to move only two fingers. With them he communicated with others by writing, but ultimately even that became illegible. On 24 May 1960 he died. It was Wesley Day, a providential occurrence that must have pleased Sangster no end. More than 1,500 people attended the memorial service at Westminster Central Hall on 3 June. Sangster's close friend Professor H. Cecil Pawson gave the address. You will find it, plus a brief biographical sketch and three sermons, in the book *Sangster of Westminster.*

Fortunately, Sangster left us at least fifteen books and many articles and pamphlets. There are two volumes of *Westminster Sermons. Sangster's Special Day Sermons* was the last volume he wrote, and in this country it was published by Abingdon. He left over a thousand sermon manuscripts when he died, but he wanted none of them published. His first book was *Why Jesus Never Wrote a Book* (1932). Other titles include: *God Does Guide Us, He Is Able, These Things Abide, Let Me Commend,* and two excellent studies in Christian holiness: *The Path to Perfection* (his doctoral thesis) and *The Pure in Heart.* But Sangster's books on preaching are, to me, more valuable than his sermons, although the sermons clearly show us how he applied his homiletical principles. Secure and read *The Approach to Preaching, The Craft of Sermon Construction,* and *The Craft of Sermon Illustration.*

Sangster's sermons have three characteristics: simplicity, clarity, and intensity. You can understand him! Early in his ministry he formed the habit of reading his messages to his wife and deleting or revising anything she did not clearly understand. He constantly sought the clearest way to express Bible truth, and nobody could describe his messages as one man described P. T. Forsythe's—"fireworks in a fog!" Furthermore, Sangster was a master of illustrations, and his book on this subject is one of the best in the field. I fear that those who have criticized him in this area have not seriously read him. Sangster did not advocate "artificial illustrations" or "sky-scraper sermons—one story on top of another." He used illustrations, and he did it well!

His messages throb with intensity. They reveal a preacher who loves people and who is desperately concerned to help them spiritually. I once heard a famous Bible teacher, now deceased, boast that he "preached only to the four square feet in front of his face!" Sangster preached to people, to both the mind and the heart, and he prepared his messages with the listener in view. His sermons were not the cold, academic productions of the learned professor (although he *was* learned); they were the warm, pastoral pleadings of a man who pursued personal holiness and who sought to make the gospel of Christ meaningful to the man on the street. In one of his lectures, Sangster suggested that the secret of "unction" in preaching is "personal holiness and . . . a passionate love of souls."[3]

No matter how you measure him, William Sangster was a big man. He had a big heart for lost souls and for all true Christians everywhere. He had a big vision of revival in his denomination and in all the churches, a vision of a nation stirred for Jesus Christ. He was happy to hear of any man's success in the ministry and never criticized a fellow pastor or envied his successes. He once prayed at a meeting of some two thousand ministers, "Lord, we don't mind who is second as long as Thou art first!" He left behind a big store of homiletical wealth for us to use. I suggest you start investigating it very soon.

Bibliography

Sangster of Westminster. London: Marshall, Morgan, and Scott, 1960.

Sangster, Paul E. *Doctor Sangster.* London: Epworth, 1962.

Sangster, W. E. *The Approach to Preaching.* London: Epworth, 1951. Reprinted—Grand Rapids: Baker, 1974.

_____. *The Craft of Sermon Construction.* London: Epworth, 1949. Reprinted—Grand Rapids: Baker, 1972.

_____. *The Craft of Sermon Illustration.* London: Epworth, 1946. Reprinted—Grand Rapids: Baker, 1973.

_____. *God Does Guide Us.* London: Hodder and Stoughton, 1934.

_____. *He Is Able.* London: Epworth, 1949. Reprinted—Grand Rapids: Baker, 1975.

_____. *Let Me Commend: Realistic Evangelism.* New York: Abingdon-Cokesbury, 1948.

_____. *The Path to Perfection.* London: Hodder and Stoughton, 1943.

_____. *The Pure in Heart.* London: Epworth, 1954.

_____. *Special-Day Sermons.* New York: Abingdon, 1960.

_____. *These Things Abide.* London: Hodder and Stoughton, 1939.

_____. *Westminster Sermons.* 2 vols. London: Epworth, 1960-1961.

_____. *Why Jesus Never Wrote a Book.* London: Epworth, 1932.

---

3. In *The Approach to Preaching,* p. 32.

Part 2

Classic Books
on the Ministry

D. Martyn Lloyd-Jones

19

The Primacy
of Preaching

Dr. D. Martyn Lloyd-Jones is one of my favorite preachers. I do not always agree with him—nor would he expect me to—but I always benefit from his sermons. His two volumes on the Sermon on the Mount have already established themselves as modern classics, and his series on Romans is destined to be a landmark in evangelical Biblical exposition. (We trust the good doctor will be spared to complete this series. He preached for over twelve years from Romans, verse by verse, and got as far as 14:17 when he resigned from Westminster Chapel in London!) Out of more than forty years' experience as a successful pastor and preacher, he wrote *Preaching and Preachers,* a book that comes as close to being a "theology of preaching" as anything I have read in the field.

As you probably know, Lloyd-Jones was associated with G. Campbell Morgan during the closing years of Morgan's second term of ministry at Westminster Chapel. Morgan had been there from October 1904 to January 1917 and had rescued the church from its dereliction, making it one of the great preaching centers of the world. After a successful ministry as an itinerant Bible teacher (and occasional pastor and faculty member), Morgan returned to Westminster in 1933 when he was nearly seventy years old. Originally, he was to share the work with Hubert Simpson, but Simpson's poor health made this arrangement impossible and Morgan took the reins alone. (Interestingly enough, there was a vocal minority in the church that opposed Morgan's return. Morgan himself admitted, "I am prepared quite frankly to say that if I had been voting as a member I should probably have voted with that minority!")

The closing years of Morgan's ministry were solid and fruitful. But if he had done nothing else during that second pastorate but bring in his successor, D. Martyn Lloyd-Jones, he would still have done a monumental thing. I do not believe the story of that event has ever appeared in print in this country, and I believe it is worth telling. I am repeating the account here, with Lloyd-Jones's permission, from his "Centenary Address," given at Westminster Chapel on 6 July 1965 when the church commemorated the one-hundredth anniversary of the opening of the building. I have abbreviated the account slightly.

"There are one or two points in connection with my coming here which will interest you. I do not pretend to be able to understand one of them. I shall never forget reading in a newspaper at breakfast one morning at the end of 1932, that Dr. Campbell Morgan was coming back from America to join Dr. Hubert Simpson in the pastorate of Westminster Chapel. I read that quite casually, but as I read it I had a strange and curious intimation. It was so definite that I called it to the attention of my wife.

"I said, 'Now, you may think that I am going mad, but I am telling you here and now that this has got something of vital importance to do with me.' Well, the thing, of course, appeared to be sheer lunacy. I had never met Dr. Campbell Morgan and there was nothing further from my mind than the idea of leaving the church where I was ministering in South Wales.

"I was taking part in a meeting in the Albert Hall, London, in December 1935. That Tuesday night proved to be a turning point in my story. Dr. Campbell Morgan came to the meeting. I shall never forget how he frightened me before the meeting! It was a typical December night and there was quite a nasty fog about. He came to me in the speaker's room before the meeting began, and he said, 'I tell you in the presence of my Maker that no one and nothing would have made me come out on a night like this but you!' How I survived that remark, I do not know. The sequel was that on the following Thursday morning I had a letter from Dr. Morgan asking me if I could preach here on the last Sunday of the year (1935). I accepted and I preached for the first time in this pulpit.

"The next interesting link between us happened in June 1937. I was in America for a preaching tour and was scheduled to preach in Philadelphia. I arrived at the house of the minister and as he received me, he said, 'Well, I don't know what sort of a congregation we can expect tonight, but this I do know: I can tell you who will be the most distinguished person in the congregation.

"I said, 'Who is that?'

"He said, 'Dr. Campbell Morgan! He arrived last night from England and the moment he heard that you were preaching here tonight, he said he was going to be here.'

"We went to the meeting and there he sat! He was the last man I wanted to see! But he did a thing which was very characteristic of him and which somehow put me right. As I was taking my text, through the corner of my eye I could see him *taking out his watch*. I saw that he was going to time me! Well, when I had finished preaching and went down from the pulpit, he was the first man to come to speak to me. Then, having spoken to me, he turned to leave the building. I noticed that he would stop every now and again and turn back to look at me. Then he would walk on, and then he would stop again and look at me. I knew exactly what was happening and I was right! He decided there and then that I was to be the man eventually to join him here. I was given that invitation in October 1938; but I did not accept it until April 1939, as I was not clear as to my duty."

In many respects Lloyd-Jones is an opposite of his predecessor. Morgan was gifted at analyzing great sections of Scripture and at expounding paragraphs; Lloyd-Jones prefers to examine the Word in detail, verse by verse. Morgan was basically a devotional preacher; Lloyd-Jones emphasizes doctrine. Morgan lived in the four Gospels and seemed to avoid heavily doctrinal books like Romans and Ephesians; Lloyd-Jones has done some of his greatest preaching from these very books. Of course, Morgan was more Arminian in his leanings; Lloyd-Jones is a staunch Calvinist of the Puritan school.

In fact, his Puritan convictions show up clearly in *Preaching and Preachers,* particularly in his emphasis on the primacy of preaching in the life of the local church. Lloyd-Jones is a keen theologian, and his theology permeates and motivates all of his life and ministry. His homiletics is rooted in Biblical theology, and any other kind of homiletics he termed "almost an abomination."[1]

He rejected books that suggest artificial techniques and man-made "preaching systems." To him, the chief end of preaching is "to give men and women a sense of God and His presence."[2] If you have ever heard the good doctor preach, you know that he accomplishes this purpose, both in what he says and the way he says it.

It is this important distinction between the sermon and the "act of preaching" that Lloyd-Jones emphasized in this series of lectures. "You can have good preaching even with a poor sermon,"[3] but this is not what he recommended! His own definition of *preaching* closely parallels that of Phillips Brooks: "A sermon is meant to be a proclamation of the truth of God as mediated through the preacher."[4] He considered it to be a "transaction between the preacher and the listener."[5] For this reason the preacher must be "a serious man" who will not use the pulpit to promote himself. Among several "abominations" that he mentioned are "pulpiteers" like Henry Ward Beecher, tape recorders, and devotional commentaries.[6] Since these lectures were transcribed from tape recordings (as are those in his books on Romans), I am sure that he was not condemning *all* uses of these machines. He probably referred to the current practice of some Christians to "worship" around a tape recorder, listening to some "great preacher," instead of attending services in their own church. If so, I heartily agree! As to devotional commentaries, I am sure he meant any books that become substitutes for the Bible and for the pastor's own serious study of the Word of God.

As to the good doctor's views of the public invitation[7] and the abolition of church choirs,[8] each reader must decide for himself.

---

1. P. 118.

2. Ibid., p. 97.

3. Ibid., p. 58.

4. Ibid., p. 222.

5. Ibid., p. 58.

6. Ibid., pp. 14, 18, and 174, respectively.

7. Ibid., chap. 14.

8. Ibid., p. 267.

Also, I hope my ministerial friends who read this book (and they ought to) will not take too seriously his advice that we read only sermons that were preached before 1900.[9] Apart from the fact that this would exclude Lloyd-Jones's excellent sermons, there is the consideration that other men in this century can also minister to us, even if we do not totally agree with their ideas. Of course here is where his Puritan blood begins to stir! He considers the nineteenth century a "devastating century" for its "innovations in the realm of religious worship," and he would rather that we go back to the seventeenth and sixteenth centuries for our spiritual roots.[10] Perhaps we should, but I fear that to follow Lloyd-Jones's advice would be to rob the church of some priceless spiritual treasures.

As you read, you will soon discover which men shine brightest in Lloyd-Jones's galaxy: George Whitefield, John Wesley, and Charles Spurgeon. If my count is correct these men are mentioned more than any others. Of course he would not agree with Wesley's theology, but he would agree with his emphasis on preaching the Word of God. You will also discover the men with whom he has minor disagreements! Their names are not always given, but if you know anything at all about sermons and preachers of the past and present, you will have no trouble identifying S. D. Gordon, William Sangster, Joseph Parker, J. H. Jowett, R. G. Lee, and Clarence Macartney. Have fun looking for these references!

The greatest value of this book is its twofold emphasis on the primacy of preaching and the importance of grounding our preaching on solid Biblical theology. This emphasis is needed today. We have too many "skyscraper sermons"—one story on top of another. We have too many "outlines without messages." Lloyd-Jones explained what kind of a man the preacher must be if he is going to preach Biblical sermons. He made it clear that you cannot separate the man from the message and that no amount of homiletical devices can manufacture a truly Biblical message. If I were teaching young preachers, I would require them to read this book, if only as an antidote against some of the shallow sermonizing that is going on. In this day of instant products, I fear we also have too many instant sermons that are the result of a process that bypasses study of, meditation on, and personal obedience to the Word, and prayer.

---

9. Ibid., p. 120.
10. Ibid., pp. 265-66.

Several times in these lectures Lloyd-Jones made it clear that each preacher must "be his own man." But he urged us to be the very *best* men we can possibly be. If he disagrees with another preacher, it is on the basis of a definite theological proposition; and he insists that the other preacher be able to defend his position as well. Obviously there are some areas of divine truth that even the most godly do not understand alike, and in these areas we must all exercise patience and charity. But reading these lectures will force the honest preacher to take a long, serious look at his methods and motives, and this in itself can only prove helpful.

Some of us would have preferred that Lloyd-Jones not use the phrase "baptism of the Spirit" when referring to the empowering of the Spirit in preaching the Word.[11] In this same chapter he mentioned the "unction" and the "filling" as though these ministries of the Spirit were identical. There is so much that is valuable in this book that I would not allow this one matter to distract me, but I do believe it is worth mentioning. Perhaps it is a matter of semantics.

I might add too that, to the best of my knowledge, D. L. Moody was never, as Lloyd-Jones wrote in an illustration,[12] the pastor of the church that today bears Moody's name. He was the founder and a deacon, but never its pastor. Knowing Lloyd-Jones's passion for accuracy, I suggest this be corrected in any future editions of the book.

Let me close with a word of counsel to some of my brethren who will read this book and violently disagree with some of its contents, particularly the somewhat dogmatic denunciations of ideas and practices that are sacred furnishings in our modern evangelical house. Some of us have a tendency to read only those books that agree with us and to reject anything that dares to examine the foundations on which we stand. I have too great a respect for Lloyd-Jones to ignore his warnings. I will disagree without being disagreeable. I urge my fellow preachers to read this book at least twice: once to disagree and once to be helped! It took at least two readings for me to begin to receive from these lectures what Lloyd-Jones wanted me to receive, and I plan to read the book again. This book will balance your thinking, awaken

---

11. Ibid., p. 308.
12. Ibid., p. 321.

your conscience, stir your heart. In wrestling with its contents, you will enlarge your vision and exercise your spiritual muscles. What more could a preacher ask?

Bibliography

Lloyd-Jones, D. Martyn. *Preaching and Preachers.* Grand Rapids: Zondervan, 1972.

20

Preaching on the Apostles

In 1881 the Christian complacency of Victorian England was shattered by a literary explosion entitled *The Autobiography of Mark Rutherford.* Four years later, *Mark Rutherford's Deliverance* came off the press, but by that time many readers knew that "Mark Rutherford" was actually William Hale White, a humble clerk in the Admiralty. White had trained for the Congregational ministry, but his liberal views had forced him into another vocation. Instead of preaching these views from a pulpit, he recorded them in his books and upset the faith of some of God's elect. Today his books are ignored (although men discussed them from their pulpits when they were first published), but several of White's essays are still included in those delightful little anthologies issued by some of the better British publishers. His essay "Judas Iscariot—What Can Be Said for Him?" is what started this train of thought. I ran across it in *Selected Modern English Essays,* published by Oxford University Press.

White was sure that Judas had been given a raw deal by evangelical preachers and theologians. Thomas DeQuincey agreed, for he also wrote an essay defending the betrayer. They argued that the factual evidence is not sufficient to condemn the man and that there are too many loopholes in the Gospel records. Perhaps He was a scapegoat, playing the role assigned to him by divine providence. In any event, they suggested that we give the man a break and not condemn him. But one thing they fail to explain is, Why did Judas condemn himself?

The two best studies I have ever seen on Judas Iscariot are *Judas, The Betrayer,* by Albert Nicole; and *Jesus and Judas,* by S. Pearce Carey. Nicole's study is both psychological and theological and is decidedly more subjective than Carey's. You need not agree with everything in these studies to benefit from them or to have your mind opened to facets of truth that you may never have considered before. If you plan to preach on Judas, I suggest you allow plenty of time for preparation. Human nature is profound, and the personality of Judas is especially difficult to understand. Of course you will find articles on Judas in the standard Bible dictionaries and encyclopedias, so do not ignore them. I have always felt that McClintock's and Strong's *Cyclopaedia,* reissued by Baker Book House, is excellent in its treatment of Bible personalities, as is also the *Imperial Bible Dictionary,* edited by the eminent Patrick Fairbairn and reissued by Zondervan. Both of these are older works; but in some areas they simply cannot be surpassed, and one of them is Bible biography.

This leads to an investigation of some of the better books about the twelve apostles, and, unfortunately, there are not too many.

Of course Peter is the best known of the apostles, and a good number of books have appeared about him. One of my favorites is *Simon Peter* by Hugh Martin. The book contains only eleven studies, so it does not cover every aspect of Peter's life and ministry. If you want a more complete survey, purchase *The Apostle Peter* by W. H. Griffith-Thomas. He dealt with Peter's experiences in the Gospels and Acts, and also with Peter's two epistles; and often he showed the interesting relationships that exist between Peter's life and his letters. Griffith-Thomas is helpful, but beware that you do not merely repeat his material in your messages! It is far better to digest the material and write your own message. The Wilson Foundation in Denver, Colorado, has reprinted a number of books by Dr. W. T. P. Wolston, an Edinburgh physician who was widely used of God as an evangelist and Bible teacher. Among his titles is *Simon Peter: His Life and Letters,* twenty-seven studies that are spiritually refreshing and satisfying. Wolston was converted in 1862, and in spite of a demanding medical practice, he ministered the Word faithfully well into the second decade of the twentieth century. In one sense, he was the Dr. M. R. DeHaan of his generation, a "beloved physician" with a heart for souls and a gift for teaching the Bible.[1]

I assume that you have in your library the two most valuable sets of Bible-character studies, namely, *The Greater Men and Women of the Bible,* edited by James Hastings; and *Bible Characters,* written by that prince of preachers, Alexander Whyte. The Hastings set is old but valuable, and the bibliographical data will keep you busy searching through the used-book stores and building the biographical section of your library. Of Whyte's preaching, nothing more needs to be said. Another classic that will help you study and preach about the twelve apostles is *The Training of the Twelve,* written by Alexander B. Bruce. Kregel in Grand Rapids recently issued a beautiful new reprint of this work, so it will not be necessary for you to chase down a used copy. This is one book that every pastor ought to take with him on a long holiday and read carefully, not only for insights into the hearts and minds of the apostles, but also for an understanding of the Master's methods with His men. This reminds me that G. Campbell Morgan's *The Great Physician* is also useful in this area. I assume that you will automatically consult the articles in Hastings's *Dictionary of Christ and the Gospels* and *Dictionary of the Apostolic Church.*

What about books concerning the twelve apostles? William Barclay has written one of the best: *The Master's Men.* This book grew out of a series of articles Barclay wrote for the *British Weekly,* so it is both popular and scholarly. Without wasting any words (a gift we wish more scholars possessed), he presents all the important Biblical, traditional, and archaeological data about the men Christ chose. It is unfortunate that Barclay is sympathetic with the views of "Mark Rutherford" and Thomas DeQuincey on Judas Iscariot, but these few pages do not debase the value of the entire book. Any man planning to preach on the apostles must have this book on his shelf.

One of my favorite Congregational preachers, J. D. Jones, published his series of sermons on the apostles under the title *The Glorious Company of the Apostles.* Used copies of this book are often listed in the catalogs.

In 1924 Revell published *Pen Portraits of the Twelve,* written

---

1. To secure Wolston's works, write: The Wilson Foundation, 5555 West Jewel Road, Denver, CO 80227.

by Bernard C. Clausen, who was at that time pastor of the First Baptist Church of Syracuse, New York. This series of twelve messages is warm with pastoral concern.

Another helpful series of messages is *The Master and the Twelve,* authored by J. W. G. Ward, who at one time pastored the New Court Church in London's Tollington Park (Morgan pastored the New Court Church from 1893 to 1901). The author's weakness for oratory bothers me some, but not enough to rob me of the helpfulness of these thirteen sermons. His final message, "The Master of the Twelve," is one of the best in the book.

The well-known Biblical scholar Edgar J. Goodspeed wrote *The Twelve,* and this book ought to be on your shelf. While we may not agree with some of his premises and the conclusions that follow from them, we will respect his scholarship and be thankful for whatever insights it can give us. In this same vein I can recommend Asbury Smith's *The Twelve Christ Chose.*

Perhaps the most recent book on the twelve apostles—and the most fascinating—is *The Search for the Twelve Apostles,* written by William S. McBirnie. The author spent more than thirty years studying the subject, and his studies took him to Europe thirty-nine times and to the Middle East twenty-seven times! (No doubt his travel agent will get a lion's share of the royalties.) This book is not a series of sermons; it is instead a *resource book* on the twelve apostles and six other men the author terms "apostles who were not with the twelve." I suppose no other popular book published in our day contains so much material on the church traditions regarding the apostles as does this one. The author has done his homework. He has investigated what archaeology has to say, and he has drawn his conclusions. Perhaps he leans too much on tradition, but at least he gives us the data so we can judge for ourselves. And he carefully makes his disclaimer: "I am keenly aware that absolute proof of every detail recorded here is not possible."[2] McBirnie's book is a good companion to Barclay's *The Master's Men,* and perhaps the two should be used together.

How does one go about preaching about the twelve apostles? For one thing, the pastor will want to prepare his material long before announcing his series. Otherwise he may find himself at a loss to know what to say about James, the son of Alphaeus, whose name is listed in four places in the New Testament but about whom we know next to nothing! (He even seems to have dropped out of church tradition.) Do your homework carefully, and you

---

2. P. 9.

will have plenty of material to work with. And keep in mind that you may have as much trouble preparing a message about Peter as about James the son of Alphaeus, simply because an abundance of material forces you to focus on one aspect of his life.

Second, show how these men compare to people today. The average churchgoer thinks that these twelve men were exceptional people and that this is why Christ called them. We need to convince our congregations that these were ordinary men who day by day learned to trust Christ and obey Him (Judas excepted, of course). For an interesting approach to relating their lives to twentieth-century man, read *Thirteen Men Who Changed the World,* by H. S. Vigeveno.

No doubt you will want to open your series with a message on the word *apostle.* Volume 1 of Gerhard Kittel's *Theological Dictionary of the New Testament* devotes fifty pages to this word.[3] Be sure to study Mark 3:13-19 and to consult the sermons preached on this passage. And do not forget that Jesus Christ is called an apostle in Hebrews 3:1. Jesus has several important things to say about His apostles in His prayer recorded in John 17, so pay attention to this passage. Be sure to note the references to the apostles outside of the Gospels and Acts. (Goodwin's valuable *Harmony of the Life of Saint Paul* is very helpful for locating the persons mentioned in the Epistles). And do not forget that apostles are also mentioned in the Book of Revelation (2:2; 18:20; 21:14). If you open your series with a message on the meaning of *apostleship* and devote one sermon a week to each of the apostles, you will probably want to close with a summary message that ties together the key lessons of the series.

In short, live with these men for weeks, until they become real to you. Listen as the Master teaches them; watch as He sends them out to test them. Put yourself in their shoes and then transfer the footprints from the dusty lanes of Palestine to the concrete sidewalks of your town or city. Find the one key truth that motivated each life; discover that one great lesson each had to learn; and share with your waiting people what God has given you. No doubt in every congregation there is an impulsive Peter, a doubting Thomas, a helpful Andrew, and, even, sad to say, a pretending Judas.

One final suggestion: plan also to preach a series on the apostle Peter alone. You could focus on the key events in his life, or the miracles he shared (start counting them—you will be amazed!), or

---

3. (Grand Rapids: Eerdmans, 1964), 1:407-45.

the questions he asked, etc. Were it not for Peter's interruptions and questions, we might not have some of the most wonderful statements from the lips of Christ; so don't criticize Peter too severely. The account of how Jesus turned the shifting sand of "Cephas" into the rock "Peter" is certainly an exciting one, and your congregation deserves to hear it.

If at any time in your series on the apostles you find yourself in need of something to prime the pump, turn to the biographical sermons of Charles H. Spurgeon, and also to those of Clovis Chappell. George Matheson's series on *The Representative Men of the Bible* and *The Representative Women of the Bible* are helpful, and Joseph Parker's biographical sermons in *The People's Bible* always excite the imagination. Give yourself time; give yourself to the Word and prayer; give yourself to discovering the problems of your people—and you will be led by the Holy Spirit to prepare a series of messages on the apostles that will enrich your own heart and meet the needs of the hearts of your people.

Bibliography

Barclay, William. *The Master's Men.* New York: Abingdon, 1959.
Bruce, Alexander B. *The Training of the Twelve.* Edinburgh: Clark, 1871. Reprinted—Grand Rapids: Kregel, 1971.
Carey, S. Pearce. *Jesus and Judas.* London: Hodder and Stoughton, 1931.
Clausen, Bernard C. *Pen Portraits of the Twelve.* New York: Revell, 1924.
Fairbairn, Patrick, ed. *The Imperial Bible Dictionary.* 6 vols. 2nd ed. London: Blackie, 1888. Reprinted—Grand Rapids: Zondervan, 1957.
Goodspeed, Edgar J. *The Twelve.* Philadelphia: Winston, 1957.
Goodwin, Frank J. *A Harmony of the Life of Saint Paul.* New York: American Tract Society, 1895. Reprinted—Grand Rapids: Baker, 1951.
Griffith-Thomas, W. H. *The Apostle Peter.* Grand Rapids: Eerdmans, 1946.
Hastings, James, ed. *Dictionary of the Apostolic Church.* 2 vols. New York: Scribner, 1916-1922. Reprinted—Grand Rapids: Baker, 1973.
———, ed. *Dictionary of Christ and the Gospels.* 2 vols. New York: Scribner, 1906-1908. Reprinted—Grand Rapids: Baker, 1973.
———, ed. *The Greater Men and Women of the Bible.* 6 vols. New York: Scribner, 1913-1916. Reprinted—Edinburgh: Clark, 1954.
Jones, J. D. *The Glorious Company of the Apostles.* New York: Doran, n.d.
———. *The Gospel According to St. Mark: A Devotional Commentary.* 4 vols. London: Religious Tract Society, n.d.
McBirnie, William S. *The Search for the Twelve Apostles.* Wheaton, Ill.: Tyndale House, 1973.
McClintock, John, and Strong, James. *Cyclopaedia of Biblical, Theological, and Ecclesiastical Literature.* 12 vols. New York: Harper, 1867. Reprinted—Grand Rapids: Baker, 1968.

Martin, Hugh. *Simon Peter.* London: Banner of Truth, 1967.

Matheson, George. *The Representative Men of the Bible.* London: Hodder and Stoughton, 1902.

_____. *The Representative Women of the Bible.* London: Hodder and Stoughton, 1907.

Morgan, G. Campbell. *The Great Physician.* London: Marshall, Morgan, and Scott, 1937. Reprinted—Westwood, N.J.: Revell, 1972.

Nicole, Albert. *Judas, the Betrayer.* Grand Rapids: Baker, 1957.

Smith, Asbury. *The Twelve Christ Chose.* New York: Harper, 1958.

Vigeveno, H. S. *Thirteen Men Who Changed the World.* Glendale, Calif.: Regal, 1966.

Ward, J. W. G. *The Master and the Twelve.* New York: Doran, 1924.

Whyte, Alexander. *Bible Characters.* 6 vols. Edinburgh: Oliphant, Anderson, and Ferrier, 1898-1902. Reprinted—1 vol. Grand Rapids: Zondervan, 1968.

Wolston, W. T. P. *Simon Peter: His Life and Letters.* London: Nisbet, 1893. Reprinted—Denver: Wilson Foundation, 1962.

21

Humor in
the Pulpit

Charles H. Spurgeon was standing in the hall of his house when there came a knock at the front door. The famous preacher opened it himself, and there stood a man with a huge stick in his hand. The man sprang into the hall and announced that he had come to kill Spurgeon!

"You must mean my brother," the preacher said, trying to calm the fellow. "His name is Spurgeon."

But the man would not be dissuaded. "It is the man that makes the jokes I mean to kill!"

Fortunately Spurgeon was able to get the man out of the house! Later the police picked him up and returned him to his room at the asylum. But it is interesting that even a madman identified Spurgeon as "the man that makes the jokes."

This brings to mind another Spurgeon story, one which may be apocryphal but is still worth repeating. An irate woman approached the pastor and scolded him for his humor in the pulpit. Spurgeon replied: "Well, madam, you may very well be right; but if you knew how much I held back, you would give me more credit than you are giving me now!"

Is there a place for humor in the pulpit? I suppose the only answer we can give is: it depends on the man and on what you mean by *humor.*

Certainly there is no place for what Phillips Brooks called the "clerical jester": "He lays his hands on the most sacred things, and leaves defilement upon all he touches. He is full of Bible jokes. . . . There are passages in the Bible which are soiled forever by the touches which the hands of ministers who delight in cheap and easy jokes have left upon them." Brooks was not against the pastor having a sense of humor and using it because he knew only too well that the pastor who cannot laugh at life is going to have a difficult time. "Humor involves the perception of the true proportions of life," he explained. "It is one of the most helpful qualities that the preacher can possess. There is no extravagance which deforms the pulpit which would not be modified and repressed, often entirely obliterated, if the minister had a true sense of humor."[1]

In other words there is a difference between humor, on the one hand, and jesting, buffoonery, farce, and comedy, on the other, to cite but a few aspects of the art of laughter. The pompous, solemn preacher may be funnier than the clerical jester! A man can be serious and still smile or even laugh out loud; but the man who is somber and solemn is perhaps taking himself too seriously, and that in itself may be funny. Certainly the pulpit is a serious place, and the preacher who is fighting Satan and battling for souls is not going to joke about it. But neither is he going to abandon his sense of humor—if he has one.

The experts disagree on Spurgeon's use of humor in the pulpit. After the great preacher's death his friend W. Robertson Nicoll wrote: "Mr. Spurgeon is thought by those who do not know his sermons to have been a humorous preacher. As a matter of fact there was no preacher whose tone was more uniformly earnest, reverent and solemn." Since Nicoll had read all of Spurgeon's printed sermons and heard him preach many times, his judgment can be trusted.

However, a modern student of Spurgeon, Helmut Thielicke, in his *Encounter with Spurgeon* took a slightly different view of the matter: "When Spurgeon was cheerful and humorous in the pulpit, he was putting himself into his preaching; he was entering into the sermon with his whole nature. . . . A church is in a bad way when it banishes laughter from the sanctuary and leaves it to the

---

1. *Lectures on Preaching,* pp. 55-57.

cabaret, the night club and the toastmasters."[2] The German professor (who himself is a very popular preacher) felt that
Spurgeon's humor was not something outside himself, something
brought in to spice up the discourse, but a part of the preacher's
God-given equipment; therefore it could be dedicated to God. *The
whole man must be in the pulpit,* and if this includes a sense of
humor, then so be it.

Obviously some men ought never try to be humorous in the
pulpit. Their humor is borrowed or (worse yet) forced. They stop
in the middle of an important point to "tell a joke," and thereby
erase from the minds of the listeners whatever truth they were
getting across. But when a humorous aside, or a humorous way of
saying something, is natural to the preacher and fits naturally into
the message, then it certainly can be used of God.

John Broadus said it perfectly in his Yale Lectures: "When
humor is employed in preaching, it ought to be an incidental
thing, and manifestly unstudied. It is so natural for some men to
indulge in quaint, and even in very odd sayings, they so promptly
and easily fall back into their prevailing seriousness that the
humorous remarks are unobjectionable and sometimes, through
the well-known relation between humor and pathos, they heighten
the effect. But an effort to be amusing, anything odd that appears
to have been calculated, is felt to be incompatible with genuine
seriousness and solemnity."

One of the almost-forgotten Yale lecturers, William Jewett
Tucker, summarized it like this in the lectures of 1898: "It is
impossible to discuss the question of the introduction of humor
into the pulpit apart from the knowledge of the man. The humor
of one preacher may be as reverent as the solemnity of another."[3]

Our great American humorist Mark Twain wrote something
similar in 1906: "Humor is only a fragrance, a decoration. . . .
Humor must not professedly teach and it must not professedly
preach, but it must do both if it would live forever. . . . If the
humor came of its own accord and uninvited, I have allowed it a
place in my sermon [Twain referred to his public lectures as
"sermons"], but I was not writing the sermon for the sake of the
humor." For all his foolishness, Mark Twain understood the place
and power of humor in influencing mankind. "The human race has
only one really effective weapon," he wrote, "and that is
laughter."

---

2. Pp. 23-24.

3. *The Making and Unmaking of the Preacher,* p. 122.

Even the "gloomy dean" of St. Paul's, William R. Inge, admitted: "I have never understood why it should be considered derogatory to the Creator to suppose that He has a sense of humor."

And did not wise Solomon write, "A merry heart doeth good like a medicine" (Prov. 17:22)? Even a somber book like Ecclesiastes informs us that there is "a time to weep, and a time to laugh" (3:4). Thus a preacher can be humorous not because he is *not* serious but because he *is* serious. "Even in laughter the heart is sorrowful; and the end of that mirth is heaviness" (Prov. 14:13). Solomon was a good psychologist.

The records indicate that John Wesley was not given to using humor in his preaching. "Beware of clownishness," he warned his Methodist preachers. "Let your whole deportment before the congregation be serious, weighty and solemn."

I must disagree with D. Martyn Lloyd-Jones's statement in *Preaching and Preachers* that George Whitefield was "never humorous."[4] You will find little humor in the edited versions of his sermons, but if you go back to the originals, you will find humor. If you own the valuable set *20 Centuries of Great Preaching*,[5] check the biographical essay on Whitefield in volume 3 and read the unedited sermons that follow.

Even Zwingli, the great reformer, knew how to use humor in his messages; since he usually preached for an hour, no doubt the congregation appreciated the opportunity to laugh!

I was amazed to discover that some of his contemporaries thought John Bunyan a bit too frivolous! In his "Author's Apology" that introduces the second part of *Pilgrim's Progress,* Bunyan wrote:

> *But some there be that say,*
> *He laughs too loud:*
> *And some do say, His head*
> *is in a cloud*
> . . . .
> *Some things are of that nature,*
> *as to make*
> *One's fancy chuckle, while his*
> *heart doth ache.*

---

4. P. 241.

5. Clyde E. Fant, Jr., and William M. Pinson, *20 Centuries of Great Preaching,* 13 vols. (Waco, Tex.: Word, 1971).

Bunyan suffered for Christ's sake, and he knew that sorrow and joy usually go together. (A modern humorist has suggested that perhaps Jewish people are so funny because they have suffered so much. There is food for thought there.)

It is interesting that Carl Sandburg combined these two topics in chapter 50 of his one-volume biography, *Abraham Lincoln:* "Lincoln's Laughter—and His Religion." Lincoln admitted during the Civil War, "With the fearful strain that is on me night and day if I did not laugh, I should die." A story made the rounds during Lincoln's administration telling about two Quakers who were discussing the war. One said, "I think Jefferson Davis will succeed."

"Why?" asked his friend.

"Because he is a praying man," the first replied.

"But Abraham Lincoln is a praying man," the second argued.

"True," said the first Quaker, "but the Lord will think Lincoln is joking."

One of the most interesting studies of humor is Elton Trueblood's *The Humor of Christ.* The author listed thirty passages in the synoptic Gospels that he considered "humorous."[6] He maintained that humor was part of Christ's strategy and that we cannot fully understand several of His parables apart from His humor. Trueblood listed several other titles that the interested student might want to secure.[7]

What, then, is the conclusion of the matter? First, humor is a definite part of life and the ability to laugh (at the right things, of course) is an evidence of maturity. The man who has been wounded and gone through the flames knows the true meaning of laughter. Second, if humor is a natural part of the preacher's equipment, then he dare not eliminate it completely from the pulpit. *The whole man must preach.* But his humor will not be studied and artificial: it will be spontaneous and natural; it will be acceptable because it belongs. Third, humor will always *assist* the message and not detract from it. If it becomes a distraction, then it is sin. Jesus made some of His most telling points on the waves of laughter. Finally, the preacher needs to cultivate his sense of humor, if for no other reason that to help maintain his own balance in a difficult world. If humor indicates contact with reality, and if contact with reality is a mark of mental health, then the happy man ought to be mentally healthy.

On 16 August 1900 G. Campbell Morgan delivered an address in

---

6. P. 127.

7. P. 27, note 14.

memory of his dear friend Dwight L. Moody, who had died on 22 December 1899. Morgan listed eight qualities that characterized Moody, and the second of them was humor. He said: "Is it not, invariably, the man of tears who is the man of laughter? With what relish Moody would listen to, or tell a good story! His merriment was constant and contagious. Yet none can charge him with having worked up to a point to make his audience laugh. The seriousness of the business of preaching was too real to him. Nevertheless his addresses always sparkled with humor, and, as I have sat by his side and watched the eager crowds, I have marvelled at the power with which he touched the fountain of tears and then immediately lit the tears with a flash of humor. The supreme gladness of the man will abide as one of my most cherished memories of him."[8]

Morgan could have said the same thing about his good friend Gipsy Smith, whose bubbling humor and deep pathos were often blended into a heart-stirring message. These men, Moody and Gipsy Smith, were not comedians: they were ambassadors—but joyful ambassadors. And because of their sanctified humor they were able to touch men for Christ. Not every preacher can do this, but those who can use humor should not bury their talent. It remains for each preacher to assess his own abilities and to be willing for God to use the other man as He sees fit.

Bibliography

Broadus, John. *A Treatise on the Preparation and Delivery of Sermons.* Philadelphia: Smith and English, 1870. Reprinted—New York: Harper and Row, 1944.

Brooks, Phillips. *Lectures on Preaching.* New York: Dutton, 1877. Reprinted—Grand Rapids: Baker, 1969.

Harries, John. *G. Campbell Morgan.* New York: Revell, 1930.

Lloyd-Jones, D. Martyn. *Preaching and Preachers.* Grand Rapids: Zondervan, 1972.

Thielicke, Helmut. *Encounter with Spurgeon.* Philadelphia: Fortress, 1963. Reprinted—Grand Rapids: Baker, 1975.

Trueblood, Elton. *The Humor of Christ.* New York: Harper and Row, 1964.

Tucker, William Jewett. *The Making and the Unmaking of the Preacher.* Boston: Houghton Mifflin, 1898.

---

8. John Harries, *G. Campbell Morgan,* pp. 157-58.

Henry Ward Beecher

22

The Yale
Lectures

On 31 January 1872 Henry Ward Beecher stood in the Marquand Chapel of Yale University Divinity School and opened the famous "Lyman Beecher Lectures on Preaching," better known today simply as the Yale Lectures. Each year for the past century, with few exceptions, someone has been lecturing in this series, which is certainly some kind of record in church history.

There have been other lectureships devoted to preaching—the Warrack Lectures in Scotland, for example—but none of them can claim the scope and influence of those delivered at Yale. The various lectures are uneven in value and some are downright failures; but for wealth of material, depth of insight, and breadth of vision no series on preaching can be compared to it. I must confess that I do not own all of the published volumes of this series nor have I read all of them. But I have read enough to know that the preacher who ignores this treasure house of homiletical currency is only robbing himself and the people to whom he ministers. Several of the volumes are especially important and should be read by every pastor.

Not every pastor will agree with my selections of the best books from this series. The ones I highlight are the ones that have excited me and helped me in my own ministry. Someone else might have a different list, and I would not argue with him. But I do recommend these to you.

Of course Henry Ward Beecher just had to be the first lecturer! (In fact, he gave the lectures for the first three years.) To begin with, the lectureship was founded by his close friend Henry W. Sage in honor of Beecher's famous father, Lyman Beecher. The elder Beecher was great in his own right as a preacher, educator, and a father of preachers—seven of his sons went into the ministry! At one time he was president of Lane Seminary in Cincinnati. But Henry Ward Beecher deserved the honor of being the first Yale lecturer: he was perhaps the most popular and successful preacher of his day. By this time he had reigned from the pulpit of the Plymouth Congregational Church in Brooklyn for a quarter of a century. He was preaching to at least 2,500 people each Sunday, and he claimed to have the largest congregation in the United States. Perhaps he did. He was sought after as a special speaker, and no man could doubt his oratorical skill. He knew how to meet an audience head-on and lift it higher.

I want to return to Beecher and his lectures later; but first I want to introduce you to two books that will help give you a working knowledge of the Yale Lectures and the people who participated in them.

The first is *The Royalty of the Pulpit* by Edgar De Witt Jones. This work focuses on the men who gave the lectures during the series' first eighty years. Jones, a distinguished preacher himself, had the additional advantage of knowing personally several of the later lecturers. His great appreciation for the craft of preaching made his writing sympathetic and kind. Instead of following the series chronologically, he categorized the men on the basis of their lives and their lectures. He has ten "Olympians," nine "Titans" (and it pains some of us to see John Henry Jowett in the same category as Harry Emerson Fosdick), seven "theologians and philosophers," six "prophets of social change," and so on. Some of us might question his system and whether he followed it consistently, but whatever its weaknesses, it did not hinder the author from making the lecturers very real and personable men.

It staggers me just to recall the great men who participated in this series. Here we find Phillips Brooks, R. W. Dale, William M. Taylor, Henry Clay Trumbull (who lectured on the Sunday school), John A. Broadus, James Stalker, John Henry Jowett, and

James S. Stewart, to name but a few. Of course the lectureship has been ecumenical from the beginning, covering a wide spectrum of doctrinal beliefs. The lectures for 1923-24 were Fosdick's *Modern Use of the Bible;* for 1898-99, George Adam Smith's *Modern Criticism and the Preaching of the Old Testament.*

Unfortunately, in later years the emphasis seems to be moving away from preaching. In 1966-67 Sydney Mead discussed "Aspects of Lyman Beecher's Theology." The next two series dealt with psychology, and in 1969-70 Ivan Illich spoke on "Education." A more recent series was actually a series of films! It would be tragic to see this great platform degenerate into a catchall for every variety of topic even remotely related to preaching. Perhaps this is a sign of the times.

Jones gives us many sidelights on the Yale Lectures that we probably could not find in many other books. For example, I did not know that Alexander Maclaren and Charles Spurgeon were both invited to lecture and that both of them refused. Spurgeon replied: "I sit on my own gate and whistle my own tunes and am quite content." Of course Spurgeon abhorred any "merchandising" of the gospel or his own ministry. When P. T. Barnum invited Spurgeon to come to the States to lecture, promising both large crowds and generous honoraria, Spurgeon refused in no uncertain terms (As I recall, he referred Barnum to Acts 13:10!). Spurgeon's *Lectures to My Students* compensates, however, for whatever he might have given at Yale.

Appendix 1 to Jones's book is a "Who's Who" of the lecturers, supplying a brief biography for each man. Unfortunately it is arranged in chronological instead of alphabetical order. Appendix 2 is a complete chronology of the lectures with a listing of the titles of the books in which they were published. The bibliography is helpful to the pastor who wants to get better acquainted with the men about whom Jones wrote.

The second book you should have on the Yale Lectures is *The Heart of the Yale Lectures* by Batsell Barrett Baxter, published in 1947. Baxter served on the faculty of David Lipscomb College in Nashville, Tennessee, and until a few years ago was also minister of the Hillsboro Church of Christ in that city. What Jones did for the men who lectured, Baxter did for the contents of their lectures. He has done a computer-sized job of analyzing and summarizing their lectures. He has three major divisions: "the preacher," "the sermon," and "the congregation." Under each major division he has many smaller divisions, so that each major idea has its proper category. Of course he did not quote what every speaker says about every topic, but he did quote widely from those men who really had something to say. At the close of each section is the author's summary, and in the closing chapter Baxter's "nine concluding observations" form a helpful summary of preaching principles.

Of course the great value of this book is the opportunity it gives to compare and contrast the personal views of "the royalty of the pulpit." How did Jowett define preaching? What did Burton say about the "call to the ministry"? What are the essentials for success in the ministry? How does one evaluate his ministry? I doubt if any other book on preaching contains as much helpful material as *The Heart of the Yale Lectures*. I prefer to read the original lectures, but I find Baxter's book very helpful and a great time-saver. Let me caution you, however, that this is not a "one-sitting book"—unless you happen to be confined to a wheelchair. It is a book to browse in and to read slowly, a section at a time. There is just too much here for instant digestion. It is the kind of book I like to take with me on a trip or a vacation or to keep beside a favorite chair.

At this point someone may ask the age-old question, "Why read books on preaching?" Will reading books automatically make a man a better preacher? Of course not! But if he has any ability at all, and any sense, he can benefit from the experience and counsel of other men. R. W. Dale helped to clarify the matter when he said: "Some men speak contemptuously of lectures on preaching. . . . For myself, I have read scores of books of this kind, and I have never read one without finding in it some useful suggestion. I advise you to read every book on preaching that you can buy or borrow, whether it is old or new. . . ."

The first three series of lectures, all delivered by Henry Ward Beecher, were published under the titles *Personal Elements in Preaching, Social and Religious Machinery of the Church* and *Methods of Using Christian Doctrines.* All three series were published in one volume in 1881.

Beecher did not write out his lectures, as most future lecturers would. Rather, he spoke in what he called "conversational address" and had the lectures taken down by a reporter. Beecher did not edit or revise the lectures, so they stand today as he gave them a century ago. The three series add up to nearly one thousand pages, including the reports of the question-and-answer sessions that followed. The lectures are wordy, which is what you would expect from extemporaneous speech. Someone really ought to edit these three series and give us the "meat" of Beecher's pastoral theology. In all of the lectures, Beecher leaned heavily on his personal experiences as a pastor and revivalist. This book contains no short-cut methods, but rather basic common-sense principles that are applicable today. To be sure there are cobwebs here and there, but there are also valuable insights that should be re-affirmed today.

Of course some of us have problems with Beecher's theology. "I consider myself a Calvinist," he said, "and in this way: I believe what John Calvin would have believed if he had lived in my time and seen things as I see them." When asked about the success of Spurgeon, an outspoken Calvinist, Beecher replied that Spurgeon was a success in spite of his Calvinism. Then he added a foolish statement: "I do not know that the camel travels any better, or is any more useful as an animal, for the hump on its back." It was a feeble analogy, and Spurgeon turned it right back at him! "The hump," said Spurgeon, "instead of being an excrescence only contributing ugliness to the camel's appearance, is a breast of nourishment to maintain the camel's strength." We have no record of Beecher's reply.

I must confess that I find Beecher's lectures to be tedious reading, although they must have been very exciting when heard in person. But on almost every page I find gems that I simply must underline and file for future use. "Great sermons, young gentlemen, ninety-nine times in a hundred, are nuisances." I like that! "A minister without feeling is no better than a book." I like that! I am not suggesting that you give up a meal to purchase these lectures; many other books in the Yale series are far more valuable. But since Beecher was a successful preacher and since these series did launch the entire lectureship, the book is worth owning and reading.

The second lecturer, who gave the fourth series (1874-75), was John Hall, then pastor of the famous Fifth Avenue Presbyterian Church of New York City. His lectures were published under the title *God's Word Through Preaching*. There could not have been a more dramatic contrast in lecturers! Hall was a conservative Ulsterman, a Puritan in life and theology. His manner was reserved and direct; he was not the showman that Beecher was, nor had he any desire to be. And he was a Calvinist! It is a relief to turn from the loquacious Beecher to the precise Hall and to catch once again the thrill of Biblical preaching. "We are not, gentlemen, heathen philosophers finding out things; we are expositors of a revelation that settled things." That statement calls for a sevenfold amen!

Another Scot, William M. Taylor, delivered the fifth series

(1875-76) and also the fourteenth (1885-86). He was at the time of his lectures the popular pastor of the Broadway Tabernacle in New York City. Pastors today know Taylor best as the author of several excellent books of sermons on Bible personalities: David, Moses, Joseph, Ruth, and others. His first series was on "The Ministry of the Word" and his second on "The Scottish Pulpit." Both are worth reading. And while you are enjoying Taylor's ministry, be sure to obtain his volumes of sermons on the parables and the miracles of Christ. They are among the finest you will ever read.

This brings us to the 1876-77 series delivered by Phillips Brooks, which to me simply has to be among the ten best of the entire series, if not the very best. Because I believe that Brooks and his preaching need to be reintroduced to this generation of preachers, I have devoted chapter 8 to him and his *Lectures on Preaching.*

Following Brooks was the great British preacher R. W. Dale, pastor of Carr's Lane Congregational Church, Birmingham, from 1859 to 1895. Dale was the "archbishop of Congregationalism" in his day, an accomplished preacher and a great theologian. I have always had a warm spot in my heart for Dale because he greatly encouraged G. Campbell Morgan, one of my homiletical heroes. Dale's series is simply called *Nine Lectures on Preaching,* and he covered the expected territory from the solid British point of view.

He was a devoted student, especially of theology, and he used his very first lecture to admonish his listeners: "If, however, you are to be good preachers by and by, it is necessary that you should be hard students now." So in his first lecture he emphasized study and warned against laying hold of every new theological idea that comes along. His second lecture warned the pastor to be intellectually honest. "Be sure that you know what you think you know. . . . Do not imagine that you know anything because you have a convenient formula in which you can express it. Get at the facts which lie behind the formula and live among them." But along with the intellect, Dale recommended the use of imagination, a topic not often dealt with in books on preaching. Interestingly enough, he used D. L. Moody as an example of a preacher who knew how to use imagination in his ministry. Dale said of Moody: "He talks as though Jacob had been an intimate personal friend of his . . . that he must have been in the boat with the apostles when Christ came to them over the stormy sea. . . ." He warned us to use imagination—not fancy!

I need not survey the entire book; I simply recommend it to you for careful and repeated reading. Dale was a giant of a preacher, a prolific writer, a man of power. You will not agree with all his observations (especially his statement that the Book of Numbers does not suggest many subjects for preaching), but you will grow intellectually and spiritually from the reading of his nine lectures.

James Stalker delivered the lectures in the 1890-91 series. All of us know Stalker for his classic studies, *The Life of Christ* and *The Life of Paul,* and perhaps we appreciate, too, his *Seven Deadly Sins* and *Seven Cardinal Virtues.* But there is something massive and overpowering in his Yale lectures, published under the title *The Preacher and His Models.*

Unlike the men who preceded him, Stalker found the springboard for his lectures in the Word of God. After his introductory lecture he devoted four lectures to Isaiah the prophet and four to Paul the apostle. He saw in these men the models for the Christian preacher today. Here are his titles for the first four lectures: "The preacher as a Man of God" (Isaiah's call and character); "The Preacher as a Patriot" (the ministry of criticism, denunciation, and comfort); "The Preacher as a Man of the Word" (a message from God, a message to men); and "The Preacher as a False Prophet" (not Isaiah, of course, but those he had to fight during his ministry—a powerful lecture). As you read these lectures, be careful not to get excited about preaching from Isaiah before you first apply these truths to your own life and ministry! Stalker's treatment of Paul is just as exciting: "The Preacher as a Man" (the personal qualities of a good minister); "The Preacher as a Christian" (the spiritual qualities necessary); "The Preacher as an Apostle" (the work of the ministry); and "The Preacher as a Thinker" (learning and living). By using Isaiah and Paul as his examples, Stalker incarnated the principles he wanted to teach and made it easier for us to follow his thinking.

I am tempted to quote Stalker, if only to whet your appetite.

"Let a preacher dwell always on the sunny side of the truth and conceal the shadows. . . ."

"I cannot help pausing here to say, that he will never be a preacher who does not know how to get at the conscience. . . ."

"What an audience looks for, before everything else, in the texture of a sermon is the bloodstreak of experience. . . ."

"Our sermons must rise out of the congregation if they are ever to reach down to it again."

"We stoop to conquer. It is better to feel that we belong to the congregation than that it belongs to us."

I especially appreciate the way he closed his final lecture: "This is your work; and the only true measure of ministerial success is how many souls you save—save in every sense—in the sense of regeneration and sanctification and redemption." When I read R. W. Dale, I feel like I am standing next to a huge cliff, with a gigantic waterfall cascading over it. When I read James Stalker, I find myself next to a quiet river flowing through a beautiful meadow. But in both situations, the water satisfies!

John Watson wore two hats when he brought the lectures in 1896, for he was famous both as an effective preacher-pastor and as a popular writer. Of course, as a writer he was known as "Ian Maclaren," and his *Beside the Bonnie Brier Bush* was a best seller on both sides of the Atlantic. His nine Yale lectures were published under the title *The Cure of Souls.* (Of course the word *cure* is used in the religious sense: the *care* of souls. If you remember your Latin, you will know it comes from *curare,* "to take care of." The assistant to an Anglican vicar is called a curate.) I like *The Cure of Souls* because it is a warm and friendly book, overflowing with pastoral love and studded with thinly veiled autobiographical references. The man who gave these lectures had a sense of humor and used it!

All nine chapters are helpful, but two of them are worth ten times the price of the book: "The Machinery of a Congregation" and "The Minister's Care of Himself." The first two chapters on sermon-making contain nothing especially new except the delightful way in which Watson reminds us of what we already know.

"The Machinery of a Congregation" was Watson's sixth lecture, and it was received with great enthusiasm. First, he discussed the "home" of the congregation and made some pointed suggestions about church buildings and church facilities. Some of his architectural ideas seem dull to us today, but they must have been devastating back in 1896. But he was dead right when he said: "Bad air is an auxiliary of Satan and accounts for one man sleeping, for another fidgeting, for another detecting a personal attack in the sermon, for someone smelling heresy." Poor ventilation and poor sound are the twin enemies of an exciting church service. After discussing the church building, he bravely marched into a discussion of the government of the congregation; and in spite of his Presbyterian loyalty, he defended all three systems: Congregational, Episcopal, and Presbyterian! The important thing is leadership, and the church ought to allow its pastor to exercise it. His closing topics in the lecture were the mind and the work of the congregation. He urged pastors to put only qualified people into places of leadership, particularly in the Sunday school. He then mentioned the Sunday school teacher who had told him that Herod was unable to kill Jesus during the Bethlehem massacre because Mary had hid Jesus in the bulrushes! "All machinery, however well conceived and enthusiastically worked, will be unblessed and useless," he said, "unless the church has spiritual aims, and be touched with heavenliness, unless she be cleansed from false ideals and a worldly spirit." Or to put it another way: ideas and systems don't work—people do; and those people had better be at their best for the Lord's sake.

I suggest that you read *The Cure of Souls* at one sitting (something I do not usually recommend), and that you read it not as a series of lectures but rather as a series of chatty conversations with a delightful friend. Permit yourself to smile and even to laugh out loud. After all, "A merry heart doeth good!" Just for the record, Watson died here in America, in Mount Pleasant, Iowa, on 6 May 1907; he was on his third lecture tour of the United States. He was buried in Britain. James Stalker preached the funeral message, and sixty thousand people of all denominations shared in the final tribute.

Several weighty theological volumes came out of the Yale series, books that were expansions of lectures given. *The Place of Christ in Modern Theology* by A. M. Fairbairn was the 1891 series, and George Adam Smith's *Modern Criticism and the Preaching of the Old Testament* was the 1898 series. Whether or not we agree with everything these men wrote, we must confess that these books had a tremendous influence on a whole generation of preachers. Another book in this category is *Positive Preaching and Modern Mind* by the Scottish Congregationalist Peter T. Forsyth. This book is worth reading in spite of the fact that the "modern mind" with which Forsyth dealt is now seventy-five years old. Forsyth is receiving new emphasis today, almost to the point of a cult developing around his writings. Eerdmans recently reprinted *The Cure of Souls,* an anthology from Forsyth's writings, edited by Harry Escott and originally published in Britain in 1948. Interestingly, the dedication reads: "To the growing band of disciples who have found in P. T. Forsyth inspiration for prayer, action and thought." I do not suggest you join any disciple band; I do suggest you read his Yale lectures, but be prepared to stretch your mind.

Charles Edward Jefferson, pastor of the Broadway Tabernacle, New York City, from 1898 until his death in 1937, gave the Yale

Lectures in 1909. They were published under the title *The Building of the Church*. This book ought to be handed to every new pastor at his ordination, but it is not too late for some of us who have been at it a few years to benefit from its pages.

Jefferson began with a truth that some pastors never seem able to grasp: local churches are living temples with traditions and dispositions and personalities of their own, and the pastor who ignores these—or, worse yet, insults them—is destined for failure. Said Jefferson, "Blessed is the preacher who realizes that he is only a sojourner as all his fathers were." He went on to say: "If a man loves his church and proves his love by his life, he can say to it anything which is proper for a Christian teacher to say to his pupils, anything which is fitting for a Christian man to say to his friends. . . . No man has a right to chide or condemn men unless he has won the right by loving them." More than once I have filled the pulpit of a church pastored by a man who seemed to hate both the building and the congregation that met in it! Jefferson's emphasis was this: we are not merely winners of souls or teachers of church members, but we are men involved in building the church. It is one thing to build a crowd; it is quite another to build a church. "No matter how long he stays, there will be more work to do than there was in sight at the beginning. Men who engage in the building of the church know that the work is never done."

His next six lectures dealt with various aspects of the "building process": building the brotherhood, the individual, moods and tempers, thrones, the holy catholic church (he means the church universal, of course), and the plan. The final lecture on "Building the Builder" emphasizes, of course, the pastor himself. This is a refreshing and rewarding book from the heart of a city pastor. It is saturated with common sense, an indispensable ingredient for ministerial success. I have underlined many sentences and marked whole paragraphs in my own copy, and I am sure that I will underline more when I read it again.

The famous J. H. Jowett gave the lectures in 1912, one year after he came to pastor the illustrious Fifth Avenue Presbyterian Church in New York City. In 1895 Jowett had succeeded R. W. Dale as pastor of Carr's Lane, Birmingham, and he remained there until 1911. (Dr. A. T. Pierson called that church "the finest church in the world.") He remained in New York City until 1918 when he returned to London to succeed G. Campbell Morgan at Westminster Chapel. You owe it to yourself to read Arthur Porritt's biography of this famous preacher, and you ought to have his sermons on your shelves. While I am not addicted to Jowett the way some preachers are (his sermons are a bit too refined and polished for me—almost artificially so), I still appreciate what he has to say. Jowett's series is published under the title *The Preacher: His Life and Work.* This volume is so well known and popular that I really need to say very little about it. His seven lectures cover the basic responsibilities of the pastoral and preaching ministry in a satisfying way. If a man masters Brooks, Stalker, and Jowett and practices what they say, he ought to have some kind of success in the ministry!

In 1952 the university went across the water for another Scotsman, James S. Stewart—author, professor, and preacher. Stewart's book on Paul, *A Man in Christ,* is required reading for the pastor who wants to understand Acts and the epistles. His three volumes of sermons are required reading too: *The Gates of New Life, The Strong Name,* and *The Wind of the Spirit.* His Yale series is entitled *A Faith to Proclaim,* and it is an excellent companion volume to his *Heralds of God,* a book dealing primarily with the mechanics of preaching. *A Faith to Proclaim* centers on the message rather than on the messenger or the methods for proclaiming the message. The five lectures deal with proclaiming the incarnation, forgiveness, the cross, the resurrection, and Christ Himself. Stewart's lectures, like his sermons, are a beautiful blending of Bible doctrine, contemporary insights, and sensible applications to the needs of life. Surely this is one of the best of the more recent series from Yale.

The pastor who regularly reads books on preaching is certainly a wise man, provided he practices what he learns. I suggest you not overlook the vast treasure of homiletical truth in the volumes of Yale Lectures on preaching. Your list of "the best books" will differ from mine, but neither of us will be the loser!

Bibliography

Baxter, Batsell Barrett. *The Heart of the Yale Lectures.* New York: Macmillan, 1947. Reprinted—Grand Rapids: Baker, 1971.

Beecher, Henry Ward. *Yale Lectures on Preaching.* New York: Fords, Howard, and Hulbert, 1881.

Brooks, Phillips. *Lectures on Preaching.* New York: Dutton, 1877. Reprinted—Grand Rapids: Baker, 1969.

Dale, R. W. *Nine Lectures on Preaching.* New York: Barnes, 1878.

Fairbairn, A. M. *The Place of Christ in Modern Theology.* London: Hodder and Stoughton, 1893.

Forsyth, P. T. *Positive Preaching and Modern Mind.* London: Hodder and Stoughton, 1907. Reprinted—Grand Rapids: Eerdmans, 1964.

Fosdick, Harry Emerson. *The Modern Use of the Bible.* New York: Macmillan, 1924.

Hall, John. *God's Word Through Preaching.* New York: Dodd and Mead, 1875.

Jefferson, Charles E. *The Building of the Church.* New York: Macmillan, 1910. Reprinted—Grand Rapids: Baker, 1969.

Jones, Edgar De Witt. *The Royalty of the Pulpit: A Survey and Appreciation of the Lyman Beecher Lectures.* New York: Harper, 1951.

Jowett, J. H. *The Preacher: His Life and Work.* New York: Hodder and Stoughton, 1912. Reprinted—Grand Rapids: Baker, 1968.

Smith, George Adam. *Modern Criticism and the Preaching of the Old Testament.* London: Hodder and Stoughton, 1902.

Stalker, James. *The Preacher and His Models.* London: Hodder and Stoughton, 1891. Reprinted—Grand Rapids: Baker, 1967.

Stewart, James S. *A Faith to Proclaim.* London: Hodder and Stoughton, 1953. Reprinted—Grand Rapids: Baker, 1972.

Taylor, William M. *The Ministry of the Word.* London: Nelson, 1876. Reprinted—Grand Rapids: Baker, 1975.

_____. *The Scottish Pulpit.* New York: Harper, 1887.

Watson, John. *The Cure of Souls.* New York: Dodd and Mead, 1896.

Edwin C. Dargan

23

Histories
of Preaching

"The business of the historian," wrote Henry Steele Commager, "is neither to entertain . . . nor to describe. . . . It is to ask questions and try to answer them. . . . His three questions are: what happened, how did it happen and why did it happen?" This quotation came to mind while reading the third volume of *A History of Preaching.* Edwin Charles Dargan wrote the first two volumes, published in 1905 and 1912, but did not live to complete the projected third volume; Ralph Turnbull finished it recently. These three volumes survey preaching and preachers in Europe and America from the apostolic fathers through 1950.

Edwin Charles Dargan, born 17 November 1852 in Darlington County, South Carolina, pastored several churches in South Carolina, Virginia, and California after his ordination to the Baptist ministry in 1876. In 1892 he became professor of homiletics at Southern Baptist Theological Seminary in Louisville, Kentucky.

During the last year of his teaching ministry, Dargan became pastor of the First Baptist Church, Macon, Georgia. In 1907 he resigned from the seminary to take the church full time. He remained there until August 1917, when he became editor of the

Sunday school materials for the Southern Baptist Convention. He held that position until 1927. Dargan was honored by the convention when elected to serve as its president from 1911 to 1913. Dargan's other works include the commentary on Colossians in *The American Commentary* (the set that contains John A. Broadus's masterful commentary on Matthew); an exposition of Romans; a book on ecclesiology; and two volumes of sermons. He also contributed to Hastings's *Dictionary of Christ and the Gospels,* the *Schaff-Herzog Encyclopedia,* and other publications.

Considering Commager's three questions we might wonder if a history of preaching is a valid theme and if such a history will do any good for the man in the pulpit. Obviously a man does not have to know the history of preaching to be able to preach. But if he is going to have perspective in his work, he should know the place of preaching in history. True preaching cannot be divorced from life. If I am going to appreciate fully the ministry of Charles H. Spurgeon or Joseph Parker, I need to know something about the Victorian Age in which they lived and preached. In the same manner, if I am to understand the Victorian Age, I need to know something about the preachers of that era. God usually prepares a man for an age, and the better we understand the age, the better we appreciate the man. *A History of Preaching* is basically biographical. Both Dargan and Turnbull provide helpful interpretative material, sketching the political and social events of the times, not in depth, but sufficiently to see the actors on something other than a bare stage.

The amount of material in these volumes is amazing. Dargan's successor at Southern Seminary, J. B. Weatherspoon, in his preface to the 1954 Baker reprint edition, called these two volumes "ambitious and encyclopaedic." His words can easily be applied to Turnbull's volume too.

Convinced that one of the curses of our age is imitation, I was thrilled to discover in these books that God is infinitely original. He uses many kinds of tools to build His church. While we have much to learn from the great preachers of the past, the most important lesson they teach is that they preached in the past. They preached to their age. For us to imitate them is to fail to preach to our age. Today we see a new interest in the Puritan preachers. This is good, but woe unto that pastor who tries to imitate Thomas Manton or John Owen. I have heard some admirers of the Puritans try to echo their voices, and the results have been painful. Yes, the Puritans still speak to us, and I thank God that they do. But we are not to speak as they did.

According to Dargan and Turnbull, even during the "dark days" of the church, God still works, usually preparing leaders for the next age of expansion and conquest. "The good old days" had their bad days as well. During the "bad days" somebody was on the Potter's wheel being molded as a vessel to bring the water of life to thirsty hearts. During the days of such great achievement, seeds were being sown that produced bitter fruit of division and heresy in later years. "He who does not know the past is condemned to repeat it" applies to preachers as well as politicians. Solomon was right: "There is nothing new under the sun." The preacher who has a grasp of church history in general and of the history of preaching in particular is not going to be shocked by the latest heresy or overawed by the latest victory.

Turnbull did outstanding work in writing the third volume of the series. He was eminently qualified, having ministered with great success in several pastorates, having taught preachers, and having written extensively about preaching and preachers. He knew the field, he loved the work, and he wrote from a pastor's heart. Turnbull's volume is valuable for the bibliographical information alone. It could easily be used as a guide to building a homiletical and biographical library. It includes in the thirty-nine–page bibliography a complete list of the Yale Lectures on preaching, as well as the Sprunt Lectures and the Warrack Lectures. Turnbull even provided an index of sermons mentioned in the volume. The names of preachers in the text are in bold type so the reader can locate them quickly. The sections on Black preaching, Jewish preaching, and preaching in Canada are welcome additions to the literature of homiletics. Being of Scandinavian background, I appreciated his section on preaching in that part of the world. This is an amazing volume. I cannot conceive of a preacher finding a dull page in it.

Many books are available about "great preachers of the past," most of them painfully thin and afflicted with "journalese." *A History of Preaching,* volume 3, is the one volume you need to supply information about preaching and preachers in the recent past. If you add Dargan's two volumes, you have a dependable encyclopedia of preaching. The essays that introduce a period in history or explain it can never take the place of a larger history, but they do their job well. Turnbull does better than Dargan, but both help us discover what happened, how it happened, and why it happened.

Of course, these three volumes are not the only ones you should have. I heartily recommend F. R. Webber's three-volume *A*

History of Preaching in Britain and America. Webber had Dargan's two volumes before him when he wrote, plus additional historical data that was not available in Dargan's time, so in some areas his studies are more complete. However, Webber limited himself to Britain and America (Dargan included continental preaching) and for the most part to Protestant Christian preaching.

Dargan left us a "condensed" version of his two volumes, a series of lectures given at Southwestern Baptist Theological Seminary in 1921 and published as *The Art of Preaching in the Light of Its History.* It is a simple survey of the major factors in the art of preaching throughout church history. Parts of this book are boring, particularly the reviews, chapter by chapter, of various treatises on preaching. But the volume is helpful if you want to discover how preaching has changed.

Lectures on the History of Preaching by John Ker (1888) is a helpful volume, but it is far from complete: Ker died before finishing it. The first eight lectures deal with preaching in the church prior to the Reformation. The last thirteen focus on the church in Germany. Ker (pronounced "car") was George Morrison's favorite preacher. His two volumes of sermons, while hard to find, are worth owning and reading, as is his fascinating book *The Psalms in History and Biography.*

For a more popular treatment of preaching in history, let me recommend *The Romance of Preaching* by C. Silvester Horne. These were the Yale Lectures for 1914, and they were published posthumously since Horne died three days after delivering them. Horne defended a daring thesis: "The preacher, who is the messenger of God, is the real master of society; not elected by society to be its ruler, but elected of God to form its ideals and through them to guide and rule its life."[1] Would that all our preaching had that great an effect on society. Horne himself was involved in British politics and even served as a member of Parliament. He greatly admired the Puritans, which helps explain his attitude toward preaching and its place in society.

A few more titles should be consulted concerning the history of preaching. One is the classic *Religion in the Development of American Culture* by the noted church historian William Warren Sweet. Another is T. H. Pattison's *The History of Christian Preaching.* William Taylor's Yale lectures for 1886, *The Scottish Pulpit,* are valuable for a study of that great subject. And DeWitte Holland's

---

1. P. 15.

Preaching in American History presents several sermons that played a great role in shaping the American mind.

To know the men who preached in the past and to know the times in which they preached is to acquire a maturity not granted with a diploma. If we must be better men to be better preachers and if education helps make us better men, then an understanding of history ought to give us the perspective and insight that will help us better minister to our age. Horne said it perfectly: "But for the present let me lay it down that there is nothing in Holy Writ to warrant the assumption that a man is likely to be more spiritual if he is an ignoramus; or that prophetic power in the pulpit especially attaches to the preacher whose heart is full and whose head is empty. Knowledge is really not a disqualification for the ministry; neither is there any incompatibility between the seer and the scholar."

Bibliography

Dargan, Edwin Charles. *The Art of Preaching in the Light of Its History*. New York: Doran, 1922.

_____, and Turnbull, Ralph G. *A History of Preaching*. 3 vols. Vols. 1-2—New York: Armstrong, 1905-1912. Reprinted—Grand Rapids: Baker, 1974. Vol. 3—Grand Rapids: Baker, 1974.

Holland, DeWitte. *Preaching in American History . . . 1630-1967*. Nashville: Abingdon, 1969.

Horne, Charles Silvester. *The Romance of Preaching*. New York: Revell, 1914.

Ker, John. *Lectures on the History of Preaching*. 2nd ed. London: Hodder and Stoughton, 1888.

Pattison, T. Harwood. *The History of Christian Preaching*. Philadelphia: American Baptist Publication Society, 1903.

Sweet, William Warren. *Religion in the Development of American Culture*. New York: Scribner, 1952.

Taylor, William M. *The Scottish Pulpit*. New York: Harper, 1887.

Webber, Frederick Roth. *A History of Preaching in Britain and America*. 3 vols. Milwaukee: Northwestern, 1952-1957.

24

Books of
Sermons

One of the marks of the great preachers of the past was their constant dissatisfaction with their own preaching. "I am still learning how to preach!" said Charles H. Spurgeon at the height of his ministry. Alexander Maclaren often came away from hearing another man preach, saying to himself, "I will never preach again!" Alexander Whyte toiled over his manuscripts, always aiming toward perfection and always frustrated because it eluded him. The preacher who thinks he has arrived is only confessing that he has not yet begun.

How can the busy pastor-preacher improve his pulpit ministry? Of course the first step is to improve the man, since the work that we do cannot be divorced from the life that we live. Phillips Brooks defined preparation for the ministry as "nothing less than the making of a man." A deeper devotional life, a closer touch with humanity, a greater joy in duty—these are things that help make a man a better preacher. In this sense we are always preparing messages, because we are always living. We grow in the ministry not by doing extraordinary things—such as running to seminars and conferences, helpful as they may be—but by doing the ordinary things of life in a better way.

The right kind of reading also can help a man improve his pulpit ministry. I mean reading that takes hold of the whole man: the mind is enlightened, the heart is stirred, and the will responds with action. Too many preachers read as a diversion instead of a discipline; they have no intention of taking the lessons to heart and doing anything about them. In fact, some men substitute this kind of reading for action. They are "hearers of the word" and not doers. Like the man in the parable, immediately with joy they receive the truth, but alas, there are no roots and consequently no fruits. A pastor can own a big library and yet have a shallow ministry.

Books about preaching are important. Every pastor ought to own the best, read them regularly, and practice their principles. I find that it does me good to read Phillips Brooks's *Lectures on Preaching* as an annual "pastoral inventory." I have read the book dozens of times, yet I am ashamed to say that much of it I forget, and some of it I am still seeking to totally understand. Most of the Yale Lectures on preaching are worth reading at least once, and a few titles are worth reading again. D. Martyn Lloyd-Jones has given us a valuable book in his *Preachers and Preaching,* and nothing will replace John H. Jowett's *The Preacher: His Life and Work.* No doubt you have your own favorites; I only hope you read them regularly.

But we can do more than read books *about* preaching: we can read preaching. Books of sermons are teachers in themselves, and every minister ought to increase that section of his library systematically. I realize that this is the "audio age" and that listening to tapes of sermons is the popular thing. (A friend of mine comments, "Some preachers are book worms, and some are tape worms!") There is certainly great value in listening to master preachers like James Stewart of Scotland, Martyn Lloyd-Jones, John Stott, and some of the well-known preachers here in the States. But, sad to say, we do not have recordings of G. Campbell Morgan, A. J. Gossip, J. D. Jones, Charles Spurgeon, Joseph Parker, or any of that glorious army of gospel ambassadors who conquered from their pulpit and who can still teach us how to preach the Word.

So, this is a plea for the pastor to read sermons. I try to read one sermon a day, either as a part of my devotional exercises or just for "spiritual relaxation" at the end of a day, but always with the intent of building my own spiritual life and sharpening my vocational skills. Of these, the first is the more important, since I do not often get to hear other men preach. One of the penalties of preaching is having to listen to yourself week after week! I find that it does my soul good to "listen" to somebody else preach. If it were announced that Morgan or F. B. Meyer was to preach in my area, I would be the first to arrive at the church. This announcement will never be made, so I turn to their books instead.

There are several advantages to reading sermons as opposed to hearing them. For one thing, there is less chance for misunderstanding or missing something. By the time a sermon gets into print, it has been carefully read by the preacher and represents his best utterance. I can read a sermon at my own pace and reread statements that "capture me" or that I may not clearly understand. Unfortunately, we do not yet have "instant replay" in our worship services. Granted, the printed sermon lacks the forcefulness of the preacher's personality, but there is one way you can partially overcome this handicap. Andrew W. Blackwood, in his *Preaching from the Bible,* suggested reading at least one good biography of the preacher before getting into his printed sermons, and also reading any books he has written on preaching and pastoring.[1] I have followed this advice for years and agree that the printed sermons come alive when you know the man better. I had read many of George H. Morrison's sermons before securing and reading the two biographies of him. Since then I have discovered meanings in his sermons that did not appear when I first read them.

I cannot encourage you enough to read sermons as a devotional exercise, simply for the good of your own soul. Read them as a sinner needing to see more of Christ. Read them as a saint needing to grow in grace. Do not read them to find ideas and outlines to share with others but to find manna for your own soul. And if you think you do not need this, you are desperately in need! "I am rich and increased with goods, and have need of nothing." Spurgeon saturated himself with the sermons of the Puritans. Alexander Whyte read Thomas Goodwin's sermons so much that the books fell apart. George W. Truett gladly confessed his debt to Spurgeon's printed messages: "Week by week, I read these sermons, often reading them over and over again until they became a part of my inmost life." Mrs. Morrison, in her biography of her gifted husband, wrote that he "read a sermon every day

---

1. (New York: Abingdon-Cokesbury, 1941), pp. 235ff.

however busy he might be. Newman, Spurgeon, Ker, Robertson, Maclaren, were taken in rotation. And he did this, not for the sake of learning 'style,' but, as he said, for his own soul's good, and to see how the great masters got their message home."

We need to read sermons for the help they can give us in sharpening our own sermonic skills, but it is here that a warning from J. H. Jowett is needful: "While I am advising you to consult other minds I must further advise you not to be overwhelmed by them. Reverently respect your own individuality. Be yourself, and slavishly imitate nobody."

Two dangers we must avoid as we read the sermonic literature of the past: imitation and plagiarism. Imitation robs me of my individuality, and plagiarism robs me of my character; both are insidious. One young preacher was so taken with the sermons in a certain book that he decided to preach them as a series. What he did not know was that one of his members owned the same book and had read it. As the member left the service one Sunday, he said to his pastor, "That was a fine sermon this morning!" Then he added with a smile, "Next week's is good, too!" The problem, of course, lies not with the character of the printed sermon but with the character of the preacher reading it. Blackwood was rather blunt in his counsel: "If one is tempted to steal the fruits of other men's labors, one ought to let such books severely alone. . . ."[2]

Francis Bacon, in one of his essays, compared students to spiders, ants, and bees, and we may justly apply the illustration to preachers. Some preachers never study but, like the spider, spin everything out from within, beautiful webs that never last. Some are like ants that steal whatever they find, store it away, and use it later. But the bee sets the example for us all: he takes from many flowers, but he makes his own honey.

One of the best books on the study of sermons is *The Protestant Pulpit* by Andrew W. Blackwood. This is an anthology of thirty-nine sermons, from Martin Luther to Leslie Weatherhead, a full spectrum of preachers and theological and ecclesiastical schools of thought. Some of the classic sermons are here that every preacher ought to read: "The Expulsive Power of a New Affection" by Thomas Chalmers; Spurgeon's "Songs in the Night"; Bushnell's "Every Man's Life a Plan of God"; and A. J. Gossip's masterpiece, written after the sudden death of his wife, "But When Life Tumbles In, What Then?" In two helpful appendices, the editor tells you how to study a sermon and what

---

2. Ibid., p. 235.

books to add to your library to help you in this enterprise. Even apart from the biographical, bibliographical, and homiletical data here, this book is valuable for the sermons it contains.

Other helpful anthologies are *Famous English Sermons,* edited by Ashley Sampson; *A Treasury of Great Sermons,* edited by Daniel A. Poling; and *Best Sermons,* edited by G. Paul Butler and appearing intermittently from different publishers since 1942. The foreward to the 1951-52 edition is by Willard Sperry, dean of Harvard Divinity School, and is titled "On Reading Other Men's Sermons." It is a classic! Of course there are larger collections of sermons such as the thirteen-volume *20 Centuries of Great Preaching.* There are less expensive ways to buy sermons, but the biographical essays are helpful and the index is useful for homiletical studies. An older set, *The World's Great Sermons,* edited by Grenville Kleiser, was published in 1908 and is often available where used religious books are sold. These ten volumes take you from St. Basil to Jowett, a span of about sixteen centuries. The books are pocket-size, convenient for carrying and reading any time.

I advise you to purchase the individual volumes of sermons by the great masters, indexing them in your file and reading them carefully. The best set of Spurgeon's sermons is *The Treasury of the Bible,* which gives you the best of his preaching and covers the entire Bible. It is carefully indexed and packed with some of the greatest preaching in modern times. However, do not limit yourself to Spurgeon, great as he is. Meet some preachers who may be new to you and who, because of that, may have something different to say to you.

If you do not yet know George Morrison of Glasgow, start with him. Baker Book House has reprinted seven of his books that are worth adding to your library. His other titles are often seen in used-book catalogs, and I trust that either Baker or some other publisher will eventually give us all of Morrison. One of the best British series is "The Scholar as Preacher" published in Edinburgh by T. & T. Clark. I think there are twenty-six titles in the series, and, like all series, the books are of uneven quality and represent many theological viewpoints. My favorites are *The Gates of New Life* and *The Strong Name,* both by James S. Stewart, and *The Hero in Thy Soul* by A. J. Gossip. I do not always agree with the interpretations in these sermons, but I still find myself enlightened and encouraged. The "Great Pulpit Masters" series from Baker is another good place to begin a sermon library. Men like A. J. Gordon, F. B. Meyer, D. L. Moody, R. A. Torrey, and others are included in this series, which was originally published by Revell. Of course every pastor will want Morgan's *Westminster Pulpit.* Joseph Parker's *The People's Bible* is one of the greatest collections of sermons in the English language, and the prayers before the sermons are often a greater blessing than the messages themselves!

One piece of counsel about Spurgeon: avoid the "Kelvedon Edition" of his sermons. They are beautifully printed volumes, but the sermons have been edited; we must have our Spurgeon complete and without surgery! In fact, avoid sermon collections that give edited versions or digests of the originals. It is too bad that several volumes of Truett's sermons have suffered under the editor's pen. His two finest collections are *A Quest for Souls* and *"Follow Thou Me,"* because they were printed just as he preached them—and that is Truett at his best!

Try to read men you disagree with; it will not undermine your convictions and it will give you a breadth of vision. Dorothy Sayers once wrote, "There's nothing you can't prove if your outlook is only sufficiently limited." Preachers cannot afford to have tunnel vision, and wide reading helps to prevent that dangerous malady. I disagree with them in some matters, but I find great help in the sermons of Brooks, F. W. Robertson, Henry Liddon, and even Cardinal Newman (who was a favorite of Alexander Whyte).

I would not be without Jowett and Macartney, Chappell and Sangster, Wesley and McCheyne, or Maclaren and Bunyan. One of my favorite contemporary preachers is the late J. Wallace Hamilton, whose books are published by Revell. Start with *Horns and Halos* (on the prodigal son), then *Who Goes There?* and *The Thunder of Bare Feet.*

"Reading sermons is like listening to an echo," said Brooks in his great Yale lectures, and perhaps he is right. But even an echo can say something to us. Since the original voices are silent, we can be thankful for the echoes and make the most of them. Jesus Christ is the Word; John the Baptist was content to be a "voice" pointing to the Word; and perhaps printed sermons echo voices that have pointed to God. They are to me; I trust they will be to you.

Bibliography

Blackwood, Andrew W. *The Protestant Pulpit.* New York: Abingdon-Cokesbury, 1947.

Butler, G. Paul, ed. *Best Sermons.* New York: Harper, 1944ff.

Fant, Clyde E., Jr., and Pinson, William M. *20 Centuries of Great Preaching.* 13 vols. Waco, Tex.: Word, 1971.

Gossip, Arthur John. *The Hero in Thy Soul.* Edinburgh: Clark, 1928.

Hamilton, James Wallace. *Horns and Halos in Human Nature.* Westwood, N.J.: Revell, 1954.

_____. *The Thunder of Bare Feet.* Westwood, N.J.: Revell, 1964.

_____. *Who Goes There? What and Where Is God?* Westwood, N.J.: Revell, 1958.

Kleiser, Grenville. *The World's Great Sermons.* 10 vols. New York: Funk and Wagnalls, 1908.

Morgan, G. Campbell. *The Westminster Pulpit.* 10 vols. Westwood, N.J.: Revell, 1954-1955. Reprinted—5 vols. Westwood, N.J.: Revell, 1975.

Parker, Joseph. *The People's Bible.* 25 vols. London: Hazell and Watson, 1886ff. Reprinted—*Preaching Through the Bible.* 14 vols. Grand Rapids: Baker, 1971.

Poling, Daniel A., ed. *A Treasury of Great Sermons.* New York: Greenberg, 1944.

Sampson, Ashley, ed. *Famous English Sermons.* London: Nelson, 1940.

Spurgeon, Charles H. *The Treasury of the Bible.* 8 vols. London: Marshall, Morgan, and Scott, 1933-1937. Reprinted—Grand Rapids: Zondervan, 1962.

Stewart, James S. *The Gates of New Life.* New York: Scribner, 1940. Reprinted—Grand Rapids: Baker, 1972.

_____. *The Strong Name.* New York: Scribner, 1941. Reprinted—Grand Rapids: Baker, 1972.

Truett, George W. *"Follow Thou Me."* New York: Long and Smith, 1932. Reprinted—Grand Rapids: Baker, 1973.

_____. *A Quest for Souls.* Dallas: Texas Baptist Book House, 1917. Grand Rapids: Eerdmans, 1961.

John Bunyan

25

Christian Classics

"A classic," wrote Mark Twain, "is a book which people praise and don't read." His definition applies to the Christian classics as well as to any other variety, so that it is very easy for the preacher to use an apt quotation from Rutherford, Augustine, Bunyan, or Calvin without ever reading what these great men wrote. I once heard a preacher use a scene from a certain novel as an illustration in his sermon. It was obvious that he had never read the novel, or he would not have used the illustration as he did. He was the victim of that dangerous crutch, the illustration book.

The mere mention of the word *classic* is enough to give the average reader a case of the jitters. We tend to associate the word with "classical music" that few people understand, or "classical books" that are ancient and ponderous, the museum pieces of the library. I think it was Ruskin who said that there are "the books of the hour, and the books of the ages," and it seems that the books of the ages need a champion to defend them in these days of speed-reading and the digests. Too many preachers (and other students of truth) turn up their noses at the classics and ask with inspired eloquence, "Why seek ye the living among the dead?" Why, indeed?

For one thing, the classics have endured, and that in itself ought to attract our attention. Instead of being literary meteorites, they have been morning stars that go right on shining no matter what men may be doing to each other. Some of them, when they first appeared, were either ignored or opposed, yet they are still with us. What the Matterhorn is to an Indiana sand dune, a classic is to the books on "the top ten" list in the newspaper. To be sure, durability is not always proof of dependability. Great books may contain great lies as well as great truths. But the books that have lasted are usually the ones that really have something to say, and we had better pay attention.

This leads to a second mark of the classic: it is a timeless, universal book that appeals to the reader in spite of time, place, or culture. You do not need to be a New England whaler to appreciate *Moby Dick* or a literary scholar to benefit from Boswell's *Life of Johnson.* Books like these belong to humanity, to man as man, and not to some limited slice of history. Carl Van Doren defined it perfectly: "A classic is a book that doesn't have to be rewritten." It is rooted in something more substantial than the latest fads and fashions. We need footnotes to explain some of the vocabulary in Shakespeare, but we need no footnotes to understand the very human qualities that his characters portray. Don Quixote rides a broken-down horse and not a Volkswagen, and yet what happens to him *essentially* is happening to people in our world today.

That word *essentially* directs us to the third characteristic of a classic: it is an essential book, a seminal book, that so comes to grips with reality that anyone who later deals with this subject must take this book into consideration. It is a book from which other books spring. It is a key that opens exciting new doors, or a seed that regularly produces a fresh harvest of thinking. Thousands upon thousands of books have been published, enjoyed, and forgotten, but a few volumes down through the ages have so captured men's minds that these books have been the basis for a continuous interchange of ideas. (Robert Hutchens has termed this interchange "the great conversation.") "The best book is not one that informs merely," wrote A. W. Tozer, "but one that stirs the reader up to inform himself." That's it exactly! A classic helps you think, and it focuses your thinking on the important issues of human experience, not on the peripheral things. It is an essential book. The Christian who becomes acquainted with the classics (both the religious and the secular) is going to grow and have roots and not be exploited by every literary promoter who is anxious to have a best seller.

This kind of reading is not popular today. We prefer "how-to-do-it" books to books that ask such dangerous questions as *"Why* are we doing it?" and *"What* should we be doing?" Ours is a pragmatic era, dominated by the activist and measured by computers. If it works, it must be good; if it does not work, do not waste time trying to find out why—get back to the drawing board! And what thou doest, do quickly! Is it any wonder that shallowness and pettiness characterize our ministries when we drink at the broken cisterns of the best-seller list and ignore the fresh waters that spring from the books of the ages?

I am convinced that most people avoid the classics because of prejudice. Some have the idea that it is sinful for the Christian to read "secular writers," and yet Paul quoted from pagan philosophers (Acts 17:28; Titus 1:12; I Cor. 15:33). When he asked for "the books, but especially the parchments" (II Tim. 4:13), he was undoubtedly referring to secular as well as sacred writings. In recent years Francis A. Schaeffer has reminded us that the Christian had better know what the world is thinking if he is ever to win today's sinner to Christ. To be sure, some believers are afraid of the classics, lest their faith be shaken; perhaps this is a valid fear. McCheyne's advice here is excellent: handle the classics as you would poison—know how to use them, but don't let them get into your system.

It is unfortunate that you and I were first exposed to the classics at a time when we were least prepared for them. *Moby Dick* is just a slow-moving sea story to a junior high school student, and what high school student gets excited about *Paradise Lost?* We carry these prejudices with us into adult life, little realizing how much we are robbing ourselves. The Christian, above all others, ought to be able to understand these two great masterpieces, because they have a strong Biblical foundation. What does the average reader do with the opening sentence of *Moby Dick:* "Call me Ishmael"? He can reach for his dictionary or literary encyclopedia, but the Bible-taught Christian has already met Ishmael and knows that he is much more than a character in Genesis. I note in successive pages of the novel other references to the Scriptures: Euroclydon, Lazarus, Canaan, Bildad, Ahab, "the sons of God and the daughters of men," and many more. Granted, the literary unbeliever can identify these references, thanks to our scholarly books; *but he can never fully understand their spiritual meaning.* It is the Christian with the light of God's Word who best can learn from the classics.

There is one Christian classic that, to my amazement, many believers—including pastors—have never read. I speak of *Pilgrim's Progress* by John Bunyan, the man that *Britannica* calls "the greatest literary genius produced by the Puritan movement." I have often asked congregations in various places whether or not they have read this immortal allegory, and I have usually been embarrassed by the statistics. *Pilgrim's Progress* is a book Christians talk about but do not read, and yet it stands next to the Bible as an all-time religious best seller and has been translated into scores of languages. That eminent literary czar, Samuel Johnson, once asked, "Was there ever yet anything written by mere man that was wished longer by its readers, excepting *Don Quixote, Robinson Crusoe* and *The Pilgrim's Progress?*" Most of the secular critics praise the book for its style (Robert Louis Stevenson called it "homespun yet impassioned"), but the Christian reader, while enjoying the style, understands the deeper meaning of the book. Bunyan was an uneducated tinker, but he knew more practical theology than many preachers do today!

Think, for instance, of the influence of this book on great preachers. J. H. Jowett's biographer, Arthur Porritt, said that this master-preacher's style was influenced more by Bunyan than by anyone else. "He [Jowett] was *par excellence* the stylist of the English pulpit—an expert in the perfect use of words." But more than Bunyan's style got into Jowett's ministry. His imagery captured the great preacher's heart. *"The Pilgrim's Progress,"* wrote Porritt, "crept into almost every sermon." The preacher who refers to any of Bunyan's characters today would send his congregation home wondering what he meant by "the slough of despond," "Mr. Ready-to-Halt," "Vanity Fair," or "the interpreter's house." Alas, there has arisen a generation that knows not Bunyan!

That delightful Methodist preacher Dinsdale Young had a lifelong love affair with *Pilgrim's Progress.* "Of all books next to the Bible," wrote Harold Murray in the official biography, "I believe he loved *The Pilgrim's Progress.*"

But of all the preachers who drank from Bunyan's well, Charles H. Spurgeon must head the list. While a young child, living with his preacher grandfather, he discovered an old copy of *Pilgrim's Progress* in an attic cupboard. Immediately he began to devour both the text and the quaint woodcut illustrations. In later years he claimed that he had read the book over one hundred times.

Since he was about six years old when he first discovered the book and he died at the age of fifty-eight, he must have read *Pilgrim's Progress* an average of twice a year! (I have read that Spurgeon usually read six books a week! Often he preached eight to ten times a week, so he was a busy man. Perhaps Bunyan was a source of inner calm for him and undoubtedly a mine of spiritual truth for sermons.) When Spurgeon fell in love with Susannah Thompson, he sent her a copy of *Pilgrim's Progress,* which shows how greatly he valued the book. She reciprocated by sending him a complete set of the works of John Calvin, a deed that proved she knew what her beloved's theology was!

During Spurgeon's early years he was the focal point of much bitter criticism, and the newspapers were filled with "letters to the editor" about the young preacher. One anonymous correspondent wrote: "Mr. Spurgeon institutes a new era, or more correctly, revives the grand old style of Bunyan, Wesley and Whitefield—men whose burning eloquence carried conviction to the hearts of their hearers—men who cared nought for the applause of their fellow-mortals, but did all for God's glory. In the steps of these apostles does Mr. S. follow, and who could desire more noble leaders?"[1]

Spurgeon steeped himself in the writings of the Puritans: Thomas Brooks, Thomas Goodwin, John Owen, Thomas Manton, Thomas Watson, and, above all, John Bunyan. These men wrote to *express,* not *impress,* and Spurgeon assimilated their style. But he also borrowed the imagery from Bunyan and often used it in his sermons. In fact he wrote a book called *Pictures from "Pilgrim's Progress"* that he hoped would introduce the great classic to the people that appreciated his own ministry.

But Spurgeon, Jowett, and Young are not the only preachers who have found spiritual help in Bunyan. Alexander Whyte's name belongs on the list too. "Bunyan's great gift was imagination," said Whyte in a lecture. "That was the sphere of his genius. . . . You will be astonished to see how often he says 'I saw.' " Whyte loved to lecture on Bunyan, and he even preached a series of sermons on the personalities in *Pilgrim's Progress* and *The Holy War.* The series, *Bunyan Characters,* appeared in four volumes and is still available in used-book stores. *Bunyan Characters* deals with every character and major event in the two Bunyan classics and is perhaps the finest work on this subject from an evangelical preacher. Bunyan was more than a great writer to Whyte. He was a

---

1. Quoted in Charles H. Spurgeon, *Spurgeon,* ed. Susannah Spurgeon and Joseph Harrald, 2 vols. (Edinburgh: Banner of Truth, 1962-1973), 1:317.

great expounder of Puritan evangelical truth. Whyte used to quote Rutherford, "Fore-fancy your deathbed!" Whyte said that, among other writings, he wanted Bunyan's "Crossing of the Jordan" from *Pilgrim's Progress* near at hand when "the darkness began to gather."

One of Whyte's assistants, John Kelman, wrote two helpful volumes on *Pilgrim's Progress.* The volumes are titled *The Road: A Study of John Bunyan's "Pilgrim's Progress,"* and they are a good supplement to the sermons of Whyte. Whyte's preaching was surgical; he majored on exposing and condemning sin. Kelman's approach is a bit brighter and more practical, so I would suggest you secure both sets of books.

But before you start hunting for books about Bunyan, please take time to read *Pilgrim's Progress.* Read it leisurely, with your heart and mind wide open. Let the book become spiritual medicine to your soul. And please do not tolerate an edited version, a modern version, or an adaptation: read the original Anglo-Saxon with all of its purity and potency. I suggest a pocket edition that you can carry with you and turn to during those extra moments when the mind is free. Or, plan to read several chapters a day after your evening meal or before going to bed. But, however and whenever you do it, *read the book!* Once it has gripped your soul you can turn to Whyte and Kelman and the other students of Bunyan, whose investigations can never improve on his book but can (if we permit them) improve our understanding of the book and ourselves.

Is Bunyan's classic still meaningful to men today? Of course! Men are men, whether they live under a seventeenth-century monarchy or a twentieth-century democracy. It is worth noting that Francis Schaeffer, in his book *The God Who Is There,* a book certainly written for modern man, when he wanted to explain what it means to trust Jesus Christ, quoted *Pilgrim's Progress.*[2] To find Bunyan in the same book with Barth, Bultmann, Camus, Freud, Picasso, and Sartre (to name but a few) suggests that the old Puritan knew how to deal with timeless truths that men need today.

Even if you have already read *Pilgrim's Progress,* get it off the shelf and read it again. If you have never read it, then please lay aside whatever you are presently reading (except the Bible) and acquaint yourself with the greatest religious classic in the English language. Meet "Mr. Worldly-Wiseman" and "Mr. Timorous"; visit

---

2. (Downers Grove, Ill.: Inter-Varsity, 1968), p. 135.

"Vanity Fair" and "the interpreter's house"; fight with the "Giant Despair"; and walk through "the delectable mountains." Enjoy comparing scripture with scripture as you move from character to character and place to place. You will be amazed at the practical theology you will learn! Keep your Bible at hand and look up the references that are unfamiliar to you. What an adventure, with saintly John Bunyan as your guide!

Then, let this experience be but the first of many such experiences in the classics. Do not permit your adolescent prejudices to rob you of the pleasure and profit you can find in the great books. You are better prepared to appreciate them now than at any other time in your life, so do not wait too long! Visit your local library and borrow a copy of Augustine's *Confessions,* Bacon's *Essays, Moby Dick,* or *Gulliver's Travels* (which is *not* a children's book), and plunge right in. Do not let any of the classics frighten you: they were written for ordinary people to understand, in spite of what some scholars say. Your librarian probably can suggest a list of the finest titles. One popular program is *The Lifetime Reading Plan* by Clifton Fadiman. *A Reader's Guide to Religious Literature* by Beatrice Batson is another helpful bibliography. But do not permit someone else to determine your diet. Browse in the library, give yourself time to get into a book, and stay with it until you complete it. Once you have done this, the classics will no longer be strangers or enemies but friends you will wish you had cultivated a long time ago.

Bibliography

Batson, Beatrice. *A Reader's Guide to Religious Literature.* Chicago: Moody, 1968.

Bunyan, John. *Pilgrim's Progress.* London: Ponder, 1678.

Fadiman, Clifton. *The Lifetime Reading Plan.* Cleveland: World, 1960.

Kelman, John. *The Road: A Study of John Bunyan's "Pilgrim's Progress."* 2 vols. Edinburgh: Oliphant and Anderson, 1911-1912.

Spurgeon, Charles H. *Pictures from "Pilgrim's Progress."* London: Passmore and Alabaster, 1903.

Whyte, Alexander. *Bunyan Characters.* 4 vols. Edinburgh: Oliphant, Anderson, and Ferrier, 1893-1908.

26

Dictionaries

When the bombs were falling on London, 29 December 1940, an explosion hurled a drum of printer's ink onto the roof of a red-brick Queen Anne house in Gough Square. A drum of printer's ink was the perfect missile to hit that house because, years before, its master had been Samuel Johnson—writer, critic, conversationalist, and editor of the famous *Dictionary* published in 1755. There had been dictionaries prior to Johnson's two huge volumes, but when his appeared, they seemed to disappear.

I once visited Johnson's house in Gough Square (providentially it had escaped the blitz, though it was threatened half a dozen times) and enjoyed seeing the rooms in which the great man had worked on his dictionary. He had six clerks in the upstairs attic, filing words and copying references and quotations, while he labored below writing the definitions and assembling the materials.

It took him nearly ten years to complete, much to the annoyance of his backers, but once the *Dictionary* appeared, it met with immediate success and maintained its high position for nearly a century. His volumes would be practically useless to us today, but they helped stabilize the English language and set an example for future dictionaries.

Since we preachers are users of words, we had better be users of dictionaries. I have mentioned in previous chapters that many great preachers of the past were readers of dictionaries—G. Campbell Morgan and John Henry Jowett, to name only two.

Did you know that the Brothers Grimm did more than collect and write fairy tales? In 1840 they began to compile a definitive German dictionary, which was completed by others and which (according to an expert, Ludwig Denecke) "set an international example for the historical dictionary of language." Remember that the next time you read "Hansel and Gretel."

Some kind of memorial ought to be established to honor Thomas Cooper, an English lexicographer who in 1565 published a Latin-English dictionary after almost losing his wife in the process. Apparently she resented her husband sitting up late each night working on his dictionary. So, when his work was half finished, she burned his manuscript. The devoted scholar simply started again and eventually finished his work.

The man who works with words needs good dictionaries to assist him, and we are fortunate that so many are available today. You ought to have an up-to-date desk dictionary for handy reference—and use it. Never permit an unfamiliar word to get by you. Look it up, note its meaning and etymology, and start using it. This is the best way to build both your reading and speaking vocabulary. Of course this does not mean that we start seasoning (or poisoning) our sermons with every new word we discover, but it does mean we grow in understanding and expression as we acquire new words. How tragic when our thoughts are too big for our words. We find ourselves unable to say what we want to say the way it deserves to be said. We must preach in language our people can understand, but we must be able to grasp language that perhaps many of our people cannot understand. The larger our vocabularies, the easier it will be for us to wrestle in the study with the great themes that must be the center of our preaching.

Perhaps the greatest English dictionary ever published is *The Oxford English Dictionary,* which appeared in twelve large volumes from 1888 to 1928. Both in size and price it was out of reach of the average student, but in 1971 the *OED* was brought out in a "compact edition" of two large volumes. Thanks to a micrographic process, these volumes give you on one page four pages of the original edition. You must use a magnifying glass to read the material, but this is not at all difficult. What a magnificent piece of literature is the *OED*. It not only gives the serious student the meanings of words, but it also traces the history of each word and illustrates it with illuminating quotations. This is not the dictionary that you reach for to learn the meaning of some unfamiliar word; you turn to it when you really want to get acquainted with a word—its origin, history, and use in the English language over the centuries. To be sure, you can get some of this information in an unabridged dictionary (and you ought to own one if possible), but even an unabridged is not nearly as complete as the *OED*. I keep my volumes on a shelf right above my typewriter and refer to them often.

Of course there's more than one kind of "dictionary," and perhaps you ought to add some of these variants to your library. I have received a great deal of help from *A Dictionary of Contemporary American Usage* by Bergen and Cornelia Evans. For many years Bergen was chairman of the English department at Northwestern University in Evanston, Illinois, and he is widely recognized as a gifted writer and teacher. *A Dictionary of Contemporary American Usage* is the kind of book you turn to when you want to know the difference between *debar* and *disbar*, or to brush up on the use of *analogy* or *hyperbole*. You can find these words in a standard dictionary and get the same results, but the Evans's neatly put them together and illustrate them, and they do it in such an entertaining way that using their dictionary is a delight. Bergen's *Dictionary of Quotations* is a favorite of mine. In fact, I prefer it to the standard *Oxford Dictionary of Quotations*. Since they supplement each other, perhaps one should have both. But the background material in the Evans volume makes it much more useful.

If you have ever wondered at the meaning or background of some literary or historical reference (such as "brain trust" or "the golden fleece" or "rob Peter to pay Paul"), then reach for *Brewer's Dictionary of Phrase and Fable*. This amazing book was first published in 1870; you will want to purchase the recent edition revised by Ivor H. Evans. Look up the innocent word *eye,* and you will find over fifty references; twenty-eight are listed under "break." The ten columns devoted to "Bible" contain a wealth of literary information, including a list of "odd editions." Have you ever heard of "The Idle Bible" or "The More Sea Bible"? I enjoy paging through this handy volume and picking up odd bits of information that come in handy in both studying and preaching. Some of us who failed to learn our English and American literature as we should can find in these pages the answers to the questions "Where did this phrase come from, and what does it mean?"

Just recently I was reading a book about F. W. Robertson and noted that he attended Brasenose College. This seemed an odd name for a college, so I checked *Brewer's Dictionary* and discovered that *brasenose* is a corruption of *brasenhuis,* a brewery, which was the site of the original school. Perhaps little details like this never interest you, but they interest me; and I appreciate the tools that reveal them.

Even though you may own an encyclopedia, be sure to purchase also a *Webster's Biographical Dictionary;* you will use it often. I use mine to identify quickly people and their times and also to learn the correct pronunciation of names. The preacher who pronounced *Sartre* to rhyme with *smarter* proved that he was not; likewise the man who managed to say *Socrates* in two syllables and *Goethe* in one. Minor matters? No. The man who expects people to listen to God's truth at least ought to be accurate in matters of pronunciation and identification. (I once listened to a man preach a moving evangelistic message in which he managed to confuse all the Herods of the New Testament. A biographical dictionary and a Bible dictionary are indispensable for identifying persons and places accurately.)

A helpful little volume I refer to regularly is *A Dictionary of Contemporaries* edited by A. F. Launay. Each section covers twenty-five years and is divided into sections for writers, artists, rulers, prominent people, etc. The preacher who wants to enrich his historical references can make good use of this book. The editor lists only names and dates, but you can get the rest of the information from your encyclopedia or *Webster's Biographical.* The book begins with 500 B.C. and closes with persons born from 1875 to 1900. Over sixty pages are devoted to the index.

Two handy volumes in the area of history are *An Encyclopedia of American History,* edited by Richard Brandon Morris, and *An Encyclopedia of World History,* edited by William L. Langer. These are not collections of articles arranged alphabetically, but collections of historical facts and events arranged chronologically. The Langer volume covers the history of the world. I often refer to it to verify some date or event for a sermon illustration, and it has never failed me. The Morris volume is in three sections: basic chronology, topical chronology (such as expansion, population, agriculture, etc.) and the biographies of "three hundred notable Americans." For quick reference in the area of history, these two stand supreme.

The latest addition to my dictionary shelf is *The New International Dictionary of the Christian Church,* edited by J. D. Douglas and published by Zondervan. (You may have *The New Bible Dictionary,* also edited by Douglas.) When my copy arrived, I sat up until midnight completely captivated. There are other dictionaries in this field, of course, but this one has the advantage of being written and edited by scholars of definite evangelical conviction. The contributors are from various parts of the world and represent many different ecclesiastical backgrounds. But there is, in addition to variety, vitality: this is no dry-as-dust tome. It is the kind of scholarly tool that you will enjoy.

The bibliographies are helpful, although in some cases they seem a bit brief. To list just one title for D. L. Moody—and perhaps not the best one at that—is unfortunate. And Jill Morgan's excellent biography of G. Campbell Morgan is not even listed. This is a minor defect in a book of this kind, in which full bibliographies are not possible.

To my shame I am weak in the important area of church history, and perhaps this is why *The New International Dictionary of the Christian Church* excites me. I can look up "Grotius" and "Socinianism" and like topics and brush up on what I learned (or should have learned!) in seminary.

I appreciate too the articles that explain ecclesiastical and political terms relating to groups with which I am not too familiar. Words like *prebend* and *metropolitan* and *provost* show up in our reading, and we ought to know what they mean. This new dictionary does a far better job than the standard English dictionary. I plan to keep it near me when I read the biographies of British churchmen because in these I am often greeted by such unfamiliar terms.

Let me warn you that this is not a Bible dictionary. There are no articles on "Isaiah" or "Noah." The topics have to do with the history of the Christian Church, so that any doctrine, event, or person that falls into that classification will probably be in these pages. I was amazed to find an article here about John Alexander Dowie, the founder of the Christian Catholic Church in Zion, Illinois, a man almost forgotten by this generation of preachers. The article on the Niagara Bible Conference also surprised me, and there is even a brief paragraph on Youth for Christ International. The missionary information in the book is helpful for historical background, as is also the material on various denominations. Of course I especially appreciate the biographical material. *The New International Dictionary of the Christian Church* will be used a great deal in my study, and my ministry will be the better for it.

One other title is *A Dictionary of Foreign Terms,* edited by C. O. Sylvester Mawson, the man who also edited everybody's favorite word book, *Roget's International Thesaurus.* The book lists about fifteen thousand phrases from fifty languages—phrases like *chi tace confessa* (Italian for "he who keeps silent admits he is guilty"), *inter spem et metum* (Latin for "between hope and fear"), and *en grande tenue* (French for "in full uniform"). If you are up on your languages, Mawson's handbook will be of little use. If foreign phrases elude you, his book is just what you need. Most modern writers avoid using foreign phrases, but if you read any of the older writers, you will meet foreign phrases on almost every page. Even Spurgeon was not above dropping in a Latin phrase or two. Expect them on almost every page of the sermons of Lancelot Andrewes or John Donne.

I enjoy dictionaries. Perhaps you do not. I will not make it a test of orthodoxy or fellowship, but I would like to encourage you at least to become acquainted with these tools. You will find most of them in the public library where you can decide whether or not they are worth the investment. In his *Dictionary* Samuel Johnson defined a lexicographer as "a writer of dictionaries, a harmless drudge." No doubt much editorial work of this type is drudgery, but it saves the rest of us from wasting valuable hours tracking down a fact or a term. Dictionaries cost money, but they save time and "time is money" (Benjamin Franklin said that, according to Evans's *Dictionary of Quotations*).[1] Imagine our plight if we had to write our own.

Bibliography

Brewer, Ebenezer Cobham. *Brewer's Dictionary of Phrase and Fable.* Revised by Ivor H. Evans. New York: Harper and Row, 1970.

Douglas, J. D., ed. *The New International Dictionary of the Christian Church.* Grand Rapids: Zondervan, 1974.

Evans, Bergen. *Dictionary of Quotations.* New York: Delacorte, 1968.

————, and Evans, Cornelia. *A Dictionary of Contemporary American Usage.* New York: Random, 1957.

Langer, William L., ed. *An Encyclopedia of World History.* 4th ed. Boston: Houghton Mifflin, 1968.

Launay, A. F., ed. *A Dictionary of Contemporaries.* London: Centaur, 1967.

Mawson, C. O. Sylvester. *A Dictionary of Foreign Terms.* New York: Crowell, 1934. Reprinted—New York: Apollo, n.d.

---

1. P. 694.

Morris, Richard Brandon, ed. *An Encyclopedia of American History.* Rev. ed. New York: Harper, 1961.

Murray, James A. H., ed. *The Oxford English Dictionary.* 12 vols. Oxford: Clarendon, 1888-1928. Reprinted—2 vols. Oxford: Clarendon, 1971.

The Oxford Dictionary of Quotations. 2nd ed. London: Oxford University, 1953.

Roget, Peter M. *Roget's International Thesaurus.* 3rd ed. Edited by C. O. Sylvester Mawson. New York: Crowell, 1962.

Webster's Biographical Dictionary. Springfield, Mass.: Merriam, 1966.

Alexander Cruden

27

Bible
Concordances

One January day in 1869, Charles H. Spurgeon wrote on the flyleaf of his *Cruden's Concordance:* "For these ten years this has been the book at my left hand when the Word of God has been at my right." Three years later he added this note: "This half crazy Cruden did better service to the church than half the D.D.'s and L.L.D.'s of all time."

It comes as a surprise to modern students that Alexander Cruden, if not "half crazy," was certainly very eccentric. We have grown up with his *Concordance* and, no doubt, have replaced it with more serviceable concordances—James Strong's, Robert Young's, G. V. Wigram's *The Englishman's Greek Concordance,* or perhaps one of the more scholarly works. But it shocks us to discover that the man who in just one year produced a great concordance was also confined in three different asylums. It is an even greater shock to learn that Alexander Cruden tried to force his affections on three different women, all of whom refused to marry him; that he threatened to put his own sister in jail; and that he considered himself the "Corrector" of public morals in

England, traveling from place to place to straighten everybody out. Nobody ever proved that Cruden was crazy, but that he was very odd, nobody will deny.

He was born in Aberdeen on 31 May 1699, the second of William and Isabel Cruden's eleven children. His father was a well-to-do merchant who saw to it that the family followed the traditional Calvinistic worship and way of life. Except for twelve holidays during the year, the children attended school every day but Sunday. Sunday was perhaps the hardest day of all, with its church services, strict discipline, and absence of games. But perhaps the hand of the Lord was in it all, for Alexander spent many Sunday afternoons playing his favorite game of tracing words through the Bible. No doubt during these Sunday afternoons the seeds were sown that later bore fruit in his famous *Concordance.*

When he was thirteen, Cruden entered Marischal College, taking his M.A. when he was nineteen. He planned to become a tutor and for several years was moderately successful. But then he experienced the first of three "romances"—all of which put him into the asylum. He fell in love with a minister's daughter and felt sure that his love was in the will of God. For her to refuse him was to disobey God's sovereign plan! But the father had other ideas and forbade him to enter the house. At this point a tragedy occurred: the girl became pregnant (rumor said her brother was involved), and she was banished from Aberdeen to have her child "in exile." Alexander simply could not endure this flood of troubles, and his mind left him. This was in November 1720, and his parents had him "put away" for a couple of weeks. He seemed to get well and the matter was forgotten, but from that time on, Alexander Cruden was destined to be a disappointed and persecuted man.

By 1726 we find Cruden in London working as a proofreader and enjoying moderate success. In fact he was known as the finest proofreader available. For one thing, he loved words; for another, he had the persistence to stay with a job until it was done correctly. "Alexander the Corrector" enjoyed his reputation, but he still longed to teach. A minister friend suggested that he join the staff of Lord Derby in Sussex, and Cruden jumped at the chance. He was hired sight unseen to read to the lord the latest French books, but Cruden had failed to inform his employer that he was not proficient in reading French. The first time he read to Lord Derby, Cruden followed the procedure he always used for proofreading French books: he spelled out each word, letter by letter! His lordship, besides being bored, was upset that such an incompetent reader had been secured, and he told one of his men to fire Cruden.

What his lordship did not realize was that Cruden had no plans to leave Halnaker House, Sussex, because he enjoyed being with important people. The manor house with its library and estate, the fine food, the elegant graces of the household—all combined to feed Cruden's ego. And, of course, Cruden just knew that it was God's will for him to remain. It took much pressure from Lord Derby's staff to convince Cruden that he was not wanted and that he had better pack up and leave. (The fact that Cruden was anti-Episcopalian, and openly declared it, did not help matters any.) On 7 July, after about a month of service, he left the estate, but he did not give up begging for his position. For several months Cruden followed Lord Derby and sought an audience, and Cruden pestered him with letters, some of which he wrote in French to show his former employer that he had improved in the language. It was all a waste of energy, so Cruden finally returned to London and proofreading.

In a few years he opened a bookshop in London, which fit in beautifully with his work as a proofreader. His shop soon became a gathering place for book-lovers, Calvinists of one trade or another, and people who just enjoyed a good talk. In 1835 he secured a Royal Warrant and was made a "Bookseller to Queen Caroline," a victory that inflated his ego even more. But the most important thing he did that year was to begin his famous *Concordance;* it was published in November 1737, certainly a remarkable feat. He would work on proofs (to pay the bills) from 7 P.M. until 1 A.M., at which time he would go to bed. Promptly at 6 A.M. he would get up and begin working on the concordance! Sad to say, he neglected his bookstore during these months, and his business left him. But he was not worried: his *Concordance* would bring him both fame and money.

If my researches are correct, the first English concordance was published by Thomas Gibson and John Day, sometime before 1540. John Marbeck published one in 1550, and in 1537 one Walter Lynne published a translation of a German concordance. The first English concordance that even approached being "complete" was put out by Clement Cotton in 1631. (It is worth noting that Cotton was a layman, and so was Cruden. Neither Young nor Strong, who also gave us concordances, was ordained, though both were active in Christian work.) Rev. Samuel Newman built upon Cotton's work and published his concordance in 1643, but when Cruden's appeared in 1737, it quickly replaced them all.

Although Cruden's *Concordance* did not bring him wealth, it did bring him fame—which he valued even more. On 3 November he was called to St. James's Palace where he presented a copy of the book to Queen Caroline, who promised him a grant of 100 pounds (he had been paid only 20 pounds for the entire first edition). Unfortunately, the queen died seventeen days later, and he never received his gift. Since the *Concordance* was dedicated to her, her death was an even greater blow, for who wants to buy a book dedicated to a dead monarch? Even the Royal Warrant granted to his bookstore was worthless!

Then came Cruden's second "romance" and his second visit to the asylum. He was certain that a Mrs. Bryan Pain, a widow, was God's choice for him in his hour of suffering. She worshiped at the church Cruden attended, and often Cruden had spent Sunday evenings in her home when her husband was yet living. Certain of the divine will, Alexander began to pursue Mrs. Pain, who instantly ran in the opposite direction and summoned the aid of her friends. Cruden wrote her very strong letters and then began to make scenes at church: he would give his responses in loud tones, and occasionally stand up and make dramatic gestures. The congregation was sure the man was out of his mind. Within a few days some friends of Mrs. Pain (whose motives were not entirely Christian) practically kidnapped Cruden and carried him away to "Mr. Wright's Private Madhouse" in Bethnal Green, where the unfortunate man was chained to his bed for almost ten weeks. It was a cruel way to treat a man who was odd, but not mad; but no doubt the perpetrators of the deed hoped to get an interest in Cruden's income. The whole affair was quite illegal, but no amount of pleading on Cruden's part brought him any assistance. Finally, on 31 May (his birthday), he managed to cut the bed leg and, with chain and bed leg in hand, escaped from the asylum. He tried to sue the men who had incarcerated him but lost his case; this made him even more certain that "Alexander the Corrector" was being opposed by the forces of darkness and that he still had a great work to do.

Around 1740 Cruden's spinster sister, Isabella, came to live with him in London, and in 1753 she married a Mr. Wild, whose piety (and purse) pleased Alexander. About this time, Cruden began to call himself "Alexander the Corrector" and to carry on a one-man crusade to clean up England. It was during this period that he was proofing *Paradise Lost* and *The Faerie Queen,* so it is possible that he saw himself as a courageous knight instead of a quiet bookseller. He began to intervene in street fights and occasionally (because he was so odd and amusing) succeeded in stopping them. But one evening he tried to stop a man from swearing and hit the fellow on the head with a shovel! This only made the fight worse, turning it into a regular riot which many passers-by joined. His landlord heard about the riot and, after consulting Isabella, tied the "Corrector" and took him to a private asylum where he was confined for three weeks. Alexander was so angry at his sister's compliance with the landlord's dastardly deed that he threatened to put her in jail! And he began to see himself as a modern-day "Alexander the Great."

Cruden spent almost the entire next year (1754) trying to get himself appointed the official "Corrector of the People." He tried to pursuade the king to knight him; he made a pest of himself at court; he wrote letters to members of the royal family. But his pleas fell on deaf ears. As the well-known editor of the *Concordance,* Alexander Cruden was respected. As a man, however, he was looked upon as *very* eccentric, and the court was not about to appoint an eccentric to arbitrate public morals. Cruden published booklets describing his life and works and sought to get them into the hands of as many leading people as possible. He then ran for a seat in Commons, representing the City of London. He thought that the other candidates would quietly resign once they heard his story! Alas, neither the candidates nor the voters considered him fit for office, and he lost the election.

Once again he turned to romance to solace his broken heart. This time his affections were centered on a Miss Abney, whom he showered with letters and sought to see in person week after week. He was convinced it was God's will that they marry and join forces in correcting the evils of the land. No doubt when she read the autobiographical booklets that he sent her, she was even more convinced that the man was crazy. After a year of these futile efforts, Cruden decided he would have to choose between his beloved lady and his work of correcting the nation; much to Miss Abney's delight, he chose the latter. In 1755 Alexander started touring the country as "Alexander the Corrector," hoping to bring the people back to Christian morality. Often he carried a sponge with him to wash unwanted writing off of public places. He even asked for an act of Parliament to authorize him to "restrain profane swearers, Sabbath breakers, lewd men and women, and other notorious sinners. ..." Despite a pompous address which he wrote and distributed to every member of Commons, no act was passed. It mattered little to Alexander: God had called him, and that was authority enough.

Because he was the editor of the great *Concordance,* he was received with dignity at Oxford, and many of the clergy, although they questioned his methods, applauded his ideals. Cruden interpreted their kindness as blanket approval, and this gave him courage to go to Cambridge. He accosted people who were taking walks on the Sabbath and gave serious "admonitions" to those engaged in "merry-making." He also appointed three deputy correctors, one of them a woman who, shortly after being appointed, went for a walk on the Sabbath evening! Cruden attacked Sunday feasting, card playing, dancing, and other forms of sin, but it is doubtful that anybody took his words seriously.

One good thing did result from this tour: Cruden found that there was a call for a third edition of his *Concordance.* He immediately made a revision, and the third edition appeared probably in 1760. He dedicated it to George III and subsequently was invited to court, an honor he had been seeking for years. Cruden was presented at court along with the author Laurence Sterne, whose *Tristram Shandy* was to make him famous. You could not conceive of two more opposite men than Cruden and Sterne. Sterne was an Anglican clergyman; Cruden opposed the state church. Sterne was a humorous writer; Cruden was deadly serious about life. And Sterne was not above dropping sexual innuendoes into his books, something Cruden would have been quick to condemn— and rightly so. For that matter, Sterne's reputation with women was not the best. The king was especially gracious to Cruden, almost to the point of ignoring Sterne, and "Alexander the Corrector" went home a happy man.

It would be easy to see Alexander Cruden only as an eccentric were it not for his *Concordance* and his personal love for lost souls. In spite of his strange ways, Cruden had a burden for the lost—especially those in prisons—and he spent much of his time and wealth trying to help them. He often visited officers and nobles to intercede for prisoners, and he preached each Lord's Day to the prisoners in Newgate. It is difficult to find much fault with a man that burdened for souls. One evening, while returning home from church, Cruden met a man whose family problems had driven him to the point of suicide; because of Cruden's interest and sacrifice, the man's life and family were saved. Eccentric? Yes! Insane? No! A bit fanatical? To be sure! But it would take a man with fanatical persistence to produce a book like the *Concordance.*

Cruden's final years were quiet compared with the earlier years, and his native Aberdeen paid him high honor. In 1770 he retired to Islington, living on his small income, spending his days walking, giving out tracts, and seeking to reform the nation. On 1 November 1770 a servant found him dead in his room. He was on his knees, in an attitude of prayer, his head on the open Bible. He was buried in Southwark, but do not try to locate his grave. That particular cemetery was sold, and for many years a brewery stood over Cruden's grave. Even in death, the poor man did not have a complete victory.

The Eccentric Life of Alexander Cruden, written by Edith Olivier and published in 1934, is not easy to find, but if you see a copy, buy it. Some early editions of *Cruden's Concordance* contain a brief biographical sketch by Alexander Chalmers. (Early editions also contain the strange "explanatory notes" that Cruden wrote about everything from birds to wolves. Many of these "significations," as Cruden termed them, are downright hilarious. Later editions have mercifully omitted these paragraphs and, also mercifully, improved the text. What Cruden believed about foxes and wolves would delight any reader of fairy tales!)

Maybe Spurgeon was right. Maybe Cruden was "half crazy." But his work has enriched God's people, and any book that Spurgeon kept next to his Bible is worth having around.

Bibliography

Cruden, Alexander. *A Complete Concordance to the Holy Scriptures.* London: Midwinter, 1738.

Olivier, Edith. *The Eccentric Life of Alexander Cruden.* London: Faber and Faber, 1934.

Strong, James. *The Exhaustive Concordance of the Bible.* New York: Abingdon, 1890.

Wigram, G. V. *The Englishman's Greek Concordance of the New Testament.* London: Central Tract Depot, 1839.

Young, Robert. *Analytical Concordance to the Bible.* New York: American Book Exchange, 1881. Reprinted—Grand Rapids: Eerdmans, 1955.

William Quayle

28

Books About the Ministry

Musicians read books about music, and I am sure plumbers read books about plumbing; but I am not so sure that we pastors read as many books as we should about our high calling. Not that reading a book will make a man either a preacher or a pastor, but it will certainly help point the way. In fact, the growing pastor will want to read the new books in the field and reread the older books that have earned a place on every pastor's shelf. With this in mind I would like to suggest some books about the ministry that have helped me and, I am sure, many other men in the ministry. The beginning pastor will want to add these titles to his library very soon and then read them carefully; the mature minister may want to take them from his shelf, blow off the dust, and catch their glow once again.

Let's begin with a classic, Charles Bridges's *The Christian Ministry*. Most of us know Bridges for his excellent commentary on Proverbs and his weighty exposition of Psalm 119. In this book he focused attention on the ministry and the minister, and the authority for all that he wrote is the Word of God. This is not a light, "how-to-do-it" manual that does your thinking for you, nor is it the ideal book for practicing your speed-reading. This is a book to take seriously, to ponder and pray over as you read. It was a hundred years old when the market crashed in 1929, so it has passed the test of time. (Incidentally, Robert Murray McCheyne carried a copy with him when he made his famous trip to the Holy Land. That is a pretty good endorsement!)

The book actually began as a letter Bridges wrote to a friend concerning "ministerial inefficiency." The letter was circulated, enlarged upon, and so singularly helpful to pastors that Bridges was persuaded to write an entire book. The result was *The Christian Ministry* and nearly 400 pages of solid meat for the serious-minded minister. I look upon this book as a "systematic theology" for the pastoral office because it deals with timeless principles and basic truths, not with passing methods or ideas. Bridges offered no short cuts to success (he would shrink in horror at such things!), but rather the sound, Scriptural principles that make a pastor a true minister of the Word, a winner of souls, and a builder of the church.

Chapter 1 gets the reader off to a grand start: "The Divine Origin and Institution of the Christian Ministry." In Chapter 2 Bridges packed into 2½ pages some real dynamite—"The Dignity of the Christian Ministry." Please understand that Bridges was not calling for stuffiness or dead formality, but for a man to "magnify his office" and act like an ambassador of Jesus Christ. In this day when some men clown in the pulpit, this warning is sorely needed. Bridges devoted seven chapters to a "general view of the ministry"; six to reasons for "want of success"; ten to "causes of ministerial inefficiency"—a powerful section; six to preaching (with a great section on "habits of meditation"); and two long chapters to pastoral work with specific kinds of people.

Do not ignore the many footnotes in this book, even though they are sometimes heavy with untranslated Latin quotations. The English quotations from the ancient divines are priceless! "Prayer without study is presumption; and study without prayer atheism." "Reading furnishes the mind only with materials of knowledge; it is thinking that makes what we read ours." "God sometimes, in saving His elect, makes use of instruments which He afterwards casts away." Worth thinking about? Yes, and worth praying over!

Now, to an entirely different kind of book—Bishop William Quayle's *The Pastor-Preacher*. Not that the Methodist bishop would disagree with anything his British brother wrote, but he would present it in a different style. Here are forty chapters that are as robust as a lumberjack, yet as personal and down-to-earth as a piece of apple pie after a good dinner. This is one of my favorite books for browsing; the chapters are short, for the most part, and I can read a chapter or two while the family is getting ready to go somewhere.

Quayle was born at Parkville, Missouri, in 1860 and died in 1925. He was ordained in 1886 and served churches in Kansas City, Indianapolis, and Chicago. In 1908 he was made a bishop, and in 1910 *The Pastor-Preacher* was published. Except for its "horse-and-buggy flavor" (which some readers may appreciate), this book is as fresh for today as when it came from his pen. Some publisher ought to reissue this book, possibly with the dated material edited out (although the amount is small). If you see a copy in a used-book store, buy it and read it. His chapter titles will stop you cold: "The Sin of Being Uninteresting," "The Fine Art of Loving Folks," "Pollen for the Mind," and "Trivialities of a Preacher's Craft" are but a few.

Quayle reveled in the "manliness of the ministry." The pulpit is no place for pigmies! "A preacher may not be a great man," said the bishop, "but he must preach great matters. To some men, preaching is sailing on a puddle!" (This reminds us of Frank W. Boreham's description of a certain preacher as "a lion in pin-curls.") "The lure of the gospel is the lure not of wages, not of leisure, not of prestige, but the lure of things to be done, which, if left undone, this world would be left a wreck along the shores of the universe." The ministry is a man's work—"quit you like men, be strong!"

Bishop Quayle did not take the "modern line" that a man should be a preacher but not a pastor. "Unless a man be a good lover of folks he has positively no business at all in the ministry of the Church of the Lord Jesus Christ," he stated. "The faithful minister is not drumming up a crowd as he goes from door to door, knowing the children, comforting the wounded; he is doing his duty, he is getting close to those whose servant he is, he is showing by his coming that here is a friend, a brother, a lover."

I especially like his chapter on "The Preacher and the Ages." If the word *relevant* is starting to upset (or even nauseate) you, then read this chapter—and rejoice! "A preacher must not be engulfed in the now," he counseled. "He must be at home in the now; but his real residence is in all times and in all eternities. . . . The flight of years has indeed changed surroundings, but not occupants."

His chapter on "Some Preacher 'Nevers' " contains wise counsel worth far more than the price of the book, and "The Preacher as

Appreciator" is utterly beautiful and yet so practical. "Not depreciation, but appreciation, is the working word for manly men."

In passing, let me remind you of Spurgeon's *Lectures to My Students,* a book too well known to deal with in detail. By all means purchase the complete edition; we must have the whole giant of the man and not some editor's midget version. My favorite chapter is "The Minister's Fainting Fits." But did you know that Spurgeon has another book especially for his fellow-pastors? It is *An All-Round Ministry,* a collection of twelve of his presidential addresses at the annual Pastor's College conferences. Banner of Truth Trust has published this with an excellent introduction by Iain Murray. These messages cannot help but convict careless pastors and encourage those who are fainting. Spurgeon reminded us: "The capacities of a man, when God takes him in hand, are not to be estimated by the man, but by God Himself." And again, "He who has an easy time of it in his ministry here, will have a hard time of it in the account to be rendered by-and-by."

The name A. T. Robertson is familiar to every preacher mainly because of his masterful work with the Greek New Testament. But Robertson was a preacher and a lover of men who preached. If you doubt that statement, read his *The Glory of the Ministry,* a thrilling exposition of II Corinthians 2:12-6:10, studded with scholarship but saturated with the love of Christ. "I have written this book," he wrote in his preface, "out of love for preachers of the Gospel of Jesus." It is gratifying that Baker Book House has reprinted this classic because the Revell edition of 1911 is not too readily available. Several things will happen to you as you read this book. First, you will experience an exultation that God has called you into the ministry. Even against the dark background of the Corinthian church's problems, Paul paints a picture of a glorious ministry. "Seeing then that we have *this kind of ministry,* we faint not!" Then, you will better understand the spiritual weapons God has given us to do the work of the ministry. Chapter 5, "This Treasure in Earthen Vessels—the Human Limitations," cannot but encourage the pastor who feels he is "all washed up." "Manhood is the first essential in the ministry," said Robertson. The secret to success lies not in special human abilities. "The secret of success in the ministry is very simple. It is real connection with God, vital union with Christ." His final chapter on "Taking Life as It Is" is a masterpiece of Biblical exposition and pastoral application, the kind of thing a man needs to read when he finds himself in the "slough of despond."

A little book that has been helpful to me is Ralph Turnbull's *A*

Minister's Obstacles, first published a quarter of a century ago. Turnbull dealt with the practical problems and temptations in the minister's life; "The Spectre of Professionalism," "The Vice of Sloth," "The Snare of Substitutes," "The Crux of Criticism." He was eminently qualified to write on these themes for at least three reasons: first, he knew his Bible; second, he knew the ministry from firsthand experience; and third, he knew the literature of the ministry and was able to use it to good advantage. When you read Bridges, you are sitting in a lecture hall listening to an eminent divine; when you read Spurgeon, you are in Metropolitan Tabernacle hearing a sermon; but when you read Turnbull, you are in a quiet study listening while a man of God opens his heart in a disarming manner. *A Minister's Obstacles* is a series of "fireside chats" about some terribly important topics.

The book is not long; there are twenty chapters, each chapter averaging about ten pages. And each chapter says something worth knowing! The newly ordained minister needs to read this book so he will be alert to the pitfalls that lie ahead; and the mature minister needs to read it as a spiritual inventory to stir up his soul. In fact, Turnbull seems to have the more experienced man in mind, particularly in his chapter "The Meridian Test." How easy it is to invest twenty or more years in the ministry and then begin to coast or, worse yet, to decline! "At no time of life are we tempted more than in middle age. . . . Physically, as in all men, there is a subtle change taking place and not every man can maintain the strenuous habits of youth . . . the appeal of the easy chair [is] more insistent . . . and a sluggishness of mind is experienced. There is nothing to stop it—except discipline!" This book is a spiritual x ray of the maturing pastor. Each man will take a different picture, but the light in these pages will fail no man because that light shines from the Word of God through the heart of a devoted minister.

My next title may seem out of place, but it is not—*Preachers I Have Heard* by Alexander Gammie. These fifty-two chapters appeared originally as articles on the church page of the Glasgow *Evening Citizen.* Gammie, one of Britain's leading journalists and the biographer of several famous preachers, in these "pen portraits" makes fifty-two ministers of the Word very real and very interesting. And he paints them "warts and all"!

Beginning pastors especially need to become acquainted with "the great cloud of witnesses" that has preceded them. It is tragic to attend pastors' conferences and mention such greats as J. D. Jones, William Temple, and John Ker, and discover that many men do not know who these preachers are! Some do not even know of G. Campbell Morgan! In Gammie's "chatty" volume you will meet these men—their photographs are included—and learn just enough about each one to make you want to find their biographies or autobiographies and learn much more.

Gammie was a gifted sermon "taster," in the best sense of the word. He knew real preaching when he heard it. And he was not narrow in his interests: you will find men from many denominations in this book. He began with Alexander Whyte (Where else would you begin?) and ended with Morgan. He related witty stories about some of these men; with others he revealed instead the secret thorns in the flesh that made them rely that much more on the grace of God. But all through the book he quietly emphasized the same message: God uses different men with different gifts in different churches, and yet all of them are helping to build His church. *Preachers I Have Heard* is a tender antidote to religious pride and denominational prejudice.

One final title: *The Preacher's Portrait,* by that gifted expositor John R. W. Stott. Stott probed five New Testament word-pictures of the preacher—the steward, the herald, the witness, the father, and the servant. For the preacher who sincerely wants to discover his privileges and responsibilities in the ministry, this is the book to read. This is not a long book—slightly over one hundred pages of actual text—but it is packed with spiritual truth and practical counsel. Stott wrote from a pastor's heart, so these studies are not academic lectures. My favorite chapter is chapter 4, "The Preacher as a Father." After carefully explaining what kind of "spiritual father" we are *not* to be (Matt. 23:6-7), he then explained the six ways in which a father's love should be manifested by the pastor: understanding, gentleness, simplicity, earnestness, example, and prayer. This is a short course in pastoral theology!

These eight titles I have suggested can never in themselves make a man a successful minister of the Word. They are not automobiles that take us anywhere; they are signposts along the highway to point in the right direction. The do-it-yourself preacher who is looking for instant success will get no encouragement from these volumes. But the man who takes his calling seriously, who devotes time to the study of these pages, cannot help but make progress in the ministry and thus bring glory to Jesus Christ.

Bibliography

Bridges, Charles. *The Christian Ministry.* London: Seeley and Burnside, 1829. Reprinted—London: Banner of Truth, 1961.

Gammie, Alexander. *Preachers I Have Heard.* London: Pickering and Inglis, 1945.

Quayle, William. *The Pastor-Preacher.* New York: Eaton and Mains, 1910.

Robertson, A. T. *The Glory of the Ministry.* New York: Revell, 1911. Reprinted—Grand Rapids: Baker, 1967.

Spurgeon, Charles H. *An All-Round Ministry.* London: Passmore and Alabaster, 1900. Reprinted—London: Banner of Truth, 1960.

_____. *Lectures to My Students.* 3 vols. London: Passmore and Alabaster, 1875-1894. Reprinted—London: Marshall, Morgan, and Scott, 1954.

Stott, John R. W. *The Preacher's Portrait.* Grand Rapids: Eerdmans, 1961.

Turnbull, Ralph. *A Minister's Obstacles.* Rev. ed. Westwood, N.J.: Revell, 1964. Reprinted—Grand Rapids: Baker, 1972.

29

The Minister and Discouragement

"I am the subject of depressions of spirit so fearful that I hope none of you ever get to such extremes of wretchedness as I go to." So said Charles H. Spurgeon in a sermon in 1866, and perhaps the statement shocked his listeners. Is it possible that the great Baptist preacher could go through the valley of despair? "Personally I have often passed through this dark valley," he said in an 1887 message. Perhaps one reason Spurgeon was able to bring such great comfort to his hearers was that he knew the problem of discouragement firsthand.

So did Alexander Whyte. Said his biographer, G. F. Barbour: "Resolute as was Dr. Whyte's character, he had seasons of deep depression regarding the results of his work in the pulpit or among his people. . . ."[1] And John Henry Jowett wrote to a friend in 1920: "You seem to imagine that I have no ups and downs, but just a level and lofty stretch of spiritual attainment with unbroken joy and equanimity. By no means! I am often perfectly wretched

---

1. *The Life of Alexander Whyte* (London: Hodder and Stoughton, 1923), p. 366.

and everything appears most murky." The saintly Andrew Bonar, friend of Robert Murray McCheyne, wrote in his journal on 4 July 1857: "I was very melancholy, I may say, on Saturday evening. The old scenes reminded me of my ministry, and this accompanied with such regret for past failures. . . ." In 1888, when celebrating his ministerial jubilee, Bonar wrote: "I see in the retrospect so much that was altogether imperfect and so much that was left undone." And he closed a letter to a friend: "Your affectionate, aged, frail, poor, unworthy, feeble, stupid brother and fellow-servant of a glorious Master!"

It seems that depression and discouragement are occupational hazards, if not occupational diseases, of the ministry; so it would be profitable if we explored some of the causes and cures of this dangerous malady. The melancholy John Donne called despair "the damp of hell," and surely that it is.

One of the best discussions of ministerial discouragement is in Spurgeon's *Lectures to My Students,* "The Minister's Fainting Fits." A more modern discussion is chapter 4 of J. Oswald Sanders's *A Spiritual Clinic,* "Despondency: Its Cause and Cure." Chapter 14 of *A Minister's Obstacles,* by Ralph Turnbull, deals with "The Dragnet of Discouragement." I highly recommend all three to you, not as substitutes for your Bible (which, after all, is the best medicine for a broken heart), but rather as encouraging signposts along the way. I find it helpful to enter into the "fellowship of sufferings" with my ministerial brethren; it does my soul good!

Sometimes the reason for discouragement is physical: too much study ("a weariness of the flesh"), too many meetings and late hours, pressures that develop into tensions, unwise eating, and lack of rest and relaxation. The average church member has no idea of the physical price that a faithful pastor pays to do God's work. Perhaps this was part of Elijah's problem when he asked to die (I Kings 19): he was just overtaxed and underfed! God let him sleep, fed him, and returned him to his ministry a new man. "Rest time is not waste time," said Spurgeon. "It is economy to gather fresh strength." Yet the average pastor feels guilty if he is "doing nothing" instead of investing leisure time for future ministry. For the busy pastor recreation cannot be "doing nothing." Rather, it must be doing something different, finding a change of pace or a change of scenery, in order to come back to the old job with new enthusiasm. After all, Jesus told His disciples, "Come ye apart and rest awhile"; and as Vance Havner reminded us, "If we do not come apart and rest, we may just—come apart!"

But I feel that Elijah's discouragement was caused by something more than a tired body and an empty stomach: *Elijah was sure that he had failed.* "I am no better than my fathers!" The pastor, if he is dedicated at all, is a man of ideals; he wants to achieve for the glory of God. Yet, no matter how hard he prays and works, it seems that his goals forever elude him. On the forty-seventh anniversary of his ordination, Bonar wrote, "My ministry has appeared to me to be wanting in so many ways, that I can only say of it, *indescribably inadequate.*" On the tenth anniversary of his marvelous ministry at London's Westminster Chapel, G. Campbell Morgan astounded his congregation by telling them he considered himself a failure! "During these ten years, I have known more of visions fading into mirages, of purposes failing of fulfillment, of things of strength crumbling away in weakness than ever in my life before," he said. Yet he had rescued his church from almost certain failure and had made it the focal point for evangelical Bible study in the entire English-speaking world! In all fairness to Morgan, I must add that a typhoid infection was already at work in his system. It laid him low for the next four months, almost taking his life.

The pastor is an idealist: he aims high and does not always reach his goal. Add to this the fact that he is usually the subject of criticism, and it is not difficult to see the ease with which discouragement can capture even a man of God. When a pastor decides that he has failed, Satan has found an opening; and you can be sure that the enemy will take advantage of it. Of course the answer to the problem is not for us to lower our standards or bury our ideals, but to learn to recognize our own moods and feelings and reckon with them.

"We are apt to become men of moods," Phillips Brooks said in his *Lectures on Preaching,* "thinking we cannot work unless we feel like it. . . . And so the first business of the preacher is to conquer the tyranny of his moods, and to be always ready for his work. It can be done." We must beware of self-pity, the attitude that so quickly saps our strength and poisons our outlook. The French mystic Francois Fenelon reminded us, "Discouragement serves no possible purpose; it is simply the despair of wounded self-love." His book *Christian Perfection* is a helpful guide for the pastor's "interior life," particularly the chapters entitled "Not to Be Discouraged by Faults" and "Helps in Dissipation and Sadness." Fenelon is a mystic, but he has a practical turn to his writing that is unique and helpful.

Our feelings of failure, like Elijah's, can drive us deep into despair, so we must learn to recognize and control them. My favorite preacher, George H. Morrison, said something in one of his sermons that has encouraged me when I have felt my work is in vain. He said: "Men who do their best always do more, though they be haunted by the sense of failure. Be good and true; be patient; be undaunted. Leave your usefulness to God to estimate. He will see to it that you do not live in vain."[2]

God rarely permits His servants to see all the good they are doing, so we must continue to "sow beside all waters" knowing that "in due season we shall reap, if we faint not." If we are to minister effectively, we must experience both the mountain tops and the valleys, and we cannot have mountains without valleys. Brooks expressed it this way in his interesting lectures, *The Influence of Jesus:* "To be a true minister to men is always to accept new happiness and new distress, both of them forever deepening and entering into closer and more inseparable union with each other the more profound and spiritual the ministry becomes. The man who gives himself to other men can never be a wholly sad man; but no more can he be a man of unclouded gladness."[3]

Mentioning Brooks reminds me of one simple device the pastor can use to brighten up his discouraging days. Brooks kept a few personal letters that he had received from people who had been helped by his ministry and who had been kind enough to write and tell him. One such letter was from an obscure Boston tailor, and when Bishop Brooks received it, it must have given him great joy and new strength. "I am a tailor in a little shop near your church," the man wrote, "and whenever I have the opportunity I always go to hear you preach. Each time I hear you preach I seem to forget all about you, for you make me think of God." Letters of appreciation (no matter how rare they may be!) are worth keeping and reading again, not to inflate the ego but to encourage the heart. By the same token the pastor ought to remember to write those who have helped him; they need encouragement too. A minister friend of mine writes five such letters each Thanksgiving, to the five people who that previous year were a special blessing to him. "Give and it shall be given unto you. . . ."

If Elijah was discouraged because he felt that he had failed God, then Moses was discouraged because he felt God had failed him! And perhaps we can put Jonah in the same category, although Jonah's discouragement obviously grew out of his rebellion against

2. *The Wind on the Heath* (London: Hodder and Stoughton, 1915), p. 10.

3. (New York: Dutton, 1903), pp. 191-92.

God's will. Moses was in the will of God, ministering to the people, and yet they were complaining so much that the great prophet wanted to die (Num. 11). Nothing depresses the pastor like criticism when he knows he is doing, with God's help, his best. If a man is thin-skinned and sensitive, he had better avoid the ministry. David was right when he said, "Let me fall now into the hand of the Lord, for very great are his mercies; but let me not fall into the hand of man" (I Chron. 21:13). Criticism is valuable when a brother "speaks the truth in love," but malicious criticism (usually motivated by jealousy or some other sinful attitude) can be a thorn in the preacher's flesh. If we are not successful in our work, somebody will criticize us; and if we are successful, somebody will criticize us!

Few preachers have experienced the kind of criticism that Spurgeon did when he began his ministry in London. A steady stream of magazine articles and pamphlets examined the young preacher's character, words, works, and motives, and most of them were anything but sympathetic. More than one writer expressed doubts that Spurgeon was even converted! His sermons were called "trashy," and he was compared to a rocket that would climb high and then suddenly drop out of sight! "What is he doing?" one writer asked. "Whose servant is he? What proof does he give that, instrumentally, his is a heart-searching, a Christ-exalting, a truth-unfolding, a sinner-converting, a church-feeding, a soul-saving ministry?" Reading that statement over a hundred years after it was published, we feel like laughing out loud! The writer was Rev. Charles Waters Banks. Have you ever heard of him?

At first this criticism deeply hurt Spurgeon, but then the Lord gave him peace and victory. Hearing slanderous reports of his character and ministry week after week could have led him into defeat; but he fell to his knees and prayed, "Master, I will not keep back even my character for Thee. If I must lose that, too, then let it go; it is the dearest thing I have, but it shall go, if, like my Master, they shall say I have a devil, and am mad, or, like Him, I am a drunken man and a wine-bibber."

Mrs. Spurgeon, knowing the trials her husband was going through, prepared a wall-motto to hang in their room, with Matthew 5:11-12 as the text. The Word of God did its work, and the preacher won the battle. Luther was right when he said that "the love of a woman" is a great help in days of discouragement; and blessed is that pastor's wife who knows when her husband needs that extra touch of love and understanding. (Luther's two other suggestions for overcoming despair are to exercise "faith in Christ—and get downright angry!")

Moses was wise enough to take his discouragement to the Lord, and the Lord solved the problem. In the final analysis, discouragement is a spiritual problem and can only be fought with spiritual weapons—the Word of God, prayer, Christian fellowship, and ministry. I think it was John Watson who advised the discouraged preacher to get busy if he would overcome his melancholy. Perhaps Watson borrowed the idea from John Keble, who advised: "When you find yourself overpowered as it were by melancholy, the best way is to go out and do something kind to somebody or other."

It does the pastor good to be reminded occasionally that he is privileged to share a high and holy calling. "Let us rejoice with one another," Brooks told his Yale audience, "that in a world where there are a great many good and happy things for men to do, God has given us the best and happiest and made us preachers of His Truth."

I find that reading again the biography of some great preacher or reading some godly preacher's sermons will usually lift the clouds and get me started again. It does me good to be reminded that the ministry is a wonderful calling, in spite of its dangers and discouragements. If a man does not love the ministry, he must seek some other vocation. Or, if a man in the ministry is too self-centered, he had better seek spiritual help; it is usually the self-centered pastor who suffers from chronic depression. "Do not be a spy on yourself," counseled Henry Ward Beecher. A constant spiritual autopsy can leave one bleeding and dying.

The pastor must have a confidant to whom he can turn in the hour of battle. Few church members ever ask, "Who is my pastor's pastor?" To be sure, as Psalm 23:1 affirms, "The Lord is my Pastor." But often the Lord uses another under-shepherd to help us unburden our hearts and regain our vision of the ministry. The right kind of friend can understand when we think nobody can, so cultivate among your brethren that kind of friendship.

Discouragement is an enemy we must learn to expect, face honestly, and fight with all our strength. No man can preach good news effectively if he himself is discouraged. We must try to understand the causes of our despair and, above all else, never yield to the expensive luxury of self-pity. The "I-only-am-left" complex can only lead to defeat. There are yet seven thousand who have not bowed the knee to Baal. It would be nice if one of them would step out and stand by our side, but until then, let us dare to believe God's Word and keep on going. "Never think of giving up preaching!", Alexander Whyte wrote to a Methodist pastor friend. "The angels around the throne envy you your great work. . . . Go on and grow in grace and power as a gospel preacher."

Above all else, let us live and labor for the eyes of God, not of men. If appreciation should come, be thankful for it; but if it does not come, be faithful just the same. Resign in a dark hour of discouragement and you will regret it when the sun comes out again. The preacher who said that "it came to pass" was his favorite statement in the Bible was not good at hermeneutics, but he certainly had common sense. The cloud that hovers over us today will be gone tomorrow, and it only covers the sun—it does not put it out.

These are discouraging days for our people, so let us as pastors magnify the ministry of encouragement. Let each of us be a Barnabas—a "Son of Encouragement." Let us ask the Lord to give us an encouraging attitude in our own hearts and encouraging messages from the Word. By encouraging others, we ourselves will be encouraged, and our work will prosper to the glory of God.

Bibliography

Fenelon, Francois. *Christian Perfection.* Edited by Charles F. Whiston. Translated by Mildred Whitney Stillman. New York: Harper, 1947.

Sanders, J. Oswald. *A Spiritual Clinic.* Chicago: Moody, 1958.

Spurgeon, Charles H. *Lectures to My Students.* 3 vols. London: Passmore and Alabaster, 1875-1894. Reprinted—London: Marshall, Morgan, and Scott, 1954.

Turnbull, Ralph. *A Minister's Obstacles.* Westwood, N.J.: Revell, 1964. Reprinted—Grand Rapids: Baker, 1972.

30

The Minister
as Comforter

Pity the church whose pastor does not understand the ministry of comfort. This pastor's funeral services are always "the same old thing," and rarely if ever does someone say, "When I die, *that's* the kind of pastor I want to comfort my loved ones." His ministry to mourners is "business as usual," and he seems ignorant of the fact that Jesus came "to heal the brokenhearted" (Luke 4:18). In short, he lacks a shepherd's heart; and a shepherd's heart is not discovered in the pages of a book nor mechanically conferred in an ordination service. A shepherd's heart is molded by the Spirit as a pastor walks through the valley with his people and weeps with those who weep.

But even the man who has the heart of a shepherd would do well to expose himself to the best books about death, mourning, and the funeral. Our most important lessons we read in the pages of the book of life, but many insights from the clinic and laboratory are valuable to the pastor who is always ready to improve his ministry to mourners. In fact, in the past quarter century both the psychologist and the philosopher have been confronting the awesome fact of death.

The emphasis of the existentialists on freedom, isolation, anxiety, and death, and the "great American illusion" of staying young and never dying both must be examined and answered. Our culture worships youth and denies death, and many Americans are totally unprepared when death takes a loved one. The pastor who cares will prepare himself and his people for this encounter with the last enemy.

If you have access to the annual volumes of *The Great Ideas Today*, then by all means read the perceptive essay "On Death" by Milton Mayer. "Death is the one idea that has no history," he began. "We do not know what to say about death because we do not know what to think about it, and we do not know what to think about it because we do not know what it is." James 2:26 gives us a Biblical definition of death, but what man can define it *from personal experience?* Mayer's essay is a storehouse of creative ideas based on history, philosophy, science, and a bit of theology. Like any good piece of writing, it will open the doors of your mind and lead you into avenues of study that you did not realize were there.

Now from the contemporary to the classic: by all means add *Holy Dying* to your shelf of books on death and the funeral. It was written by Jeremy Taylor, who lived from 1673 to 1746, and was one of several books to come from his pen during a "forced retirement" in Wales during the period of the commonwealth in Britain. Granted, the book is antique and certainly lacks the insight of modern psychology; but its practical insights and suggestions are really worthwhile. Where else could you find a theological treatise on "Impatience in Sickness" or "Remedies Against the Fear of Death"? *Holy Dying* was originally written for the parishioner, but today the pastor would get the most benefit from it. "It is a great art to die well!" said Taylor, and his book shows us how.

Perspectives on Death is a collection of nine essays edited by Liston O. Mills. The evangelical Christian will want to correct some of the exposition of the Hebrew and New Testament views of death, but he will still gain much from these essays. There are chapters on death in church history, views of death in contemporary literature, and death as seen in modern psychiatry. "Death as a Social Practice" by Ernest Q. Campbell and "Ethics and Death" by James T. Laney deal with topics not discussed in the average pastoral theology seminar. The final chapter, "Pastoral Care of the Dying and the Bereaved," written by the editor, is one of the finest treatments of this subject I have ever read.

The problem of terminal illness is dealt with in *Death and Contemporary Man: The Crisis of Terminal Illness,* written by Carl G. Carlozzi. The foreword is by the well-known Walter C. Alvarez. Every pastor has faced the question "Should we tell the patient his illness is terminal?" The question tests not only the patient's faith but also the pastor's! Not every man is able to face this kind of storm and weather it. The book is brief (seventy-nine pages), but it is packed with helpful insights, not all of which you will agree with but none of which you can lightly dismiss.

The philosophically minded pastor who wants some background material will want to read *Death and Western Thought* by Jacque Choron. Interestingly enough, the author's purpose (as he stated it) is to help "those who, at a time when the consolations of religion have lost their force, seek to come to terms with death." As a survey of thinking about death from Socrates to Sartre, the book is excellent. As an answer to the problems men face, the book leaves something to be desired. If you are pastoring in a college or university community, the book is a must.

Most pastors read and were shocked by Jessica Mitford's *The American Way of Death* and Ruth Mulvey Harmer's *The High Cost of Dying,* both published in 1963. The dust has pretty well settled now, and the extreme statements in both books have been answered by sane judgment. But some of the problems still remain. Can a person afford to die? Are there profiteers in the funeral profession? Is the American public too "corpse conscious"?

One of the best treatments of these problems from the pastor's point of view is *The Funeral: Vestige or Value?* by Paul E. Irion. (I trust you have Irion's book *The Funeral and the Mourners* in your library; it is one of the best books available on the psychology of death and the ministry of comfort.) In *The Funeral: Vestige or Value?* he took up the problem of the "secularization of death." He saw three types of funerals today: (1) the religious funeral; (2) the conventional funeral with religious rites but no Christian meaning, and (3) the secular or humanistic funeral. Every pastor has faced the problem of conducting a service for a family not religiously oriented and has wondered how to do it without being either hypocritical or judgmental. Irion has some suggestions, and he helps to put the ideas of *The American Way of Death* and *The High Cost of Dying* into proper perspective. He acknowledged that both books make some helpful contributions, but he also pointed out their limitations and blind spots.

The pastor needs to be a student of the psychology of grief. He must take the insights of psychology and, after testing them with the Word, put them to use. *Understanding Grief* by Edgar N. Jackson is a good book to start with, and after you have read it, get Jackson's smaller book, *For the Living.* The latter book is made up of questions and answers that grew out of the author's seminars with professional people on the topic of death. You might say that in the larger book Jackson gave the theory and in the smaller book the application; and they belong together. By the way, Jackson also has authored a little book for mourners called *You and Your Grief.* One wishes that there were more of a positive Christian message in this book, but the pastor can read it for his own profit and incorporate some of its ideas into his funeral messages. A similar little book by Granger E. Westberg is called *Good Grief.* It is an excellent summary of the psychological stresses and strains involved in bereavement and also of some of the processes involved in healing.

All of us know C. S. Lewis as the witty author of *Screwtape Letters* and the profound defender of the faith who wrote *Mere Christianity, Miracles,* and a host of other essays and books. Perhaps, however, you have missed one of his finest books—*A Grief Observed.* The book was originally published under the pseudonym of N. W. Clerk shortly before Lewis himself died in 1963. Married late in life, Lewis and his wife Joy (referred to as "H" in the book), were very happy together. Then cancer moved in. After her death Lewis began to vent his honest feelings and thoughts in four book manuscripts that were found in the house. His writing was "a defense against total collapse, a safety valve," and the sympathetic reader shares with him the deep emotions of those dark hours and weeks.

As an honest record of a dedicated Christian confronting grief and isolation, *A Grief Observed* stands almost alone. "No one ever told me that grief felt so much like fear," he wrote. "And no one ever told me about the laziness of grief." Please read *A Grief Observed* not as a short course in grief psychology but as a personal encounter with a great Christian man struggling with the realities of life and death.

Those of us who know Joseph Bayly as a friend know that he has a keen mind and a tender heart, an appreciation of the past, and an awareness of the present—certainly a rare combination for an evangelical Christian. He has been through the valley; he knows the Shepherd. His little book *The View from a Hearse* he dedicated "to the memory of three sons—Danny, John and Joe—who introduced us to death—its tragedy, its glory." That dedication assures you that the author knows whereof he speaks. As a personal witness to the power of God to heal the brokenhearted, *The View from a Hearse* is almost without peer. You will especially appreciate the author's treatment of the problems involved when a child is dying. I recommended this book to my entire congregation; many of them followed my suggestion, and (to my knowledge) none of them felt disappointed.

The Christian Way of Death by Gladys Hunt contains chapters on death, reality, triumph, deliverance, grief, sympathy, children, funerals, and God. Here we have nine quiet essays that seek to understand death *in a contemporary setting* and from a Christian perspective. (It is really too bad that we do not have some new songs and poems to use at funerals. So many of the "funeral anthologies" are covered with cobwebs. Here is a vast field for our contemporary poets and composers.) Hunt's chapter on telling children about death is most helpful; in fact, this is the kind of book the pastor can recommend to young couples, who probably are not thinking about death but who need to!

One of the best source books on the funeral is the one by Andrew Blackwood simply called *The Funeral.* In twenty-two chapters the author told the pastor how it ought to be done. I like Blackwood's treatment of the funeral sermon; I confess that his ideas have governed my own funeral preaching for over twenty years. "The appeal should be mainly to the imagination," said Blackwood. "In a few minutes there is time for only a single truth. It should be luminous." Blackwood gave suggestions for "problem funerals" and for military funerals. He showed the pastor how to use the time of mourning for the benefit of the people and for the glory of God. This is the one funeral book I would not be without.

Loraine Boettner's excellent book *Immortality* is one of the best theological discussions of death, the intermediate state, and immortality. No pastor preaches heavy theology at a funeral, but what he says had better be based on solid Biblical truth. The pastor who wants to preach about death and grief may want to read *Home Before Dark* by Bryant M. Kirkland, and Lettie Cowman's devotional book *Consolation* contains many fine seed thoughts that the creative pastor may use.

Finally, for a psychologist's thinking about suicide, read *Suicide and the Soul* by James Hillman. There is not much theology in this book, but it is still worth reading and pondering. Why hasn't some capable evangelical given us a Biblical treatment of this perplexing topic?

"If you would endure life, be prepared for death," said Sigmund Freud, who himself offered no counsel on how to be prepared. But the Christian pastor who understands death and grief and who knows the truth of the Word can minister to men's hearts and help them to live—and to die.

Bibliography

Bayly, Joseph. *The View from a Hearse.* Elgin, Ill.: Cook, 1970.

Blackwood, Andrew. *The Funeral.* Philadelphia: Westminster, 1942. Reprinted—Grand Rapids: Baker, 1972.

Boettner, Loraine. *Immortality.* Grand Rapids: Eerdmans, 1956.

Carlozzi, Carl G. *Death and Contemporary Man: The Crisis of Terminal Illness.* Grand Rapids: Eerdmans, 1968.

Choron, Jacque. *Death and Western Thought.* New York: Collier, 1963.

Cowman, Lettie (Mrs. Charles E.), ed. *Consolation.* Los Angeles: Oriental Missionary Society, 1944.

Harmer, Ruth Mulvey. *The High Cost of Dying.* New York: Crowell-Collier, 1963.

Hillman, James. *Suicide and the Soul.* New York: Harper and Row, 1964.

Hunt, Gladys. *The Christian Way of Death.* Grand Rapids: Zondervan, 1971.

Irion, Paul E. *The Funeral and the Mourners.* Nashville: Abingdon, 1954.

————. *The Funeral: Vestige or Value?* Nashville: Abingdon, 1966.

Jackson, Edgar N. *For the Living.* Des Moines: Channel, 1963.

————. *Understanding Grief.* New York: Abingdon, 1957.

————. *You and Your Grief.* New York: Channel, 1964.

Kirkland, Bryant M. *Home Before Dark.* New York: Abingdon, 1965.

Lewis, C. S. *A Grief Observed.* Greenwich, Conn.: Seabury, 1963. Reprinted—New York: Bantam, 1976.

Mayer, Milton. "On Death." In Hutchins, Robert M., and Adler, Mortimer J., eds. *The Great Ideas Today: 1965.* Chicago: Encyclopaedia Britannica, 1965. Pp. 107-49.

Mills, Liston O., ed. *Perspectives on Death.* Nashville: Abingdon, 1969.

Mitford, Jessica. *The American Way of Death.* New York: Simon and Schuster, 1963.

Taylor, Jeremy. *The Rule and Exercises of Holy Dying.* London: Royston, 1651. Reprinted—Cleveland: World, 1952.

Westberg, Granger E. *Good Grief.* Rev. ed. Philadelphia: Fortress, 1971.

E. M. Bounds

31

The Minister
and Prayer

Imagine yourself in Glasgow, Scotland, at the end of the Lord's Day, 30 December 1866. The pastor is reviewing the day's ministry in his journal. He writes: "Yesterday worn out in body and not able to pray much, so today did not get very close to the Lord's presence, nor to the people's consciences." Six years later he writes: "Morning interruptions are a great hindrance to continued devotion. Lord, give me more leisure for prayer!"

That preacher was the saintly Andrew Bonar, friend and biographer of Robert Murray McCheyne, and a minister of the Word whose life was saturated with prayer. "I see that prayerlessness is one of my great sins of omission," he wrote early in his ministry, and he set himself with the Lord's help to remedy that weakness. "Another time of nearness in prayer," he wrote in 1872. "And now may every sermon of mine be first laid on the altar of incense, and sent forth breathing its fragrance." What a tremendous spiritual ideal for any preacher of the gospel!

And listen to one of Bonar's contemporaries, Charles H. Spurgeon: "The minister who does not earnestly pray over his work must surely be a vain and conceited man. He acts as if he thought himself sufficient of himself, and therefore needed not to appeal to God. Yet what a baseless pride to conceive that our preaching can ever be in itself so powerful that it can turn men from their sins and bring them to God without the working of the Holy Ghost." So speaks the prince of preachers in "The Preacher's Private Prayer," one of his *Lectures to My Students,* and so speaks the Holy Spirit to the heart of every honest pastor who wants his ministry to be owned of God. *There is no power apart from prayer.*

One of the most moving experiences of my own life was stepping from John Wesley's bedroom in his London house into the little prayer room adjacent. Outside the house was the traffic noise of City Road, but in that prayer chamber was the holy hush of God. Frankly, I am not one who is easily moved by atmosphere, but in that little room I was moved. The only furnishings are a walnut table with a Greek Testament and a candlestick, a tiny prayer stool, and a chair. It was here that Wesley would come early each morning (when he was in London), read God's Word, and pray. "This little room was the powerhouse of Methodism," the guide whispered. No wonder Wesley wrote in his *Journal,* "I began visiting the Classes and found a considerable increase in the Society. This I impute chiefly to a small company of young persons who have kept a Prayer Meeting at five in the morning."

Mentioning Wesley reminds me of another Methodist whose life was a ministry of prayer—Edward McKendrie Bounds, author of some of the greatest books on prayer ever published in this country. If you have not read *Power Through Prayer,* then begin today. Then read *Purpose in Prayer* and *Preaching and Prayer.* "What the church needs today is not more machinery or better," wrote Bounds, "not new organizations or more and novel methods, but men whom the Holy Ghost can use—men of prayer, men mighty in prayer. The Holy Ghost does not flow through methods, but through men. He does not come on machinery, but on men. He does not anoint plans, but men—men of prayer." By the time you have read the first chapter, you are ready to lay the book down—*and go off and pray!* Then you pick up *Purpose in Prayer* and cannot get past the title of the first chapter, "God Shapes the World by Prayer." "Prayer is no fitful, short-lived thing," he wrote. "It is no voice crying unheard and unheeded in the silence. It is a voice which goes into God's ear, and it lives as long as God's ear is open to holy pleas, as long as God's heart is alive to holy things. God shapes the world by prayer. Prayers are deathless."

Bounds was born in 1835 in Shelby County, Missouri, and died in Washington, Georgia, in 1913. After practicing law for three years he entered the ministry and served in the Civil War as chaplain of the Fifth Missouri Regiment. Twice during that conflict he was held as a prisoner of war. During the last seventeen years of his life, living with his family in Georgia, he wrote his books. He used to rise at 4 A.M. and pray until 7 A.M. When he wrote about the power of prayer, he wrote out of the holy experiences of a full heart.

I must warn you that reading *Power Through Prayer* is something like opening a blast furnace! Chapter 10, "Under the Dew of Heaven," is especially convicting, dealing with that indefinable necessity that men call *unction.* "This unction comes to the preacher not in the study but in the closet. It is heaven's distillation in answer to prayer. . . . This unction is not a gift of genius. It is not found in the halls of learning. No eloquence can woo it. No industry can win it." I suggest that we pastors read through E. M. Bounds's books at least once a year, especially during those barren seasons when our souls become dry and our ministry lacks power. And may there be fewer such seasons!

Volume 7 of the *Library of Spurgeon's Sermons* published by Zondervan is devoted entirely to sermons on prayer. (If you own the larger set, *The Treasury of the Bible,* you will already have many of these messages.) His sermon on Philippians 1:19, entitled "The Minister's Plea," is especially encouraging. Some publisher ought to put this sermon in an attractive booklet for distribution to church members to encourage them to pray for their pastors. Perhaps his message on John 15:7, "The Secret of Power in Prayer," could also be included. "What a church we should be, if you were all mighty in prayer!" cried Spurgeon at the close of this sermon. "What an army would you be if you all had this power with God in prayer!" The application is just as relevant today.

A classic book on prayer that for some reason is little known among pastors is *The Hidden Life of Prayer* by David Martin M'Intyre. He was born in a pastor's home in Scotland in 1859. He trusted Christ early in life, surrendered to the ministry, and went to Edinburgh for training. He was ordained at the College Park Church in 1886. In 1891 he was called to serve with Andrew Bonar at the Finnieston Church in Glasgow, and when Bonar died the next year, M'Intyre became the sole pastor, leading the church until 1915. We reproduce after our kind: no doubt the prayer habits of Bonar rubbed off on his younger colleague. Two years after Bonar died, M'Intyre married Bonar's third daughter, Jane.

M'Intyre's book, while less than 100 pages in length, is a gold mine of spiritual wealth! For example:

"The soil in which the prayer of faith takes root is a life of unbroken communion with God, a life in which the windows of the soul are always open towards the City of Rest."

"Those who pray well, work well. Those who pray most, achieve the grandest results. . . . 'In God nothing is hindered.' "

"Now, what God requires of those who seek His face is a 'right intention'—a deliberate, a resigned, a joyful acceptance of His good and perfect will."

Eight brief but profound chapters make up this book, chapters that must be read again and again for them to have their full impact upon the heart. If *The Hidden Life of Prayer* is not on your devotional shelf, put it there as soon as possible. But do not leave it there! Read it!

Two books by Andrew Murray always come to mind when I think about prayer. The first is simply titled *The Prayer-Life* and is available in a number of inexpensive paperback editions. This book grew out of Murray's messages at a pastors' conference in South Africa in April 1912. Concerned about "the state of the Church," the pastors had gathered with missionaries and students to seek the Lord's help and blessing. Apparently Murray's sermons were greatly used of God to begin a stirring; now, more than half a century later, they still stir the heart.

A companion volume is *The Inner Chamber and the Inner Life,* published originally in 1906. This book focuses on the "devotional time" (call it what you will: the quiet time, the morning watch, the prayer hour). How easy it is for that important hour to become routine! The reason? Murray pinpointed it: "There is a terrible danger to which you stand exposed in your inner chamber. You are in danger of substituting Prayer and Bible Study for living fellowship with God, the living interchange of giving Him your love, your heart, and your life, and receiving from Him His love, His life, and His Spirit." *The Inner Chamber* is a book for quiet, meditative reading. The chapters are brief; no words are wasted. Chapter 34 on soul winning gives the right emphasis to the devotional life: "The great characteristic of the Divine life, whether in God, or in Christ, or in us, is—love seeking to save the lost." The reason some so-called "deeper life" programs have waned and died is probably because they were dead-end streets: there was no burden to share the life with others.

Let me name four other titles that the pastor ought to have in his library, read carefully, and put into practice.

The Practice of Prayer is a series of messages that G. Campbell Morgan gave originally at British Keswick. When you read this book, keep in mind something Morgan wrote about prayer to a correspondent in 1927: "There are wonderful stories of men in the ministry who have devoted hours to prayer, and of others of whom I have heard who spent whole nights in the actual exercise. I have a very great respect for men who do this, but the idea has never made the slightest appeal to me and I have never practiced it. . . . I am certain that the secret of real spiritual power in the ministry is that of personal, maintained relationship with God. Whatever habits are necessary to the individual man [to maintain such relationship] he should cultivate and observe. No person can lay down rules for another in this regard."[1] Sound spiritual counsel!

Prayer, by Bishop Ole Hallesby of Oslo, Norway, is another spiritual classic that the pastor must read and digest. Taking Revelation 3:20 as his key text ("I doubt that I know of a passage in the whole Bible which throws greater light upon prayer than this one does"), Hallesby defined *prayer* and then showed that prayer is work. The two chapters on "wrestling in prayer" are excellent.

I dare not forget Alexander Whyte's great volume of sermons on prayer, *Lord Teach Us to Pray.* Who but Whyte would preach on such topics as: "The Geometry of Prayer," "Imagination in Prayer," and "Concentration in Prayer"? That Whyte himself believed in earnest prayer is revealed in a story he told in his book on Thomas Shepard. Whyte had been interceding for a friend who was ill "nigh unto death." God seemed to say to him, "If you are sincere in your prayers, will you agree to transfer to your friend *half of your remaining years?*" "I sprang to my feet in a torrent of sweat," said Whyte. "It was a kind of Garden of Gethsemane to me. But, like Gethsemane, I got strength to say, 'Let it be as Thou hast said. Thy will be done.' " You may not always agree with all that Whyte preached, but you can never accuse him of preaching what he did not practice.

Next to Bounds's *Power Through Prayer* the book that has helped me the most in my personal prayer life is *Prayer: Asking and Receiving,* by the well-known evangelist and author John R. Rice. (In fact, this is the first book I purchased for my own library after I became a Christian, and I have never regretted the investment!) You read this book with confidence because the writer tells you what prayer has done in *his own life and ministry.* (The

---

1. *This Was His Faith,* ed. Jill Morgan (Westwood, N.J.: Revell, 1952), p. 26.

man who preaches on prayer and uses "borrowed illustrations" is like a bald barber selling a hair-restorer!) This book is a powerful blending of Biblical truth and practical experience; it presents clear doctrine plus evangelistic zeal, like the sea of glass mingled with fire.

The purpose of this brief listing (and many more books could be added) is not to build your devotional library but *to stir your soul to pray.* More than any other book, the Bible *alone* ought to move us to pray. But if one of these books helps a tired, discouraged pastor find new life and power, then the labor is not in vain. Whatever else we pastors may do during any given week—and there are many good things to be done—we must regularly pray. Bounds put it so much better, so I will close with a paragraph from *Power Through Prayer:* "We put it as our most sober judgment that the great need of the Church in this and all ages is men of such commanding faith, of such unsullied holiness, of such marked spiritual vigor and consuming zeal, that their prayers, faith, lives, and ministry will be of such a radical and aggressive form as to work spiritual revolutions which will form eras in individual and Church life." Lord, teach us to pray!

Bibliography

Bounds, E. M. *Power Through Prayer.* 12th ed. London: Marshall, 1912. Reprinted—Grand Rapids: Baker, 1972.

———. *Preacher and Prayer.* Nashville: Methodist Episcopal Church, South, 1907. Reprinted—Grand Rapids: Zondervan, n.d.

———. *Purpose in Prayer.* 2nd ed. London: Marshall, 1914. Reprinted—Chicago: Moody, n.d.

Hallesby, Ole. *Prayer.* Translated by Clarence J. Carlsen. Minneapolis: Augsburg, 1931.

M'Intyre, David Martin. *The Hidden Life of Prayer.* Stirling: Drummond's Tract Depot, 1907. Reprinted—Minneapolis: Bethany Fellowship, 1969.

Morgan, G. Campbell. *The Practice of Prayer.* New York: Revell, 1906. Reprinted—Grand Rapids: Baker, 1971.

Murray, Andrew. *The Inner Chamber and the Inner Life.* New York: Revell, 1906. Reprinted—Grand Rapids: Zondervan, n.d.

———. *The Prayer-Life.* London: Morgan and Scott, 1914. Reprinted—Grand Rapids: Zondervan, n.d.

Rice, John R. *Prayer: Asking and Receiving.* Wheaton, Ill.: Sword of the Lord, 1942.

Spurgeon, Charles H. *Sermons on Prayer.* Library of Spurgeon's Sermons, edited by Charles T. Cook, vol. 7. Grand Rapids: Zondervan, 1959.

Whyte, Alexander. *Lord, Teach Us to Pray.* New York: Harper, n.d.

Index of
Persons